A Country House at Work

MAIGNEN'S PATENT

A Country House at Work

Three Centuries of Dunham Massey

PAMELA SAMBROOK

First published in Great Britain in 2003 by
National Trust Enterprises Ltd
36 Queen Anne's Gate, London SW1H 9AS

www.nationaltrust.org.uk

British Library Cataloguing in Publication Data
A Catalogue record for this book is available from the British Library

ISBN 0-7078-0344-6

Designed by Newton Engert Partnership

Printed in Italy by G. Canale & C. S.p.A

FRONTISPIECE: The kitchen sink at Dunham Massey.

Contents

Acknowledgements

My sincerest thanks are due to the many people who have contributed to this book, especially the current staff of Dunham Massey and the Stamford Estates Office. Special mention must be made of James Rothwell and Margaret Stone, both of whom have patiently answered endless questions, suggested ideas and provided solutions. Without James's long-term enthusiasm and encouragement, little would have been achieved.

I would also like to thank the staff of the various libraries and record offices visited, especially those of the John Rylands Library at the University of Manchester, where most of the Stamford Archive is deposited. In particular, the superb catalogue by John Hodgson demonstrates the value of first-class archival skills, for which there is no substitute. The owners of Enville Hall, Peter and Diana Williams, and their archivist, Sandy Haynes, have been most helpful in searching out data and allowing its reproduction. I also thank Craig Thornber, who has generously provided access to his material, both published and unpublished, and Minnie Hulme, whose reminiscences make a real contribution to my final chapter.

Several of my friends and colleagues have had the unenviable experience of having text dumped on them to read through. To them I apologise and give thanks. Finally, to everyone involved in the completion of the final product I extend my sincere gratitude, especially Nadia Mackenzie for her wonderful photographs, Martin Newton and Gail Engert for their beautiful design, and Margaret Willes and Andrew Cummins for their enduring patience and good nature.

CHAPTER ONE

Introduction

Dunham Massey is an island of peace in a busy world. The great country house and its 3,000 acres of park and estate lie on the south-westerly edge of the sprawling conurbation of Manchester, sandwiched between motorway and international airport. Shielded from the outside world by tree-lined walks, and guarded by moat and mound, the house is both austere and domestic, a presence which claims its ancient place in the landscape with understated Englishness. Inside, it enfolds the visitor in a comfortable elegance, a home rather than a stately monument.

For most of its life Dunham Massey was the residence of two great families, the Booths and later the Greys, joined by marriage in the seventeenth and the eighteenth centuries and both marked by turbulent early histories. Since 1976 the house and park have been owned by the National Trust and today a small army of administrators, conservators, craftsmen and volunteers work industriously to preserve the present tranquillity. So it has always been. Behind the easy elegance of the English country house lay a complex structure of domestic management. House, garden, park and estate were part of a hugely intricate web of connections and dependencies. How this structure worked in practice is the subject of this book, not the deeds and ambitions of ennobled men. Steward and housekeeper are our focus, not earl or countess. The incumbents of Dunham were always colourful and independent, yet if one's viewpoint is shifted their history becomes but a backcloth to other family histories. Dunham has been the focus in the lives of literally thousands of families of servants, tenants, labourers, contractors and tradesmen. It has been the means of financial support to their kin, many of whom never set foot inside its walls.

The Booths and the Greys, however, provided the context which influenced the nature of the household and its management. The Booths were committed Presbyterians and were thus heavily involved in the convulsive swings of seventeenth-century national politics, the English Civil War of 1642–9, the claims of Charles II and his subsequent restoration in 1660.[1] Three terms of imprisonment in the Tower of London and a good deal of debt were balanced by elevations firstly to the barony of Delamer, awarded in 1661, and to the earldom of Warrington in 1690. Along with these went programmes of extension and landscaping of their country seat at Dunham. It has been estimated that by 1688 Henry Booth, 2nd Lord Delamer, later the 1st Earl of Warrington, owed something in the region of £50,000, in modern terms almost £4 million.[2]

LEFT: Two aspects of Dunham Massey: (ABOVE) the south front, and (BELOW) looking from the north across the moat.

At times life back at Dunham Massey must have been grim. Whilst her husband was in the Tower in the late 1650s, Henry's wife Mary had been reduced to selling her personal silver plate to make ends meet and later she survived by borrowing from her

Timeline for Dunham Massey

1362 First recorded mention of a park at Dunham

1410–11 First recorded mention of the house at Dunham Massey, including a hall, chapel, treasury, kitchen and stable and a ruined dovecote. Also first recorded mention of the moat.

1434 First recorded mention of the Higher Park (later the New Park)

Late 1500s, early 1600s A new house built containing the Great Hall as part of a north wing flanked by two forward-projecting end wings. Substantial repairs to barns, stables and gardens.

1616 The water corn-mill built

1650s New southern range built by the 1st Lord Delamer to link the east and west wings and form an enclosed inner courtyard. Also built the chapel.

By 1697 First formal avenues of trees planted in Old Park

1720–30s John Norris built for the 2nd Earl of Warrington two new stable blocks for coach and riding horses, brew-house and bakehouse, new kitchen court on the site of old parterre and orangery, followed by rebuilding of main house retaining the courtyard plan and echoing the old house in fenestration. New parterres, new planted landscapes, avenues with sheets of water, statuary, new well-house and water supply.

1740 Deer barn and slaughterhouse built

1748–51 Park wall built

1758 Lady Stamford started to transform the Higher Park, renamed New Park by 1765

Sometime during 2nd half of 18th century New orangery built

1770s New fireplace fitted into the kitchen, floor reflagged

1779 New walls and greenhouses built in the kitchen garden. New drive called the Ash Walk created.

1783–4 John Hope altered the Great Gallery for the 5th Earl, inserting new fireplace and sash windows

1789–90 John Hope rebuilt the south front. New lawns and naturalistic planting.

1800 New wash-house built

1822 John Shaw employed by 6th Earl to create new dining room out of the old Great Parlour and withdrawing room (now the Saloon), raising the ceiling by 3ft, and providing a semi-circular bay window with screen of scagliola columns and elaborate gilt pelmets, and a massive marble fireplace. Inserted a covered passage across the inner courtyard. Altered fenestration and entrance steps of the north front. New flight of steps from the Grand Staircase to first floor of the east range.

Continued tree planting, especially in the pleasure ground. Also built home farm with octagonal dovecote, houses for farm steward and staff, and carpenters' workshop, smithy etc.

1831–3 Repainting of family rooms. Billiard table set up in the Yellow Damask Room, now the Queen Anne Room. New game larder built and ventilation to existing larders improved. Repainting and minor changes to kitchen court and stable block. New aviary for ornamental birds.

1855–6	Plate glass introduced to first-floor windows of east front and the first-floor of the east wing refurbished and refurnished. New island flower-beds, Bark House built near orangery and bridge over moat.
1860s	Corn-mill converted to a saw-mill
By 1870s	Farm and estate buildings in a poor state
1869–82	Great Gallery (renamed drawing room) redecorated for the Platts
1880s	Gas lighting installed
1880s–1917	Main estate farmlands changed from arable to dairy enterprise to meet the Manchester market. Fields enlarged. Farms renovated or rebuilt to Stamford design.
1906 alterations	Whole house overhauled by Compton Hall for 9th Earl, including: lowering roofline of the south front, replacing attic windows with dormers and new cornice. New steps to the north front, alterations to steps to the east front. New dining room closer to kitchen, with single-storey stone-clad bay, made out of the old steward's room, maids' room and back staircase. Created a suite of private day rooms on the ground floor of the south range for 9th Earl and Countess of Stamford. Expanded original entrance hall. Removed inner courtyard corridor. Created Saloon out of old dining room. Enlarged Stone Parlour by taking in old lamp room to become ante-room to new dining room. New billiard room, study. Refurbished old Velvet Bedchamber to create King Charles Room, later became Summer Parlour. Installed low-voltage electrical system, piped hot and cold water, 6 bathrooms. Modernised kitchen, larders, servery. New lavatory for kitchen staff. New butler's pantry, new servants' hall. Converted a coach-house into garage and brew-house into car wash. Removed island flower-beds, created new parterre and rose garden, badminton and tennis courts. Bark House resited. Estate cottages improved.
1942	New Park requisitioned as German prison-camp
Post 1945	Golf course in New Park
1976	Dunham Massey bequeathed to the National Trust by the 10th Earl

Note on acreages and valuations: in 1873, the 7th Earl of Stamford owned 31,000 acres over eight counties. This figure in itself represents a substantial reduction following the sale of thousands of acres mostly in Cheshire. In 2002 the estate covered around 3,000 acres, with 20 farms and 100 cottages let to private tenants.

In the mid-nineteenth century Dunham Massey Park was around 400 acres, divided into two parts, the Old and the New Parks. In the Old Park were 500 deer and there had been formerly a heronry.*

In 1784 Dunham Massey Hall was insured against fire damage at the Sun Fire Office for the sum of £8,000 plus £2,000 for coach-houses, stables and barns. Enville was similarly valued at £8,000 plus £1,000 for outbuildings. The combined annual premium was £52 3s 6d.†

* Charles Balshaw, *A Stranger's Guide and Complete Directory to Altrincham, Bowdon, Dunham, Timperley, Baguley, Ashley, Hale and Bollington* (1860s, reprinted by E.J. Morten, Manchester, 1973).

† EGR 4/1/6/11/1 Sun Fire Office Insurance Policy, 25 March 1784.

servants and from her own children's meagre pocket money. When Henry's son, George, succeeded his father in 1694 as 2nd Earl of Warrington, he inherited a decidedly mixed blessing. The household was in debt to all sorts of local tradesmen, family legacies were unpaid and servants had received no wages for many years. According to George Booth, Dunham was run down and in 'rotten condition and very barely furnished with worn out goods ... the house was so decayed as forced me to rebuild it, for it could not have lasted safe another generation'. Boding even worse for the long term, the annual income from the estates was generally reckoned to be totally inadequate to support the rank of earldom, being a mere £2,000, whereas the average income of the peerage was three times that amount. No wonder George carried with him the enduring memory of his father weeping at the size of his debts.

One of the first actions of the nineteen-year-old 2nd Earl was a vain attempt to suppress his father's will, which hung around his neck impossible bequests to his brothers and sisters. He also adopted several longer-term strategies for debt management, which eventually met with more success. Looking back to his ancestral history he saw clearly enough that public service 'must necessarily be the absolute ruine of our family.' With the tribulations of his father and grandfather ever in mind, the 2nd Earl forsook political life and remained on his country estates, dedicating himself almost obsessively to their personal management. As it turned out he sacrificed his own happiness in a desire for financial security, for he contracted an unhappy marriage to a rich heiress, the daughter of a London merchant. An extravagant wife and a careless housekeeper, Mary Oldbury nevertheless brought with her a dowry of £20,000. In 1715, by virtue of 'a great deal of care and pain' on his behalf, a large part of the family debt had been repaid. In 1724 the 2nd Earl inherited his brother Langham's estate and during the 1720s and 1730s he was able to rebuild substantially the whole house at Dunham, beginning with two stable blocks and a domestic kitchen court. He was also able to invest in what became a superb collection of silver, pictures and furniture. By the time of his death in 1758 he was a relatively wealthy man.

There was a price to pay, of course. At one level there was personal grief at an unsatisfactory marriage. In 1711 the Earl explained his departure from the London social scene in a letter to his uncle. London, he wrote, was not a 'suitable place to make a long stay in with one's Family, when a wife is so far from taking care, or ordering anything, that I believe she never bestowed one thought towards management of anything that's mine'. This unhappy marriage yielded only one legitimate offspring, a daughter, Mary.[3] There were also sacrifices to be made at another level. Intense concentration on his estates required withdrawal from political influence on both a national and local scale. Precedence within the county of Cheshire was ceded to political opponents, the Tories, especially the Cholmondeleys. After 1722 a Booth was never again to sit as an MP for Cheshire.

The awful predicament in which the 2nd Earl found himself in 1694 had a profound influence on later generations of the family. Although there is no doubt that the estate was heavily in debt, the Earl's description of the poor state of the buildings and furnishings which he inherited was perhaps exaggerated.[4] Believing that he had 'purchased rather than inherited what I have' he chose to pass on the

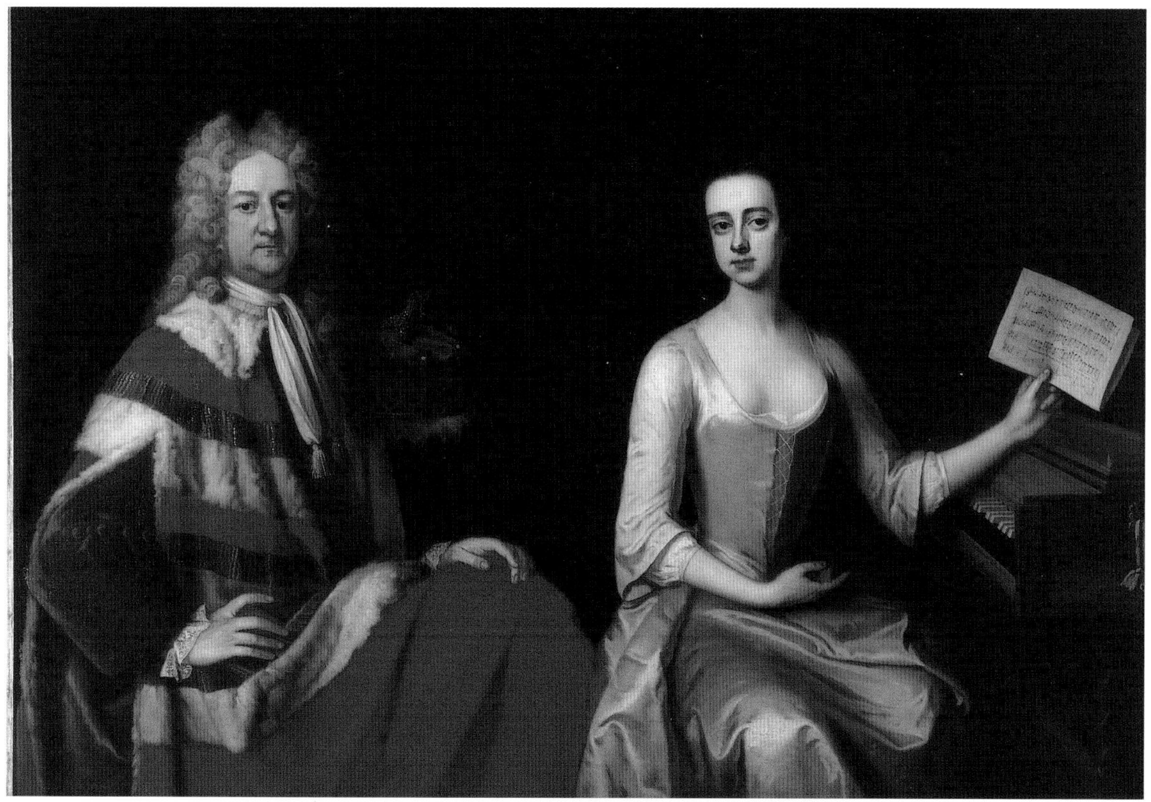

George Booth, 2nd Earl of Warrington, with his daughter and heir, Lady Mary, painted by Michael Dahl, *c.*1730.

benefits directly to his daughter, rather than to his cousin who was theoretically the male heir. This was an unusual attitude for the times. As married women could not own property, ownership of any real estate they had as single women passed automatically to their husbands on marriage, so the Earl left Dunham in trust for his daughter, ensuring her long-term legal interest. Instructed by her father in matters of house and estate management, Lady Mary became an able and formidable châtelaine of Dunham. Her marriage in 1736 to Harry Grey, the 4th Earl of Stamford, however, resulted in a profound change in the use of the house. Her husband's family house at Enville in Staffordshire became the couple's home for the first half of the year, the family and personal servants moving to Dunham in July and remaining there until late November or December. This tradition was passed on to her son, the 5th Earl of Stamford, and to later generations of the family until the 1850s.

Like his grandfather, the 5th Earl of Stamford devoted himself to the conservative management of Dunham and also to the pursuit of country sports, especially hunting and racing. In the 1780s he employed a local architect, John Hope, to remodel the south front of the house and alter the Great Gallery, as well as carrying out an ambitious scheme of planting in the garden. His son, the 6th Earl, spent a substantial sum on alterations and maintenance in the early 1820s, including inserting a corridor across the main courtyard and building a new home farm. It is during these years that we can see the Dunham household perhaps at its most fashionable, playing host to lavish house parties during the late summer and autumn.

We can also see in the 6th Earl a personification of some of the best qualities of the landed aristocrat, a practitioner of benevolent paternalism and a man greatly

George Grey, 5th Earl of Stamford, painted in Rome on the Grand Tour in 1760, by Anton Raphael Mengs.

appreciated by his tenants. Yet he was also a stern father-figure to his own family. George Harry Grey, his grandson and heir, reacted predictably. To the horror of his family he married Elizabeth Billage, the daughter of his servant at Cambridge. This unfortunate woman was totally unprepared for life as the head of a household of the size and complexity of Dunham. With his wife overwhelmed and unhappy, the 7th Earl left Cheshire to make their primary home at Enville. When Elizabeth died in 1854, he made what seemed to his family yet another disastrous marriage, this time to Catherine Cocks, a former bareback rider in a circus act. On his return to Dunham to introduce his new bride to the Cheshire tenantry, the local ladies of Altrincham and the vicar of Bowdon gave her such a frosty reception that the Earl abandoned Dunham once more and removed permanently to Enville.

After the 7th Earl's death in 1883, the Rev. Harry Grey, a distant relation through

George Harry Grey, 6th Earl of Stamford, painted by George Romney in 1790.

the youngest son of the 4th Earl of Stamford, inherited the earldom but never owned Dunham, which remained in the control of the trustees of the 7th Earl's widow, Catherine, until her death in 1905. Between 1869 and 1905 the house was either let to tenants or occupied only by a caretaker. By 1905 the house had fallen into a general state of disrepair, but on the family's return in that year the newly inherited 9th Earl and his Countess began to plan an expensive programme of refurbishment and modernisation. This turned Dunham into an interesting example of Edwardian domestic technology. With only minor changes, the house was occupied by the 9th Earl and his family and by his son Roger Grey, the 10th Earl, until the latter's death in 1976, when it was bequeathed to the National Trust.

The ebb and flow of family success and disaster over the centuries had obvious and profound repercussions on the household at Dunham Massey. It is a clear example of how the nature of the great family and their individual predilections dictated the nature of the servant administration. Under the 2nd Earl's regime, Dunham was governed by a careful master but a neglectful mistress. The day-to-day running of the house must have been largely in the hands of senior servants. The Earl might have run the estate (forty years of rental records were written in his own hand) and chosen high-status furnishings like silver or furniture, but the equipping of new kitchens, laundries and other domestic offices must have required the skills of experienced and reliable servants. A social life which encompassed absences of only two or three weeks in London each year required a more settled routine than that of other families who moved from one house to another with the progress of the annual social calendar.[5] In the next generation, the conjoining by marriage of two great houses, Dunham and Enville, created yet a different housekeeping regime, each year divided into two distinct halves, run by two sets of servants. This routine was disrupted in the second half of the nineteenth century, when the abandonment of Dunham for Enville resulted in the house being leased out. Then life at Dunham operated at a different level and only limited large-scale investment was put in place for the best part of half a century. The return of a new Earl and his family in 1905 meant renewed investment and a revitalisation of household and estate employment.

The service wing at Dunham Massey as we see it today was largely the creation of the 2nd Earl of Warrington. Substantially recovered from the crippling debts which he inherited, in 1720 he set about building himself a series of spacious, modern domestic offices, grouped around a square courtyard which was connected on one side to the main house. On the north side of the court was built a kitchen suite, complete with kitchen, scullery, pastry and larders. To the west were the dairy and the laundries, and on the south was the service entrance guarded by the porter's lodge. The east wing, connecting the court to the family's inner courtyard, provided accommodation for the upper servants, the housekeeper and the house steward.

The layout of service areas around a court had a number of qualities to recommend it. The kitchen, for example, was set to one side of the main house but physically linked to it. Yet the court still afforded a high degree of privacy for family members, who were shielded from the gaze of the lower ranks of servants, rude, ill-educated and hard-worked, by a guard of senior servants, well paid, genteel and reliably deferential. Thus there was incorporated into the physical fabric of one building not the double world of modern television mythology, upstairs/downstairs, but the tripartite structure of the classic country house: family, management and workers.

This tripartite model was complicated by all sorts of subtle and not-so-subtle intricacies. Each team of servants was ranked according to experience and status, which differentiated the work they did, the rooms to which they had entrance, even the rug on their bedroom floor. They were differentiated too by their age and their gender, in some cases even by their height. This was not the end of the story, however, for those servants to whom the kitchen court was home as well as workplace were swelled by yet other populations of outdoor servants and estate workers, day labourers and contractors. Dunham was a magnet for a veritable host of gardeners, grooms, jockeys, slaughtermen, grocers, post boys, charwomen, seamstresses, bricklayers, plasterers, painters, chimney-sweeps' boys, feather-pickers, dung-sweepers, bookbinders, surgeons and apothecaries. Fitting each person into the overall picture is like attempting a gigantic three-dimensional jigsaw puzzle. Yet such an analogy is inadequate for it has no element of change or movement built into it; a more successful image would be that of a pool, in which the central family created successive ripples of influence radiating outwards, changing and renewing themselves over both time and distance.

* * *

A bird's-eye view of Dunham Massey from the south, painted by John Harris, *c.*1750, as a record of the improvements made by the 2nd Earl of Warrington.

The affairs of great men and families are relatively well documented, but how do we gain access to the lives of this more modestly placed workforce? One of the definitive characteristics of great families is that they leave behind not only complex domestic environments which we can inspect, but also family archives which preserve the attempts of the family to control the administration and financing of their household. In this case the Stamford and Warrington family archives are housed in the John Rylands Library of the University of Manchester where they have been extensively and very ably catalogued. To these we must add more family archives kept at Enville as well as public archives created by census enumerations and ecclesiastical parish and probate records.

The evidence of bricks and mortar can be supplemented by reference to several paintings in the house and to six inventories of the movable contents of the property, taken usually at the death of one of the Earls. Thus there are inventories from 1693–4 (the 1st Earl of Warrington's death), 1758 (2nd Earl of Warrington), 1819 (5th Earl of Stamford), 1883 (7th Earl of Stamford), 1905 (the 7th Countess) and 1912 (taken for insurance purposes).[6] The inventories are highly variable in detail. The 1693–4 inventory, for example, gave only the total estimated value of each room's contents, whereas the later inventories listed individual items. In general only movable contents were included, meaning that cooking-ranges or ovens were excluded. Only three of the six inventories gave valuations – 1693–4, 1819 and 1912. The 1693–4 inventory has to be viewed with some degree of scepticism, at least as far as the valuations are concerned. The 2nd Earl himself poured scorn on his father's probate inventory, which estimated the total value of the contents to be almost £10,000. According to him the appraisal was taken by 'ignorant country men who know nothing of the value of furniture, plate, jewels or other things and accordingly set on many things excessively more than they were worth'.[7] Working with inventories as historical documents is a specialised area and one which has been well rehearsed by academics.[8] It is easy to make unwarranted assumptions about the positioning of rooms in relation to each other or in relation to interiors in successive inventories.[9] Room names changed over time, as did the description of equipment and the experience and specialist knowledge of the appraiser. Inventories took time and money to prepare. Nathaniel Pass, an auctioneer in Altrincham, began the 1819 inventory on 16 June and worked uninterruptedly for the following eight days. For this he was paid £14 8s 6d plus a personal gratuity of 4gns. In the same inventory, the pictures were valued by a Manchester firm of carvers, gilders and frame-makers, Zanetti and Agnew, who worked for two days for a payment of £3 0s 6d. The equivalent inventory at Enville was much more expensive and was made by a Dudley firm who charged £105 for valuations of everything from books to livestock.

Accounting practices within the great country houses are critical in enabling studies such as this. Even medieval households practised departmental record-keeping, whereby separate sections of the household kept an independent accounting, re-charging the goods supplied and the services rendered to other sections. Such systems lie at the core of our exploration of how the household worked, even if the values attributed were sometimes theoretical rather than realistic. At Dunham annual household accounts were kept by the house steward and other servants. Those of the house steward were kept in two books, his cash book and his account book. The cash book is single-line entry, a chronologically kept record of cash payments made personally by the house steward. In some years (1822, for example) the single-line entries are backed up by bundles of vouchers (bills) from the tradesmen carrying out the work. The account book is a totally different type of record, listing payments of cash or issues of supplies by other staff who reported to the house steward. This forms the main record of the work of the housekeeper at Dunham. The account book has survived in long runs from the 1740s to the 1840s, but the cash books are far more intermittent. Sometimes the house steward kept more specialised records of particular occurrences. In 1822, for instance, he kept a building account of the refurbishments carried out by the 6th Earl.

Other senior servants kept their own accounts but survival of these is very variable. The butlers' records of the cellar exist from the early nineteenth century, for example. The farm or land steward kept accounts which for some periods included not only those of the home farm but also those of the head gardener and the miller, and also sometimes covered records of the estate carpenters and builders. Annual stock lists recorded the numbers and types of livestock kept. A more personal record was kept by William Torry, a footman who later became butler to the Grey family at Enville and Dunham. Organised alphabetically rather than chronologically, this contains summary reports of deaths, arrivals, accidents, robberies and other notable events taking place on both estates during the 1820s and 1830s.[10]

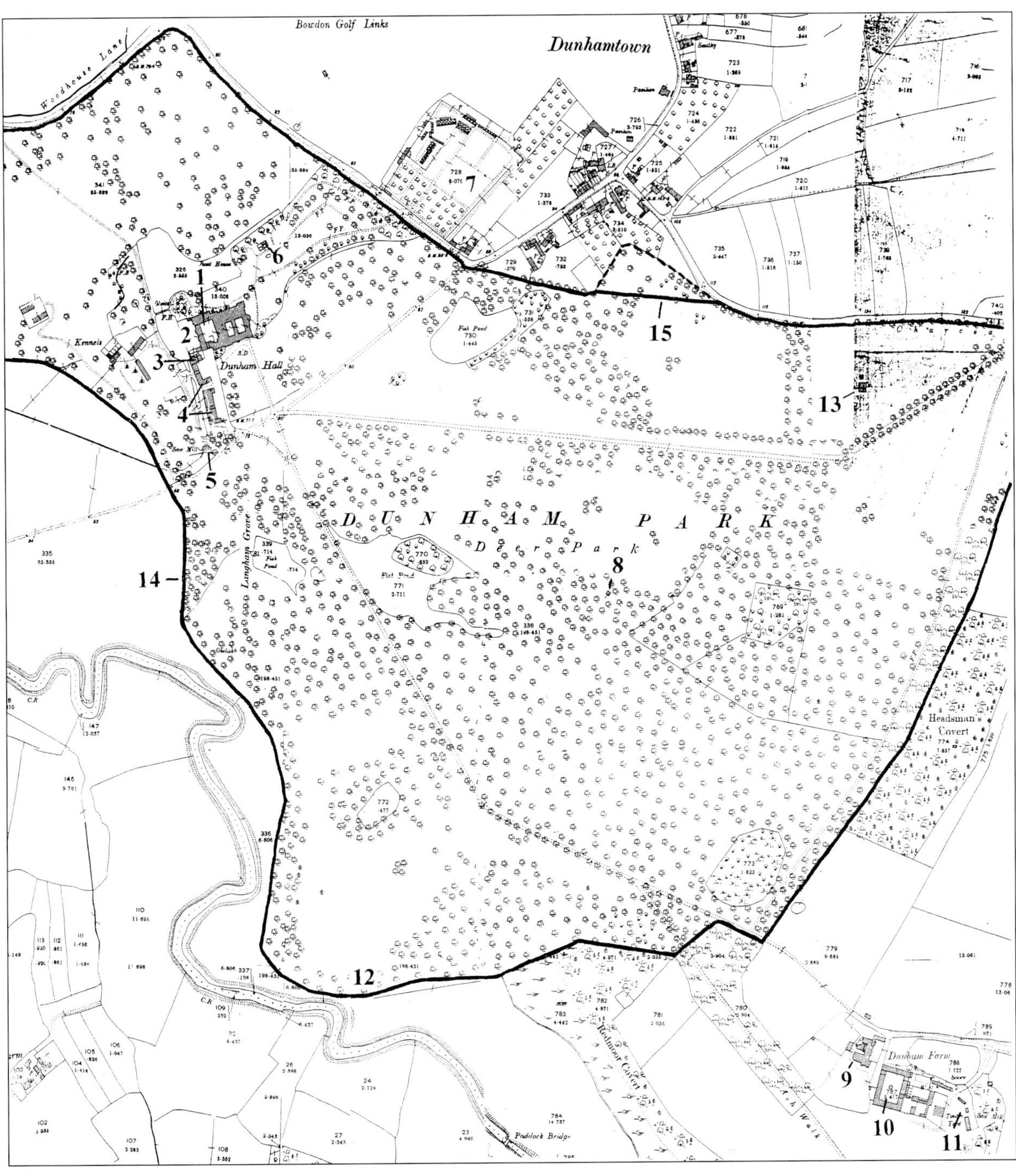

Dunham Massey and the Old Park, based on the second edition Ordnance Survey map, 1897.

1. Kitchen court
2. Drying green
3. Brew-house and bakehouse
4. Coach-house and stables
5. Mill
6. Pump-house
7. Kitchen garden
8. Slaughterhouse
9. Land steward's house
10. Home farm yard and dovecote
11. Smithy, joiner's shop, sawpit etc
12. Ice-house
13. Deer barn
14. Park wall
15. New section of park wall built post 1976 replacing original length (dotted)

Grey family members themselves kept records which occasionally help to throw light on the running of the household. At the death of the 5th Earl of Stamford, for example, there was a list made of all his bequests to servants. From the late eighteenth to the mid-nineteenth centuries the family was absent from Dunham for at least six months of each year and during this time the land agents, the Worthington family of Altrincham, sent regular letters of report about estate affairs to the Earls. Most of them deal with tenancy matters and property purchases rather than household or domestic administration but they sometimes include accounts of the deaths of servants and these can provide a very useful glimpse into the more human side of the household.

When we begin to look for consistent evidence about people, the archive is less accommodating. The Dunham wage records, for example, are very disappointing. There are no consistent runs of wage books for the indoor servants and few lists of their names survive. Only one wage book, from 1858 to 1867, includes some indoor servants and this is incomplete and often does not specify their post. The payment of salaries, as opposed to day wages, may well have been the responsibility of the land agent rather than the house steward and much of this part of the agents' record seems not to have survived. For this reason we have potentially more information about seasonal and casual workers at Dunham than about the permanent living-in staff.

To fill in such gaps we have recourse to national census enumeration records, at least from 1841, the first national census.[11] Unfortunately, the nineteenth-century census returns for Dunham are extremely disappointing. In 1841, no family members were in residence and although there was a list of eight indoor servants living at the house and several more in cottages on the estate, their functions were not specified except for the house steward and the housekeeper. Unfortunately, the 1851 census is not much better. The family was again absent, though eight servants were listed, and again the generic title of 'house servant' was used for the female servants with only the housekeeper, butler, usher and footman being specified. The enumeration for the 1861 census follows the same pattern, the family was again absent, the Earl of Stamford's twenty-eight-year-old land agent, Arthur Payne, being designated as 'head of household', which consisted of a housekeeper, two men servants and one woman servant.

We are unusually unlucky in these three censuses. The enumerator who took the information, probably from the house steward or housekeeper, was not as painstaking as many others and did not identify specific jobs. In addition, of course, the timing of censuses was awkward. For various reasons, such as the seasonality of harvest workers, enumerations have always been made in spring, usually April, just the time at Dunham when the main household, including the family, were living at Enville. Thus only those servants living permanently at Dunham appeared in the census and this gives a far from complete view of the size and nature of the servant household. The Enville census would be misleading too, since it would include, but not differentiate between, the permanent Enville servants and those who would later move to Dunham with the family.

The 1871 and 1881 census records give a different picture. The main house at Dunham was then leased by a tenant, Robert Platt, described in the 1871 census as a sixty-seven-year-old cotton-spinner and magistrate. The living-in servant household of sixteen was a fairly extensive one for what was presumably a rising middle-class family. Thus for much of the nineteenth century the only real detail of the indoor domestic servants at Dunham given by the census relates to the Platt household.

Before the arrival of the national census in 1841 genealogical sources are largely limited to parish records of baptisms, marriages and burials, which before 1837 were notoriously incomplete. To compound the problem, Cheshire is exceptionally badly served by the main surname index, the International Genealogical Index, so searching for individual servants is impossibly time-consuming. The families of locally born outdoor servants are highly complex, but it has been possible to supplement parish records with a survey of grave inscriptions in Bowdon churchyard, trade directories and a number of wills.

Later, in the twentieth century, the evidence of written archives is supplemented by oral records. Staff associated with Dunham Massey have recorded interviews with retired servants or with relations of the Grey family who visited the house as children. These have provided a useful injection of that element of the experiential which is so difficult to find in other sources, to answer the question: what was it actually like to work at Dunham? This is particularly true of the reminiscences of Minnie Hulme, who as a young girl in the 1930s worked at Dunham as a housemaid.

* * *

This book is the result of interplay between a variety of sources, especially between material goods and more conventional documentary methods. The scope and structure have been dictated by sources which are in some instances richly detailed and in others frustratingly impoverished. It is important to find a balance between mere description and more thoughtful explanation of patterns and their significance.

Like our ripples in a pool, the scope of the study gradually widened as practical research progressed. The original idea for the book identified 'household' with the physical structure of the house itself. To this was added firstly the kitchen garden and later the home farm, both important elements in household food supplies. Consideration of the home farm inevitably led on to inclusion of the park administration and to the outside contractors and suppliers. The line was drawn at the tenanted estates, which are not included within the concept of the Dunham household, though sometimes individual tenants appear in other categories. Very broadly, the structure of the book follows this expanding pattern.

To counterbalance this lateral spread, the focus has been restricted chronologically, generally to those years around the time of the death of the 5th Earl of Stamford and the first decade or so of the 6th Earl's regime. This choice was largely a pragmatic one, dictated by the survival of records. The 1820s and 1830s was a time when the house was operating at a high level, with both Earls taking an active role in record-keeping and management. The focus is not a blinkered one, though, and comparative material from both an earlier and a later date will help set the context throughout.

In Chapter Two the book focuses upon the 'domestic offices', the term often used in literature of the eighteenth and nineteenth centuries to denote service interiors.

LEFT: Dunham Massey's kitchen court, looking towards the kitchen from the main service entrance.

These have been keyed into a plan (p.27), so that the chapter can be used as a sort of guide around this part of the house. Because interiors underwent change and refurbishment, this section is tied only in the loosest way to our chosen time-frame.

In Chapter Three, when attention turns to the size and structure of the full-time servant staff, sheer scale dictates a more vigorous restriction of timescale. So many people were involved in the management of Dunham that to follow their every path over the years becomes impractical, even if the records had survived to make it possible. A snapshot focuses therefore on one short period, the two or three years at the beginning of the 6th Earl's tenure, following the death of his father in 1819. Surviving lists of servants enable us to explore issues such as hierarchy, recruitment, mobility and rewards.

In the following three chapters the viewpoint focuses even more closely on a single year. Because the 6th Earl was a careful housekeeper busy in 1822 with building alterations, the records are particularly complete, providing a richness of texture missing at other times. Accounts, stock books and consumption books from house steward, housekeeper, butler, land steward, gardener and miller are all available. The housekeeper, the house steward and the land steward are the three major players at the senior level. Each is taken in turn and the accounts of their work in this one year analysed through a wealth of detail.

Through these three senior members of staff we make the acquaintance of the many individuals connected with the community of the household. Chapter Seven uses sources from the Stamford archives at both the John Rylands Library and Enville, local trade directories, parish records, wills and graveyard inscriptions to lift a few of these people from obscurity, revealing something of the nature of the ties which bound them to the great house.

Having concentrated mainly on the early decades of the nineteenth century, the ultimate chapter brings Dunham into the twentieth century. How did it survive? The modernisation scheme which took place in 1906 provides part of the answer and oral records show something of the nature of service in the 1930s, when the whole world of the hierarchical country house was winding down.

CHAPTER TWO

'Three maidens, a bench and a stool...'

A Workplace for Servants

The 2nd Earl of Warrington's kitchen court, built around 1720, remains essentially intact today, though the interiors on the west side have been ravaged by disuse for a hundred years or more. By contrast, the great kitchen remained in more continuous use and was regularly repaired over the centuries, usually when a new Earl took charge and brought a new vigour to his custodianship. It was given attention in the 1770s, 1820s, 1830s and 1880s, and a major overhaul in 1906. As in many country houses, outmoded equipment and furniture were rarely thrown away or sold but relegated to the cellars or attics, there to await the respectability conferred by age. Change over time within the workplaces reflected changes in the requirements of the

Dunham Massey, *c.*1697, painted by Adriaen Van Diest, showing the seventeenth-century house and garden before the 2nd Earl began his improvements, including the construction of the kitchen court.

family as well as in fashion, expectation and technical innovation. Rooms are therefore puzzles to be unravelled – how have they developed over the years and what does change signify? For this reason, the time-frame of this chapter is more loosely focused than later, following the development of the site from before the 2nd Earl built his new court to the period on which we will concentrate, the first half of the nineteenth century.

We have a brief description of the kitchen at Dunham Massey in 1410–11, which tells us that it was separate from the main house but connected by a timber-roofed, screened passageway, the kitchen itself being roofed with stone.[12] There is only the sketchiest of evidence enabling us to place the domestic interiors at Dunham between this time and the 1720s, and nothing remains of these early offices except the seventeenth-century water-mill. Our information for this period comes mainly from three somewhat enigmatic sources: a painting dated around 1697 by Van Diest now hanging in the Great Gallery, an engraving by Kip of a painting by Leonard Knyff of the same date now hanging at the foot of the Crimson Staircase, and one probate inventory taken at the death of Henry Booth, 1st Earl of Warrington, in 1693–4.[13] This listed a total of fifty-nine rooms, twenty of which were workrooms. Facilities for food preparation were fairly sophisticated, consisting of a main kitchen, a pantry and mealhouse for the storage of dry goods, a scullery for the cleaning and storage of pots and pans, a pastry for baking, and two larders for the preparation and storage of fresh and salted meat. There was also a still house for making drinks, cordials and medications, a brew-house and a slaughterhouse.

In a medieval house the traditional site of the food service rooms would have been

Engraving by Johannes Kip, from a painting by Leonard Knyff, showing the house and formal garden in 1697. The kitchen court was built on the site of the orangery and adjacent formal garden.

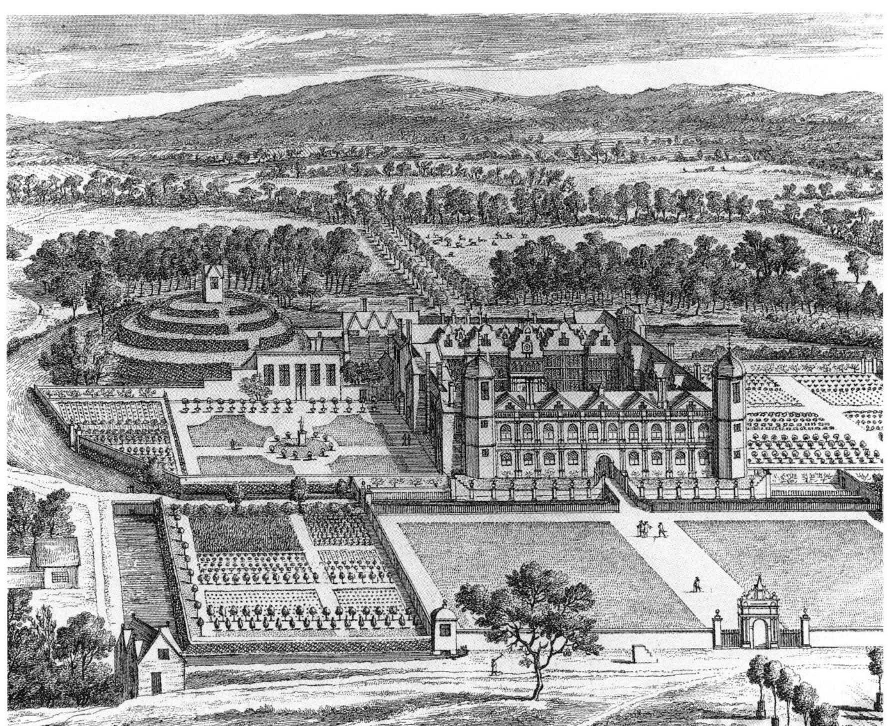

at the opposite side of the main entrance passage to the Great Hall. The old house at Dunham Massey was built probably around 1600, and consisted of a great hall flanked by two forward-projecting wings. Sometime around the 1650s, 'Young' Sir George Booth built a southern wing which joined up with the side wings to form a courtyard house. The original block of the house thus became a north wing. This evolution would position the kitchen somewhere in the north-west corner of the house. For reasons of noise, smell and fire safety, the more specialist food-processing areas such as the brew-house, bakehouse and butchery would have been in separate buildings in the same area.

Both the Van Diest and the Knyff pictures lend support to this theoretical positioning. They show that to the west of the main house, on the site of the later kitchen court, there was a formal parterre garden. West and south of the parterre there were walled kitchen gardens, whilst on the north side, where the kitchen is now, was an orangery and behind that a separate row of modest gabled buildings. It seems likely that this last was a pavilion housing the processing areas. A close-up of the Knyff drawing shows a blank wall on the ground floor of the north-west corner of the main house which may be the outside wall of the old kitchen, with two windows at first-floor level giving ventilation above a great fireplace. On the other hand, the kitchen itself may have been moved out into the separate pavilion at the rear. In any case, there appears to be a small court between the main house and the pavilion, with a wall and trees at the front, perhaps an early and smaller version of a domestic court. This seems a likely proposition. Dunham Massey has a long tradition of conservative change rather than radical upheaval and the idea of a more modest predecessor to the present court appeals.

It seems likely therefore that when the 2nd Earl of Warrington built the new kitchen court around 1720 he was expanding an older concept. The idea of arranging domestic interiors around a yard was a highly successful one adopted by many country-house architects over time. Not only did it make good use of light and space, but it allowed for appropriate forms of supervision. Because the court itself provided access, interiors like the dairy and laundry could be self-contained units with no internal linking corridor necessary. This not only saved space but also made for less time-wasting between lower servants, as well as enabling discreet supervision from the windows of the offices of the senior staff and from the private apartments of the Earl on the first floor. The seniors' offices themselves were linked internally by corridors, allowing more private communication between senior staff. They were accommodated in the east wing of the court which was also the west flank of the main house. Butlers and footmen who came into personal contact with the family were based in the adjacent part of the main house. These areas thus formed an inner service area separate from the outer service area, which provided accommodation for the more menial and smelly functions. It is noticeable that the steward's office commanded the critical point of both internal and external communications, near to the main entrance to the court and therefore easily accessible from outside, but equally convenient for the main house. By contrast, the housekeeper's room in the middle of the east wing commanded only the internal flow into the main house. A detailed analysis of the work of these two senior members of staff will show whether

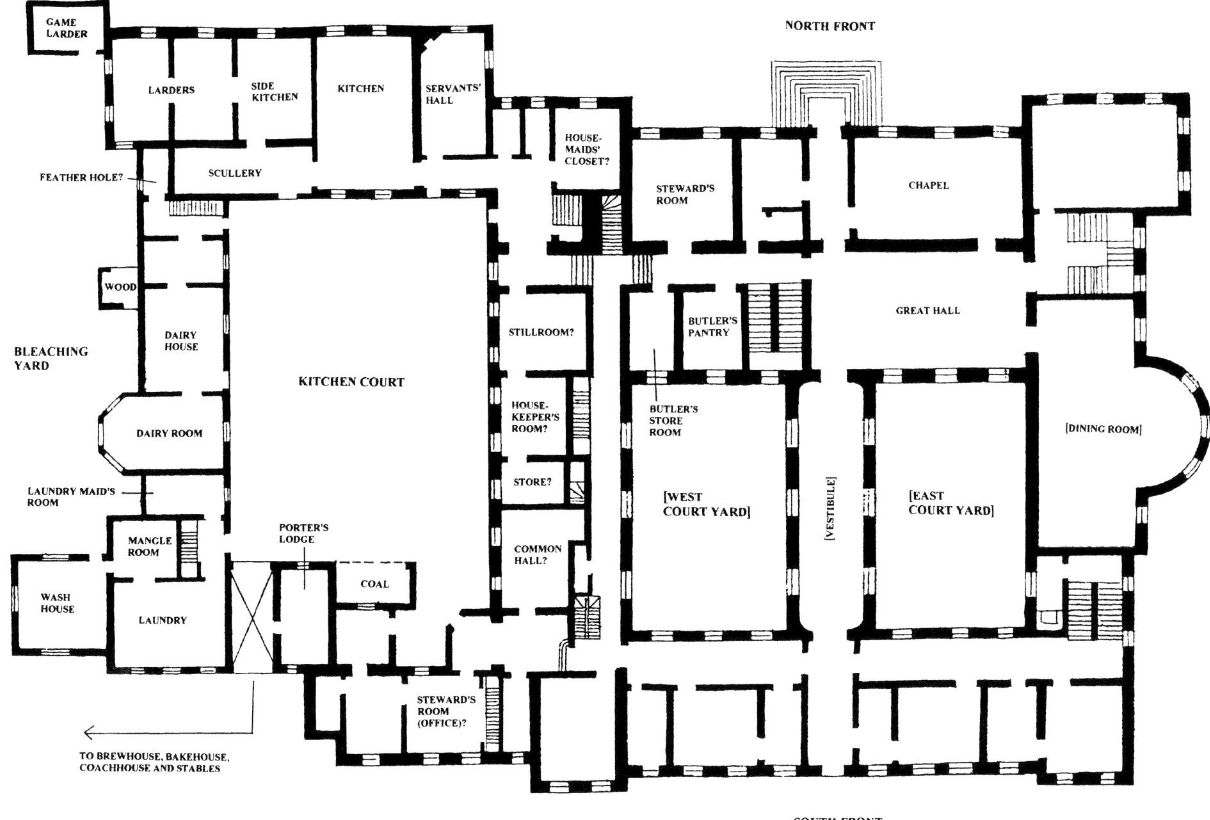

The ground floor of Dunham Massey, *c.*1820. The room functions are taken from the 1819 inventory. Those with question marks are tentative attributions. Square brackets indicate the 1822–3 alterations.

there was a perceptible distinction between the 'internal' and the 'external' as regards their responsibilities as well as their physical position in the house layout.

The way workplaces relate to each other can reveal more about the hierarchy of the household than can their contents in isolation. The layout of domestic service blocks was influenced by many different considerations. It is often pointed out that domestic offices were divided along lines of gender, men's work areas being kept separate from those of the women.[14] This principle appears to operate to some extent at Dunham, with the housekeeper's quarters and other female areas in the east and west wings, separate from the cluster of butlers' rooms in the main house. Yet issues of status and communication seem to inform the layout at Dunham as much as gender and certainly more than functionalism. It is a far cry from the beautifully planned inner service yard based on the technical requirements of different interiors that was provided in the 1830s by Charles Barry at Trentham in Staffordshire.[15]

The contact point between inner and outer service areas was a real issue during the building of the kitchen court itself. The problem was that of connecting the new court to an older house which was itself due to be rebuilt a few years later. In the first phase the court finished at the main chimney wall of the kitchen, as shown by the bricked-up window openings above the fireplace. There must have been a narrow gap separating the new kitchen from the older, inner service rooms. The connecting room, the servants' hall, was not built until work on the house itself was carried out in the 1730s, and evidence of this can be seen in the break in brickwork on both the courtyard frontage and the back elevation. When this second phase finally took place, the kitchen became fully connected and the windows were blocked up. It was at this stage that the gallery was inserted into the upper part of the kitchen, allowing inspection by steward and family without disruption to the work below. Details of a picture by John Harris dated 1750 show the finished arrangement (see p.49).

Steward's Rooms

Until the mid-nineteenth century, the house steward's quarters were the central pivot of the functional structure of the Dunham household. There must have been such a centre in the seventeenth-century house, but it is not listed in the 1693–4 inventory. In both the 1758 and the 1819 inventories two rooms were assigned to him, each of which had very different functions.[16] The room simply called 'the Steward's Room' was the dining room for the senior servants, in line with the traditional separation of the managerial from the menial staff. In 1758 this was furnished with three tables and twenty-four walnut chairs, a large mirror, clock and with the walls lined with pictures. Fifty years later it was slightly more luxurious, with carpet and curtains, a large oak dining-table and chairs, several small oak tables, a corner cupboard, a plate-warmer, salt box and both ebony- and ivory-handled silver cutlery.

According to the 1758 inventory, the steward worked from an office which was separate from his bedchamber. Fitted with a writing-table and drawers, this was clearly his private work space where he kept abreast of accounts and cash. His bedchamber was some way away in the south wing of the house. When a new steward called John Poole arrived at Dunham in 1819 he was given accommodation befitting his status: a comfortable room with carpet, fireplace and hearth rug, the windows dressed with both curtains and blinds. At one end there was a four-poster bedstead and hangings with a high-quality feather bed, a wardrobe, washstand and jug and a looking-glass. At the other end of the room he was provided with two desks, a bookcase, a corner cupboard and a barometer. No doubt it looked very old-fashioned and dark, for a couple of years later the oak wainscotting was removed, the walls replastered to a dado and a better carpet was brought from upstairs.[17]

Housekeeper's Rooms

In neither 1693–4 nor 1758 was there mention of the housekeeper's room as such, and it is possible that the still room doubled as her workroom. By 1819 the housekeeper, then an ailing Mrs Princep, was a major presence in the house, with three rooms attributed to her. One was a store for spare furniture and another was clearly her private bedroom and apartment, outside which stood a large cupboard full of glass and china. Even in 1758, the bedroom was furnished to a higher standard than the steward's, with a four-poster bed fitted with blue and white embroidered curtains and window curtains of a plaid pattern. Later the walls were papered with a pretty blue and white floral design. She had several tables, including a good walnut writing-table, and both a dressing-glass (a full-length swivel mirror) and a hanging mirror. In 1758 she was the only servant to have the luxury of an oak chest-of-drawers in which

The kitchen wing today. The join in the brickwork, where the new kitchen of the 1720s was attached to the main house, can be seen to the left of the right-hand door.

to store her clothes. She also had a number of chairs, a stool and a close-(closet) stool in her room. To warm her she had a fireplace with a full set of fire-irons.

The third housekeeper's room was her main workroom. In 1819 it was fitted up with a cast-iron hob grate, carpet, hearth rug and good mahogany furniture, a writing desk with drawers, two tables, a clock, a bookcase, fifteen chairs of various types, a draughtboard and fire-screens. Here was a place to keep up-to-date with paperwork, interview servants and offer visiting tradesmen a drink of wine.

Housemaids' Closet and Pantry

When walking around a country house we have difficulty in 'seeing' the housemaids' work. Unlike the laundry-maid or the kitchen staff, housemaids' work was done in the house itself, as quietly and as unobtrusively as possible. In the nineteenth century most houses, however, provided the housemaids with a main store, usually called the housemaids' pantry, and smaller rooms or stores on the main bedroom floors, called housemaids' closets. This last was the older term and in the early inventories at Dunham this was the name used for the main store, which was situated on the first floor. Not until 1883 does the name 'Housemaids' Pantry' appear on the inventory list.

Both the 1758 and the 1819 inventories give a good idea of the range of jobs done by the housemaids. In the closet was the standard servants' furniture, table, chairs, and a mirror to check that she looked clean and smart. It was also a store for all the equipment she needed for her work. She had to clean fireplaces and light the fires; one of the later inventories has spare grate bars in the stores. She had to service the toilet facilities in the dressing rooms, empty chamber-pots, slop the washing and shaving water into slop pails and clean the jugs and basins. Thus her closet was well provided with items of 'toilet ware' and brass kettles or water-cans for taking clean water to the bedrooms. She cleaned the rooms, swept the carpets with a hand brush every morning and rubbed the wooden floors. She was responsible for candles and candlesticks, both upright ones and the chamber-sticks issued to members of the family to light their way to bed.

The nature of the candlesticks in particular is revealing. The inventories show that those in the care of the housemaids were brass or japanned metal, never silver. The housemaids' job was the basic cleanliness of the downstairs rooms, the servicing of the upstairs floors and the seasonal care of furniture. Strangely, the housemaids were not responsible for the routine cleaning of valuable downstairs furniture and fittings when the family was in residence. The polishing of silver, whether candlesticks or cutlery, was in the hands of the footmen and butler. This was men's work, as was the routine care of cut glass, mirrors, picture frames and mahogany, gilt and ormolu furniture, as well as the tidying of desks. When the family departed Dunham each season, the butler and his footmen would carefully store away the glass and wrap the silver in baize bags and place them in the safe before they themselves left. The maids who remained would give a thorough clean to all the rooms and their contents, including the furniture, after which every piece was shrouded in dust covers made from Holland linen, cut and sewn to fit each individual piece, even the window drapery and pelmets. Immediately before the next visit was due the covers in the family rooms were removed, those in the public rooms (used for entertaining) being left until guests arrived. Once the family was back in residence, the household reverted to the demarcation between cleaning by housemaids and cleaning by footmen.

Not only was housework structured along lines of gender, but each individual housemaid had her own area within the house, defined according to experience and status. The 1st housemaid had more complex interiors to clean than the 2nd or 3rd, and the 4th learnt her trade by cleaning servants' rooms. The rougher work, such as scrubbing floors and cleaning fireplaces, was done only by the lower-ranking maids. This was brought out very clearly in reminiscences of the 1930s by a housemaid at Dunham, but no doubt the system then in operation had altered very little from previous years.[18] Each hour of each day was scheduled, enforcing a rigorous, unchanging routine which made sure that every room in the house was given appropriate attention, as illustrated in the written timetables which were handed to servants when they took up work.

The Still Rooms

At Dunham the workplace known as the still room appeared in all the inventories. Traditionally this was very much within the domain of the housekeeper rather than the kitchen staff and it seems to have been always situated adjacent to the housekeeper's room and china store in the east wing of the kitchen court. Even in the earliest inventory, 1693–4, the still room was next to the housekeeper's store of 'cheany ware', the combined value of which was put at £200. In the 1758 and 1819 inventories there was also a room called a 'Stilling Room', later called the still house, clearly separate from the still room, probably situated on the opposite side of the court near to the dairy and further away from the main house. The reasons for this duplication become obvious when the contents and functions of the two offices are considered.

In origin, the still house was the older of the two and existed in English country houses from Elizabethan to Georgian times.[19] This was the distilling room, fitted with a furnace and a variety of stills for the extraction of the essential oils, flavours and medicinal properties from herbs, flowers, seeds and roots. The early versions were a detached or semi-detached building, relatively isolated because of the problem of smells, security and risk of fire. A still house was not mentioned in the 1693–4 inventory of Dunham, though in 1758 it was well equipped, with four cold or 'common' stills for making simple flower and herb waters such as orangewater and rosewater, which were widely used to flavour sweet dishes, and one hot still for distilling alcoholic spirits.

The still house was certainly in use in the 1740s, when the housekeeper bought poppies to make sedatives, and in 1774 when it was given a major refurbishment. New oak floorboards and a new hearthstone were fitted and a bricklayer's bill paid.[20] It probably remained until the early nineteenth century. According to the 1819 inventory it had some basic furniture, a still and forty-eight bottles of vinegar, which might well have been home-made. But even in 1758 the inventory included a clue to the later development of the still house, for one of its contents was a sweetmeat cupboard.

BELOW LEFT: A cold or 'common' still and furnace, from A. Cooper, *The Complete Distiller*, 1757. Despite its name, the cold still required gentle heat, either from being fitted into the top of a furnace or stood in a warm-water bath. It was used for making simple flower and herb waters, which were widely used to flavour sweet dishes.

BELOW RIGHT: A hot still used for making alcoholic distillations, from J. H. Walsh, *A Manual of Domestic Economy*, 1857. After heating, rapid cooling was needed to condense the alcoholic vapours. This was done using a serpentine tube, usually called a 'worm', immersed in a barrel of cold water. Hence this arrangement came to be called a 'worm tub'.

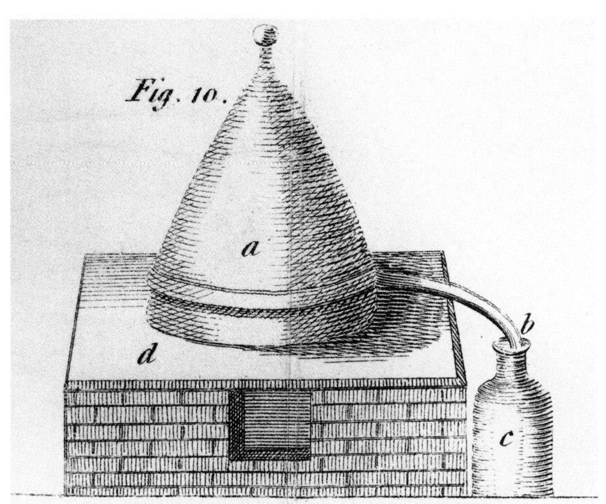

A still house with stills and furnaces near the door, from N. Bailey, *Dictionarium Domesticum*, 1736.

As the world became more commercialised, great households became less self-reliant and more inclined to buy cookery ingredients from the grocer and medicines from the apothecary. The skills of the distiller were forgotten by housekeepers and the function of the still room moved more and more to that of making sweetmeats, biscuits, delicate cakes, fruit conserves and the new high-status drinks, tea, coffee and chocolate. At the same time the still-room maid's function changed subtly to take on the role of personal assistant to the housekeeper. By the nineteenth century she had become the supplier and organiser of small-scale meals, freeing the main kitchen to concentrate on dinner. The still room, for example, made up the early-morning calling trays, colour-coded to the décor of each bedroom, on which footmen and housemaids delivered tea and bread and butter to the family bedrooms. The still-room maid also made most of the ingredients for the new mid-afternoon meal of tea – sandwiches, conserves, small cakes, biscuits and the tea itself.

We can see these functions reflected in the changing inventories of the Dunham still room. By 1758 it contained an oven and hearth, equipment for making tea, coffee and chocolate, for weighing ingredients, for making jam and pastry and 'plates to bake cakes on'. In the 1758 inventory there was also mentioned a second 'nearer Still Room' which by 1819 had become a store room for the housekeeper.

The brushing room at Penrhyn Castle, Gwynedd. Inventories of Dunham do not identify a separate brushing room until 1883, and in the eighteenth century clothes brushing equipment was kept in the servants' hall. By 1833 the brushing room must have been sizeable as William Torry noted that the servants dined in there because of a fall of soot in the servants' hall.

Butlers and Footmen

The early inventories of the butler's pantry at Dunham show that at that time the butler's role primarily involved the serving of food and drink. In 1758 his pantry was equipped for the washing and storage of tableware and napkins, whilst the 1819 inventory listed in detail the drinking-glasses. Like the silver, glass was removed from the table to the butler's pantry for washing and was not entrusted to the scullery. Adjacent to the pantry would be a plate room fitted with cupboards and a silver safe for the more valuable pieces.

The butler's pantry was a base not only for the butler himself but also for under-butlers and footmen. Under-butlers were simply assistant butlers, primarily concerned with food presentation and the reception of visitors. Footmen were lower in the hierarchy than under-butlers and like them they served meals, but they were also personal servants who inherited from the past a variety of other jobs: 'waiting' on the family, carriage duty, answering the calling-bells, delivering messages, cleaning silver, glass and furniture, and valeting for junior male members of the family.[21] Theirs too was the job of cleaning the family's outdoor clothing. Footmen and valets would work hard all evening, staying up until midnight or later, sponging, drying and brushing, and then getting up before dawn to work on the nap of the

1

Bell-pulls

Line drawing of a bell-pull system adapted from Cassell's *Household Guide*, showing both the lever pull mechanism (A), usually sited to one side of the fireplace, the crank (B), fitted in the wall, enabling the wire to change direction, and the bell (C) with its long, horizontal, spiral spring (D).* Fitting such a system was a major upheaval as the wires had to be embedded underneath the plaster. Lilian Bond remembered the bells at Tyneham: 'Along the lobby wall the house bells hung in a row, each with coiled metal spring and metal crank above it and the name of its room in painted letters below... When one was set in motion, its rattling and grating squeaks were audible in all the rooms along its route ... they never went out of order and ... were not dependent on an evanescent battery. They could be recognized by their individual tongues, or, failing that, by the plainly visible swinging of the bell itself.'† Experiments show that a bell will keep moving for ten minutes after being rung.

At Dunham there were two sets of bells. One served the south end of the house, one the north end. They were strategically placed so that they could be heard in both male and female workplaces as well as the Servants' Hall. The wire-operated bells were replaced by an electric system in 1906.

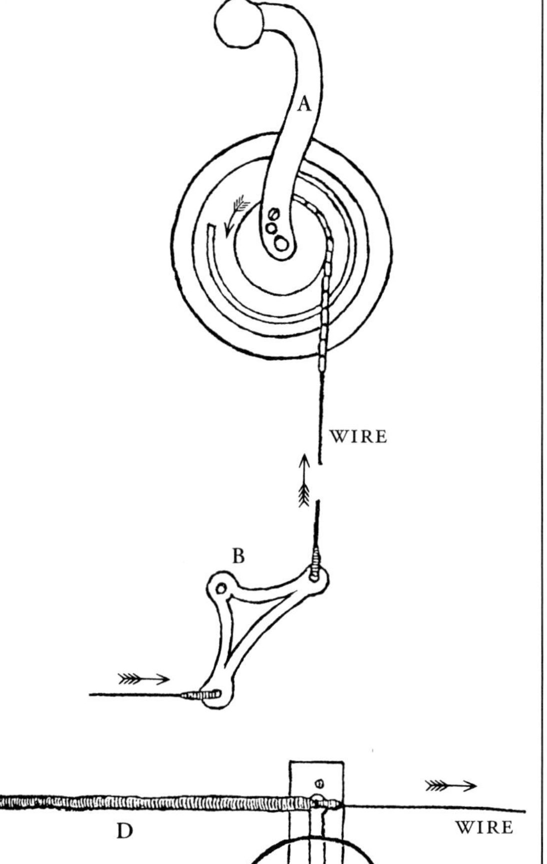

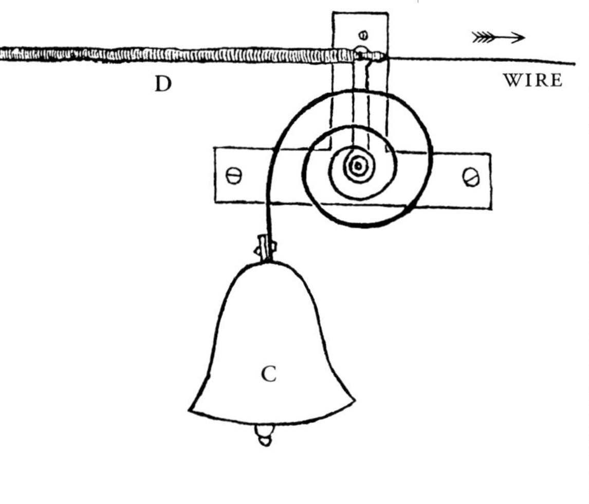

Bell-pulls at Dunham Massey in 1830

A list from EGR 4/2/12/9/17

ROOMS	NUMBER OF BELLS
Stairfoot Room	1
Velvet Room	1
Lord and Lady Grey's Rooms	3
Maroon Bedroom	1
Dressing Room to above	1
West Apartments	2
Chintz Room	1
Lord Grey's Room	1
Lord Stamford's Bedroom	1
South Apartments	2
Museum	1
South-West Bedroom	1
Dressing Room to above	1
South Bedroom	1
Dressing Room to above	1
Blue Bedroom	1
Dressing Room to above	1
Billiard Room	1
Chaplain's Room	1

* Cassell's *Household Guide*, Vol. 1 (Cassell, Petter and Galpin ed, n.d.), p.181.

† Lilian Bond, *Tyneham: a Lost Heritage* (Dovecote Press, 1956), p.27.

cloth. In the early days this was carried out in the common hall but later many Victorian households provided a separate room for brushing. A 'Brushing Room' is mentioned at Dunham in 1833 when the servants had to dine there because of a fall of soot in the servants' hall, and the name also appears in the 1883 inventory.[22]

An inner corridor connected the corner of the kitchen court with the butler's area and the main house. In the 1758 inventory this was called the 'Fire Engine Corridor' and was an important communications centre for the house, as it contained the internal bell-pull system (Box 1, opposite). It also housed the fire engine. As early as 1819 the house owned a hand-operated water-pump with leather hoses, probably the one which now stands under the laundry stairs. A full complement of thirty-six leather fire buckets hung on pegs above the engine. Manned by a team of menservants and estate labourers, the machine was used primarily for the protection of the house and estate, no doubt turning out when the laundry roof caught fire in 1824 and the farm hayrick burnt down the following year.[23] But the engine and its crew also assisted at any fire in the locality. In 1814, for example, it was sent to help fight a serious fire on Hale Moss. The turf on the Moss had been deliberately set ablaze to a considerable depth by some boys and it took a while to extinguish it.[24]

Another corridor ran the length of the east wing, and off this opened a number of closets or small rooms. One was probably the powder closet of the 1758 inventory. It contained two wig stands, a wig block and a powder tray, equipment for the storage, repair and powdering of wigs. At this date, wigs were fashionable for general wear and all senior servants, both male and female, and the footmen would have worn grey powdered wigs when on duty. From this developed the long tradition of powdering footmen's own hair which lasted well into the twentieth century, being retained even when their formal wear was a morning suit.[25]

The Servants' Hall

The servants' hall was the social and recreational centre of the indoor servants' world. It defined more clearly than any other interior who was inside the household and who was outside. The coachman, for example, was included, but other outdoor servants, gardeners and farm labourers, were excluded. A servants' hall as such was not mentioned in the pre-1720 house, but there was a 'Common Hall', a name which was left over from the time when the medieval 'Great Hall' was the common living-area for the whole household. It had a large oak table and forms for dining, pegs to hang clothes on and a stand on which to brush uniforms. In the 1720 rebuilding the room underwent a radical repositioning and renaming. The last part of the kitchen court to be finished, the new servants' hall, slotted in east of the kitchen, connecting it to the main building. Here it stayed until 1906.

In 1758 the servants' hall had a hob-type fireplace and was lit with glass sconces (wall-mounted candle-holders) and furnished with a long dining-table and forms, around which the servants sat in order of gender and rank. Food records show that large quantities of meat were consumed by the servants, probably in the form of roasts, and a carving set was provided for this, wielded by the senior male servant present who would sit in the only armchair at the head of the table. Meat continued to be issued even when the family was away from Dunham, though by general traditional practice the servants were not entitled to full board in such circumstances, but were paid board wages. These were cash sums of several shillings a week, variable according to status, in lieu of meal and drink allowances. Whilst on board wages, servants had control over their own food arrangements. Sometimes they pooled their cash and paid a kitchen-maid to cater for them. Sometimes, however, they fed themselves singly or in small groups. Either way it was useful to have the means of making snack meals and the fireplace was equipped with a salamander for toasting cheese or bread.

The 1819 inventory shows that the servants ate from pewter plates and dishes, then too old-fashioned for any other use. They also had use of a wagon, a miniature wheeled tray which was pushed up and down the centre of the table, carrying a coopered barrel (probably the 'wooden can' of the inventory) which contained the meal's ale allowance. These are commonly found in hall inventories within large servant households, but they have rarely survived in actuality. Dunham's now sits slightly incongruously in the south corridor. As the barrel passed along the table, each servant helped themselves, pouring the ale into horn or copper cups or 'jacks'.[26] This method of distribution was a traditional one, ensuring the allowance was meted out fairly and no one could surreptitiously take more than they were allowed. By 1819 the allowance would probably have been about a pint of ale at dinner for the men and half that amount for women, plus more generous amounts of weaker beer.[27]

The Kitchen

The most important of the surviving domestic offices at Dunham, and the one most redolent of the past, is the kitchen and its ancillary rooms. The earliest inventory, of course, relates not to this room but to its seventeenth-century predecessor, of which little is known. Only high-status goods such as jewellery were listed individually in

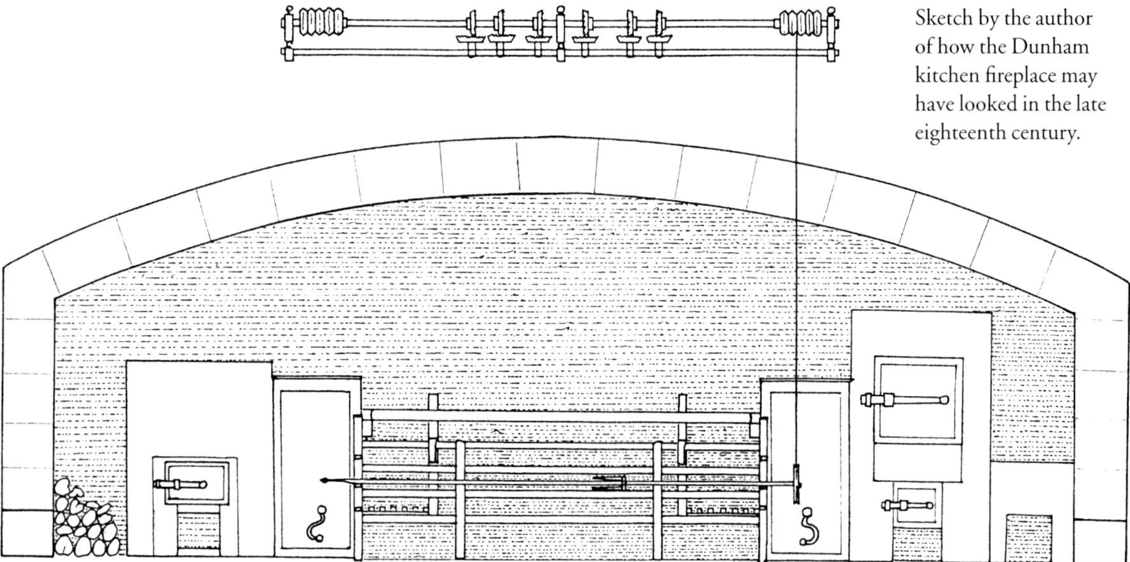

Sketch by the author of how the Dunham kitchen fireplace may have looked in the late eighteenth century.

The kitchen at Kedleston Hall, Derbyshire, built *c.*1760, shows a similar structure to that at Dunham Massey. In the photograph taken in the 1920s, a 'hastener' can be seen standing in front of the fireplace.

the 1693–4 inventory so that for utilitarian metalware we have to be content with the usual tradition of giving valuations by weight. The utensils throughout the house reflect the fashion and metal technology of the late seventeenth century, especially a reliance on brassware and pewter rather than copperware and iron. Goods in the kitchen were valued at £20, but the copperware saucepans were valued separately, 28lb at 5s per pound, a total of £7 worth. Two copper cisterns were valued at £10 and three warming-pans £1, giving a total value of copperware in the house of £18. By contrast, the total brassware in the house was valued at over £31 and the pewter at over £36. With a much lower value-per-pound weight than the copper, both of these must have been numerous. An item at the very end of the inventory mentions ironware such as jacks, sieves and shovels, valued at only £5. So the majority of the utilitarian fittings around the house such as candlesticks, basins, pots, chamber-pots and closet-stool pans were made of brass and pewter. The copper was limited to items which would be heated, while the limited development of iron-smelting technology meant that there were very few iron goods.

An inventory of the new kitchen taken in 1758 at the death of George Booth, the 2nd Earl, provides more detail, and from it we can reconstruct a fairly full picture. The floor was of stone flags. In the centre of the main fireplace arch, which spans twenty-three feet, there was a huge open range, made up of a wide bar grate, probably flanked by two cast-iron hobs. Above the grate was fitted a smoke-driven fan built into a small chamber within the chimney itself. This powered a set of jack chains, the drive for a choice of four spits. The heat thrown into the room from the fire would have been intense, so it was reflected back on itself by a movable screen (usually called a 'hastener' but in the Dunham inventories called a 'haster') which could be wheeled in front of the fire. This was made of wood but lined with tin and fitted with shelves. Besides acting as a reflector it served as a hot cupboard for cooked food, plates and serving dishes. Between the fire and the haster were the iron spits for roasting meat, turning slowly above a huge copper dripping-pan which stood on the floor. All the other bits and pieces needed to service the fire stood nearby, shovels, fire-tongs, pokers and a rack to hold the spits when not in use.

The open range was used primarily for roasting and the records of the housekeeper's work show just how important meat, especially beef, was in the household diet (see Chapter Four). The quantity consumed was prodigious. The aristocratic lifestyle of the Booths and Greys, however, demanded a sophisticated level of cooking, requiring delicate sauces, gravies and glazes, so to supplement the roasting equipment the kitchen was fitted with a length of small charcoal hearths set into a worktop, rather like a set of barbecue grids. These were used for saucepan cooking, simmering and frying. The 1758 inventory includes a set of twelve trivets to stand on top of the grids as supports for copper pans. Charcoal stoves have survived in the large recessed arch opposite the main fireplace, but if these are the original ones they have been altered substantially since. It is even possible that sometime in the late eighteenth or early nineteenth century the stoves were moved to their present site from under the window, though their position within a recessed arch is similar to those in the Windsor Great Kitchen.

The suite of copper pans listed in the 1758 inventory was impressive though not outrageously extravagant. It clearly represents an expansion from the copper in the old kitchen and there were also more iron implements such as gridirons, tongs, forks and skewers. The kitchen still possessed the earlier items of brass and pewter and there is also a quantity of tinware. More pieces of metalware were added to the inventory nine years later, a few copper saucepans, stockpots and moulds, and long-handled iron spoons for basting the roasts. In 1758, the furniture in the new kitchen consisted of two tables, two dressers, a cupboard, a chair for the chef and stools for the rest of the kitchen staff, and various other functional items such as a pestle and mortar and a chest for storing salt. The present mortar is probably one bought later in 1790. Most importantly for the chef was a clock mounted high up on the wall, complete with ladder for access.

By 1819 we see levels of comfort in the kitchen improving and more equipment being fitted. There were, for example, fewer stools and more chairs for the staff. The two tables had been replaced by one long one, but not, however, by the table which survives, which is later. The basic cooking technology had been refined. There was still an open bar grate for roasting, with jacks, spits and hastener, but an item in the house steward's accounts for 1774 records the purchase of 'three hundred fire Bricks for Kitchen fireplace', indicating a major refit. Around the same time the floor was reflagged and shortly afterwards two new grates were purchased for the room, along with a new smoke-jack and new cord for the spit-drive.[28] According to the 1819 inventory the kitchen also had an iron oven, with its own furnace underneath, and a boiler. These could all have been part of a new fireplace, installed around 1770, which incorporated a new central bar grate as well as an oven and side boiler. Bits of this may well have survived to be depicted in a photograph taken of the kitchen in the 1880s. (p.177) This shows a late nineteenth-century 'closed' range replacing the

RIGHT: The kitchen at Dunham Massey, looking south towards the kitchen court and showing the inspection gallery.

open bar grate, but flanking the range are hot closets and ovens, some of which carry the distinctive early decoration still seen today on the stoves on the west side of the kitchen. The thinness of the existing cast-iron plates, their embellishment and the plain edges to the bottom archways of the stoves suggest a late eighteenth-century date, though they have certainly been substantially repaired and modernised since, as the bottom arches show bricks of a much later period.[29] In short, it seems likely that the kitchen underwent a major modernisation around 1770, which involved the fitting of a new range complete with bar grate, smoke jack, oven and boiler, a run of cast-iron charcoal stoves, a hotplate in an adjacent archway, and a new flagged floor. According to the 1819 inventory the smaller equipment seems largely unchanged, though much of the existing pewter dates from this period, bought by the 5th Earl. An innately conservative but practical man who clung to the old ways, he perhaps bought unfashionable pewter for servant use as a means of reducing breakages.

On the death of the 5th Earl, minor refurbishment of the domestic offices was carried out during the period 1822 to 1825. A new iron oven was fitted up somewhere, and more pieces were added to both the copper and the pewter collections. The kitchen itself was whitewashed and the cupboards were painted to simulate dark mahogany, then fashionable.[30] A new hastener was bought in 1839 and a new centre table in 1840, a date which is cut into the end of the present table.[31] This measures 3ft 8in wide by over 12ft long, with two drawers in the sides, a pair of cutlery drawers at one end and a lower shelf for saucepan storage. A long work-table like this was central to the organisation of the kitchen routine throughout the Victorian period. Different menus for the family, nursery and servants were prepared by different kitchen staff at separate work stations on the table.

Bills from the estate blacksmith to the housekeeper show how much maintenance was needed to keep a traditional roasting-range in good order.[32] In November 1822, when the kitchen was working flat out, Daniel Parsons cleaned and oiled the smoke-jack three times in a month, on the 2nd, 11th and 26th, at a cost each time of 2s 6d for labour and 6s 6d for two flasks of oil. Two years later the jack was replaced with a new one, an awkward job which took two days.[33] Parsons also mended a trivet and repaired five spits, the spit holdfast and rack, a pair of stake tongs and twenty 'squers' (skewers) as well as providing twenty new ones. The chimney-sweep was also required regularly. In 1842, for example, the main kitchen flue was swept twice, at a cost of 7s to the sweep plus 1s to the sweep's boys. The second occasion, in mid-December, was part of the annual sweeping of the house flues, when seventy-three room chimneys were also cleaned at a total cost of £3 15s plus meals.[34]

Ancillary Rooms

The names of some of the ancillary rooms have changed over the years. The original scullery was built at the same time as the kitchen, around 1720, and probably occupied the site of the present scullery. According to the 1758 inventory it contained equipment for washing-up: a lead sink for the disposal of waste water, wooden tubs for washing smaller items, and a boiler for scalding pots and pans and providing hot water. This last was probably sited under the right hand of the two arches at the end

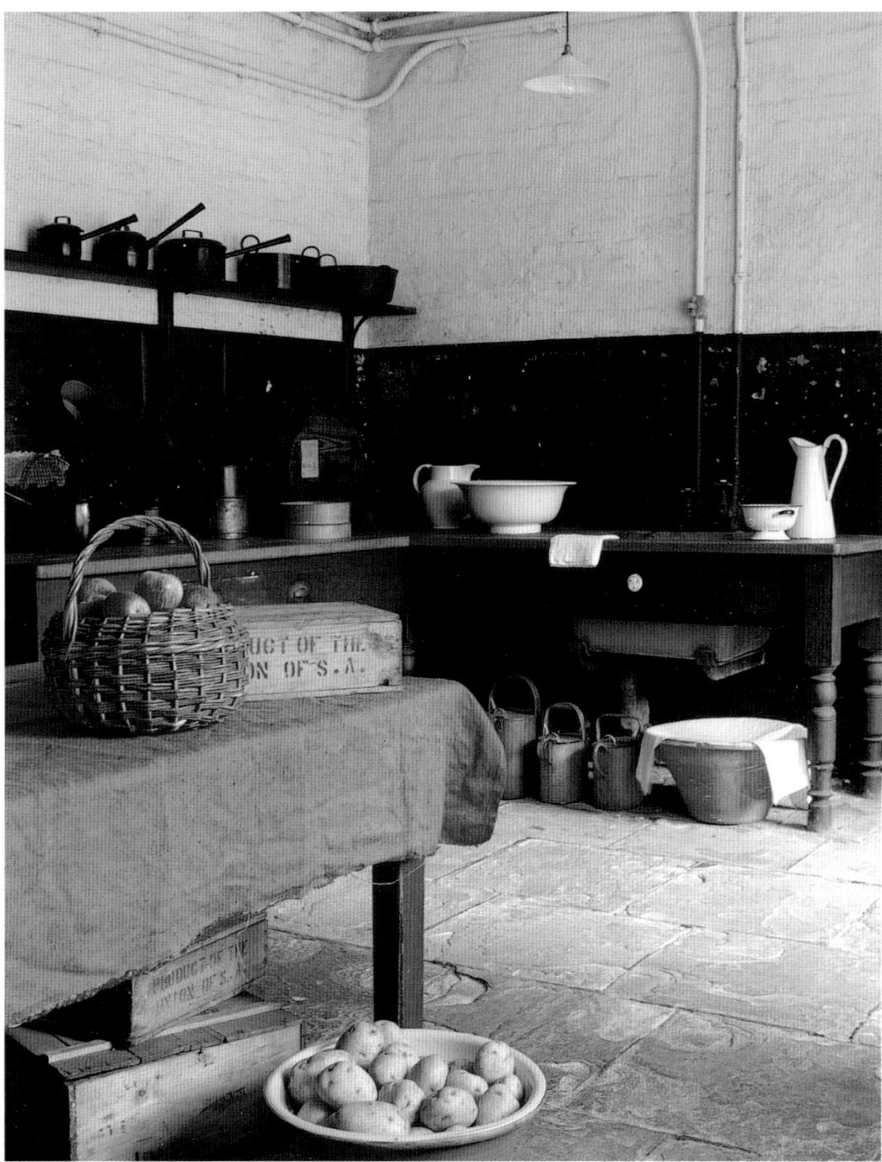

The scullery at Dunham Massey, showing the new sink fitted by Clements Jeakes, *c.*1906.

of the room, now removed to make a corridor. The other arch housed a brick-built oven which survives today, but because it was built into the fabric it has not featured in any of the inventories. The scullery also contained furniture for the storage of metalware. Only cookware and servants' ceramics were stored here; china was stored in the still room. In 1819 we are given one or two extra details about the scullery equipment. One tub collected swill to be taken to the farm to feed pigs whilst the main washing-up tub was oval and probably stood on a wooden bench.

The 1758 inventory also lists items in the pastry, which provided baking facilities for the kitchen, although the main bread-baking was done in a bakehouse adjoining the brew-house. Almost certainly the pastry was sited in what is now called the chef's room. Ovens were not included on the list, but there must have been one as

there were oven peels and an axe for the firewood. The pastry also had facilities for the provision of hot water and small-scale equipment for pastry-making. In 1819 a side kitchen was mentioned for the first time, almost certainly the old pastry, as this was no longer listed. It had a boiler, cistern, tubs and buckets, suggesting it was used as a second scullery of some sort, though the surviving internal window indicates it was used as a chef's room, from which he could both guard the larders and monitor events in the kitchen. A repair bill dated 1822 from the estate blacksmith supports earlier evidence that there was an oven in this room.[35]

In 1758 there were listed an indeterminate number of larders, presumably the two existing at present. They were fitted with tubs for salting meat, hanging storage shelves to protect food from rats and mice, and facilities for jointing, trussing and general meat preparation. By 1819 the first of the two larders mentioned had undergone a decided change and was now more of a storeroom for ceramic tableware for the chef, containing more furniture, tables, chests, shelves, cupboards, plates, serving dishes and cups. Amongst them were only a few 'odd pieces' of plain china, suggesting the rest was earthenware. The inner larder, later known as the meat larder, remained as before, a workroom fitted with stillages, salting and hanging facilities. The substantial framed rack was suspended from the roof crossbeams by metal rods, carrying hooks for cattle and deer carcasses. The room must have been very cool, as the windows were originally covered only with wire, now augmented by glazed shutters on the inside. Even so, air circulation was inadequate, for in 1832, new wooden ventilated partitions were built between the larders and new air grids were put into the outside walls of the meat larder.[36] At the same time a new game larder was built onto the outer north-west corner of the kitchen court, a completely separate building with no internal access to the other larders. It was designed with a well-ventilated coved ceiling to make the most of its height and had a system of wooden and metal pulleys on the walls and ceiling, controlling wooden racks for hanging the game birds. The walls were fitted with 'a range of pheasant hooks'.

Plucking birds of various sorts must have been an endless and aggravating chore and somewhere near the scullery was a 'Feather Hole', a tiny room provided with a form to sit on and a tub for the feathers. These would be collected periodically, sorted, washed in a net or sheet and dried in the scullery oven for use on servant beds.

The Dairy

Nowadays it takes a great leap of the imagination to see through the grime to the sparkling whitewashed suite of the eighteenth and early nineteenth centuries when the Dunham dairy was at its peak. It was made up of two rooms. The larger room was called the 'Dairy House' in 1819 and formed the core of the operation. Here there was a large cast-iron grate complete with a wind-up clockwork jack and two boilers or 'furnace pans', fitted into either side of the fire. One was made of iron for scalding equipment, the other was copper for heating milk for cheese-making. The shelf on the wall opposite the fireplace carried the maturing cheeses. This was also the room where butter was made, and here too the early-rising dairymaids could make their own breakfasts of pancakes or oatcakes on a griddle.

LEFT: The chef's room at Dunham Massey, previously the side kitchen. The wooden screen to the left divides the room from the larders.

Both milk and cheese required long hours of standing and settling and this would be the main function of the room next door, the milk room or 'Dairy Room' of 1819. Here stood the wide but shallow brass and copper settling-pans in which the fresh milk was left to stand so that the cream would separate out to the top. Far from being heated like next door, this room was cooled by cold water standing in the slate sinks. The cream was taken off the top of the pans with brass skimmers and small wooden dishes and then carried through into the dairy house to be churned into butter. At Dunham Massey most of the cream was made into butter. When the household needed to serve fresh cream it had to buy it in from elsewhere. As in other great houses, the cold environment of the dairy room would also be used to make a variety of cold puddings such as junket and ice cream.[37]

The milk which had been skimmed of its cream was made into cheese. In the eighteenth century the Dunham dairy produced four or five Cheshire-style cheeses every week and the inventories list equipment for this: cheese-tubs in which rennet was added to heated milk to make curds, and cheese-vats (in 1758 called 'chesfords') into which the curds were piled. Curds were then weighted, at first by a board on top and then in the two stone presses which stood side by side in a single frame in the dairy house. After pressing, the cheeses were wrapped in muslin and left to mature.

The Dunham dairy was definitely a hard-working enterprise, far from being a fashionable aristocratic plaything, and was much more important in the eighteenth century than in later years (see Chapter Four). For most of the nineteenth century cheese-making ceased, though butter-making continued and was still an important element in kitchen supplies.

The Laundry

Near to the entrance of the kitchen court and further away from the main house than the kitchen or dairy was built another major service area, the laundry. Before 1720, Dunham had two separate 'Landries' and a wash-house, but no record remains of their position except that one was described as being 'higher'. There are no details of contents, apart from the total value, which was £14. The wash-house was probably somewhere near to the moat and its only equipment would be some sort of boiler and individual coopered wash-tubs for steeping, hand-agitating and rinsing, the main processes used by early washerwomen. The wash-house would not be used every week. Washing took the form of large-scale intermittent cleaning of household textiles such as bed, table and kitchen linen, together with the larger and simpler items of personal 'body linen' such as shifts, shirts and underskirts. Before the mid-seventeenth century, washing was a seasonal occurrence organised like many other features of life around the annual quarters, winter, spring, summer and autumn. By the late seventeenth century, in most great houses this had developed into monthly washing, with perhaps an especially large wash in spring and autumn.[38]

After washing, most of the linen would be dried outside, bleached by sun and wind. Household linen such as sheets or tablecloths would not be ironed but simply hand-smoothed and folded in a linen press. High-status linen would be starched and smoothed with irons in one of the laundries. The 'Higher Landry' may well have

The dry laundry at Dunham Massey. In 1822 this looked little different: there were candleholders on hooks in the walls and the windows were curtained. Large items were ironed on the long 'dresser', smaller items on narrow boards propped between the table edge and a chair-back or trestle.

been in the house itself, on one of the upper floors, convenient for the washing and ironing of small items of personal linen by the lady's maid or the valet. Even in the realm of laundering there was a clear division of status between the 'wash maid', who came in periodically to do the heavy work, and the 'landry maid' or the body servant who could starch and shape high-quality items of clothing.

The laundry built in the 1720s in the kitchen court replaced all of these laundries. At first the new facilities consisted of only two rooms. The processes used would have changed little. The main room doubled as both a wash-house and an ironing room. It had a single copper for heating water and a dozen washing-tubs. These were wooden, cooper-made, varying in size from a large bucket upwards. There were seven

2

Washing with lye

Before the nineteenth century, most domestic and body linen was made of flax fibres and the techniques used in washing evolved from processes used in linen manufacture. These were familiar to servants since many of the larger households grew and processed their own flax for domestic use. The 1693–4 inventory of Dunham, for example, implies that the house still made its own linen, though probably only for servants' or children's sheets.

Washing involved cold-soaking (often called 'bucking') in an alkaline liquid called 'lye', followed by boiling in diluted lye. Lye was made by steeping wood or bracken ashes in water, perhaps strengthened by pigeon or chicken dung and human urine. A barrel was kept topped up with this mixture and the strong yellow liquid was run off through a tap in the bottom. It had a very powerful bleaching action.

After soaking and boiling, the linen was rinsed in clear water and laid out on a drying-green, a walled area of lawn where the grass was kept fairly long. The linen was spread out on the grass to bleach and dry in the sun and wind. The process was helped by oxygenation caused by the process of photosynthesis in the grass. If necessary the linen was repeatedly dampened by throwing water or diluted lye over it. If the area was too windy, a length of hedge was provided to hang the linen on. Box and holly were usual for this, though the latter required care if the clothes were not to be ripped.

When almost dry and sufficiently whitened, the linen was dampened by sprinkling with water and rolled up for the moisture to 'regulate', that is, to spread evenly throughout the piece. Whilst still damp it was shaken and pulled vigorously to straighten the yarns and edges, otherwise it would not be 'squared'. It was folded and mangled whilst damp (but not wet) in a box mangle, which smoothed the linen and gave it a slight polish. It was then thoroughly aired, folded and stored for use.

Washing with soap

Household inventories from elsewhere show that throughout the seventeenth and eighteenth centuries linen goods increased in both quantity and quality. The eighteenth and nineteenth centuries saw more textile imports from Europe and the ownership of cotton fabrics widened, along with coloured and printed patterns. Lye was too strong for these and was thus replaced by hot-water washing with soap. Laundry soap was hard, yellow and resinous; it was bought in foot-long bars which were later cut into tablets and then either grated into water to form a jelly, or rubbed whole onto the garment for scrubbing.

The 1819 inventory of Dunham Massey implies that lye-washing had largely been superseded by the new soap method. The presence of a dolly and a 'suds tub' shows that washing with soap had taken over, even for some of the large items. At this time soap was bought by the house in quantity; in one of the storerooms the inventory listed four boxes of soap, each weighing a hundredweight and valued at £4 each. After the 1820s, it became usual to pre-soak dirty items in a solution of washing soda, then beginning to be manufactured commercially for the first time. By 1842 the Dunham housekeeper was able to buy ready-made 'bleaching liquid'.

stools, stands for the smaller tubs in which the washing was soaked, rubbed and rinsed. Larger tubs stood directly on the floor and were used mainly for soaking linen in lye (Box 2, above). There was also a 'slop cistern', a stone trough leading into a drain for the disposal of dirty water, probably the stone quadrant sink which can still be seen today in the corner under the cupboard.

For ironing, the laundry was fitted with two tables and a dresser surface. There was also a stove for heating irons and nine smoothing irons, later increasing to twelve. It also had numerous racks for airing (one was called a 'wood jane', probably what we would call a clothes maid), baskets and a pan for mixing starch. The room was lit by wall candle-holders.

The second room was the drying room, fitted with a stove, tables and chair and a linen press for storing linen. Today the remains of hooks high up on the walls show

RIGHT: The laundry corridor at Tyntesfield, Somerset. This was obviously used as a drying room, and still retains some of the smaller pieces of equipment that no longer survive at Dunham.

3

The box mangle

Handwork and dexterity played a larger part in early laundry methods than machines, but mangling was one area where a machine was important. One of the most difficult jobs was smoothing large linen tablecloths and sheets, which could be four yards long. Before the nineteenth century, most of these would not have been ironed, but smoothed whilst damp in a box mangle.

- Early box mangles were driven a simple rope or leather strap, attached to a weighted box running on rollers over a flat bed.
- Later, gearing systems were introduced which automatically reversed the direction of movement of the box.
- The most commonly surviving pattern is that shown by the mangle in the Dunham Laundry today. This uses a cogged wheel and a large flywheel to ease the motion of the heavy box. Although made by Thomas Bradfords of Salford, the pattern was known as the 'Baker's Patent'. By 1832, these improved reversing machines were acknowledged to be the very best available.*
- The earliest patent for a box mangle is dated 1791, yet they were still described in a laundry manual published in the 1920s.

* J. C. Loudon, *An Encyclopaedia of Cottage, Farm and Villa Architecture and Furniture*, 1836 and 1842. For the history of mangling and washing see Pamela Sambrook, *The Country House Servant* (Sutton Publishing in association with the National Trust, 1999).

Mangling and wringing machines. — Consists in the application of polished glass surfaces to mangles, &c. Fig. 1 shows the application to a mangle. The usual travelling box *b* is faced on its underside with a plate of polished glass, preferably cemented to a slab of slate or stone secured to the bottom of the box. The frame *a* is preferably built of stone or slate, and is similarly faced with glass. The cloth or other

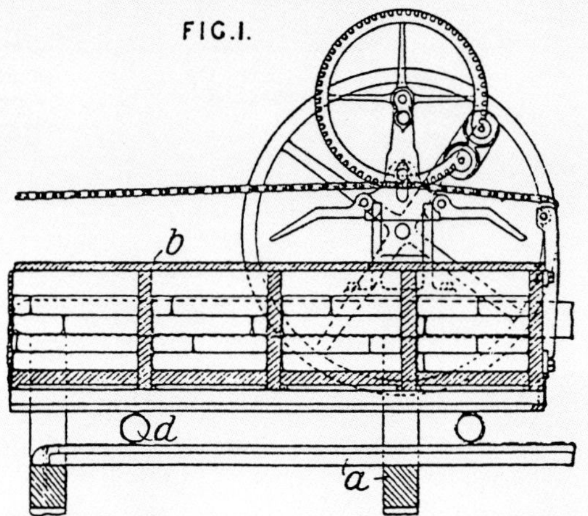

material is wound on rollers *d*, preferably formed of glass as described in Specification No. 1084, A.D, 1854, placed loosely between the box and frame *a*. As the box *b* is reciprocated to and fro, the cloth &c. is alternately unwound from and wound on the rollers.

Diagram of a box mangle taken from a patent specification dated 1854.

Using a box mangle

At Dunham the box mangle was installed in the old Drying Room. A table was used for loading the box mangle rollers; at Dunham the 1883 inventory lists mangle and table together as if they were parts of a whole.

- The sheet was folded into four and laid out on the table, then rolled onto the roller so as to be a tight, even fit. Then it was wrapped around with a mangle cloth, made of unbleached linen woven to the width of the rollers. Smaller items could be mangled inside the sheet.
- The loaded roller was then slipped under the box in such a way as to part-unroll when the box was moved back and forth. Each roller would be mangled for a few turns. The fibres of the linen would not only be pressed but would rub against each other. If the linen had been starched this produced a smooth, stiff finish.
- After mangling the pieces could be taken off the roller and either folded or stored as a cylinder. Only the best-quality sheets would need to be hand-finished with a hot iron. Best table linen was mangled twice, taken off the roller after the first time and put back on the reverse way.

Mangling with a box mangle produced a superior finish to that of an upright mangle, which required great care in order not to stretch or strain the articles.

Detail from John Harris's painting of Dunham Massey viewed from the north, *c.*1750. Beyond the mound, to the west of the house, can be seen the kitchen court and drying green. This was a large grassy area, completely enclosed by walls and crossed by four lengths of hedges. The linen could be laid out either on the grass or on the hedges.

where racks were fitted for use in wet weather. At this time there was no mention of a box mangle, though these machines were just coming into use for smoothing large items (Box 3, opposite). Neither did the 1758 inventory mention a drying-green, yet the painting of Dunham by John Harris, which is dated 1751, clearly shows such a green immediately to the rear of the laundry.

By 1800 the single-room laundry must have been inadequate for the increasing throughput of linen and cotton goods, so a separate wash-house was built onto the back. The main laundry was changed from a multi-purpose room into a large ironing room, generally called by the Victorians a 'dry laundry', and fitted with better stoves and more irons and airers[39] (Box 4, below). By 1819 all three interiors of the laundry suite probably looked much as they do now.

Smoothing irons

4

The number of smoothing irons illustrates the growth and decline of the Dunham Laundry. According to the inventories, there were nine smoothing irons in 1758. By 1819 this had increased to twenty-one, then called flat irons; a new stove had been fitted to heat them. By 1883 the number was down to fourteen and in 1905 there were thirteen, all described as 'old and imperfect'. By 1912 all small fittings had been removed.

One iron which appears generally in laundry inventories, including those from Dunham Massey from 1819 onwards, is what became known in Victorian England as the 'Italian' iron or 'tally' iron. They were used to flute the front edge of servants' caps, or to iron awkward shapes such as sleeve-gathers, by pressing the linen over a cylinder with the thumbs. They were also used to smooth ribbons, especially if made of a piled fabric such as velvet and if already made up into bows.

By the nineteenth century there were many varied irons and stands on the market. Country-house inventories rarely included many of these and Dunham is no exception. In general, it seems that Victorian country-house laundry-maids used only basic tools, usually a selection of flat irons of different sizes, one or two Italian irons, a pair of goffering tongs and a polishing iron. Laundresses preferred to show off their dexterity with simple tools rather than an array of complicated gadgets.

Above all, successful ironing required speed. A young girl starting in the laundry would be hopelessly slow, even if she had been trained at home to ordinary domestic standards. She would practise on servants' wear before being allowed to handle family linen. She passed the test when able to turn out a perfectly ironed shirt in two minutes.

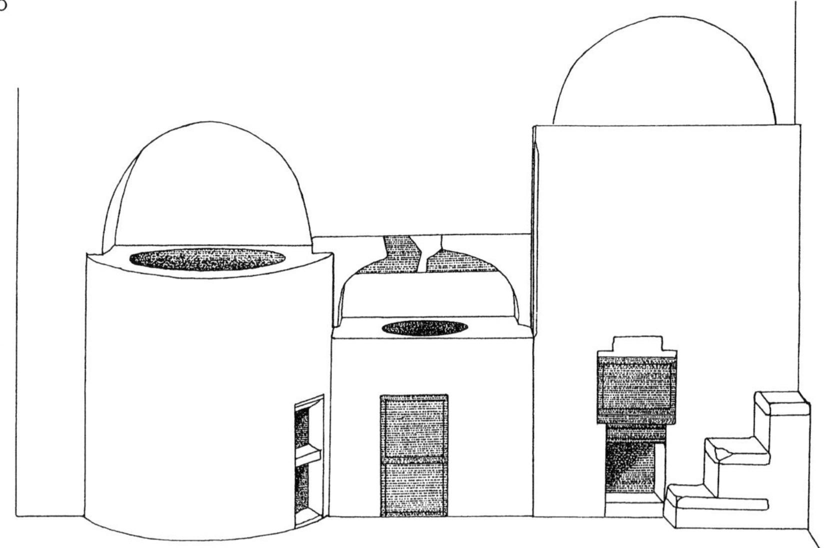

Author's sketch of the three boilers in the wash-house. The left-hand was for boiling large whites, the middle for smaller whites and the right-hand supplied hot water to the sinks.

This is not to say that changes had not taken place. By the late eighteenth century most large households had changed from lye to laundry soap with hot water, although bucking with lye was still used for some fabrics and in some old-fashioned houses. The processes of finishing were also changing. Cotton goods did not respond as well as linen to box-mangling and gradually throughout the nineteenth century ironing took over as the main finishing process, though box mangles continued in use for large items such as sheets well into the twentieth century. Thus the working area needed for ironing increased, especially if sheets were now to be ironed. The facilities provided became more elaborate, too. Early wash-houses sometimes had fixed boilers of brass or copper, which avoided having to pour hot lye from a pan over an open fire, but these non-ferrous boilers were filled and emptied by hand-ladling. Nineteenth-century laundry boilers were more usually made of iron and filled by taps. Most large laundries had at least two, sometimes three boilers, as at Dunham.

Along with these changes, the old distinction between the 'wash maid' and 'landry maid' disappeared. Laundry-maids were now full-time, living-in servants, washing once a week in a complex routine of sorting, steeping, rubbing, boiling, rinsing, starching and finishing. In many ways this modern system was more tedious and time-consuming than the old bucking with lye, but it suited the new textiles better as well as being in line with the complex domestic hierarchies so beloved of wealthy Victorians.

Linen

The Dunham inventories seem to indicate that the middle period, 1819, represents the high point of linen ownership, with almost 2,000 items valued at nearly £400. Yet the amount of linen in the early inventories was probably underestimated compared with later. A close look shows that whilst the last inventory, 1912, included items like dusters, kitchen cloths and housemaids' cloths (over 500 items), the earlier inventories did not. This seems to have been usual with early inventories, for work on records from Hardwick Hall in Derbyshire shows that late-medieval linen inventories excluded even the bedlinen, possibly because it was mostly home-made, low-status and had no monetary value put upon it.[40] It was not until 1782 that workaday items used in the kitchen were shown in the Hardwick inventories, and the Dunham inventories conform to this pattern, for even in 1819 working linen was listed simply as 'sundry coarse linen'.

In general, the large amount of domestic linen owned by seventeenth- and early eighteenth-century households is well known from probate inventories and should not come as a surprise. Linen was one of the few forms of goods which married women owned in their own right. As such it came to represent something more than a mere material possession. Fine-quality domestic linen was highly prized as an heirloom and as part of a trousseau. It was endowed with a significance which was almost religious and this was reflected in the care taken over it. Even when out of use and stored, it was regularly counted over and reorganised.

Apart from the amounts of linen, the Dunham inventories also illustrate the changing pattern of textile type. The 1693-4 list specified different qualities and weaves of linen, each of which had its own use: damask for best tablecloths, the absorbent weaves of 'dyaper' and 'huccaback' for towels, the fine-woven 'Holland' linen and coarser 'flaxon' for sheets and pillowcases. Other textiles appeared rarely, only hemp for coarser sheets and the new imported cotton fabric called 'callico' for sheets and covers for dressing-tables. This contrasts with 1819, when only damask was picked out amongst the linen weaves. In 1912 the best-quality sheets and cloths were still made of linen, but cotton was much more important than previously, as is shown by greater differentiation between the types.

The variety in quality of goods is a useful illustration of the hierarchical nature of the Dunham household. In 1912 the best cloths and sheets were decorated with drawn thread work and embroidered with the Stamford 'S' and coronet. The family were using the softer, more absorbent cotton turkish towels whilst servants' towels were still of diaper and the menservants' were coloured brown, presumably not to show the dirt. The disappearance of items such as the 'close stool cloaths' of 1693-4 also show the progress of technology, whilst others illustrate changes in fashionable nomenclature, the dinner napkins becoming 'serviettes' in 1912.

The later inventories provide a description of the linen room, where textiles were stored. The traditional method of storage was in chests and in 1883 both old oak and walnut chests were still present. By this time, however, it had become usual to store linen in purpose-built cupboards and these too were listed in 1883, made of pine with folding doors. Such cupboards were usually lined with brown glazed holland (linen) cloth or brown paper and had sliding shelves. Some cupboards like this survive at Dunham in corridors within the servants' quarters. The linen room was also provided with a large pine bin with subdivisions, presumably for dirty linen.

Brew-house

It is noticeable that in the 1693-4 inventory one of the most detailed lists of domestic contents related to the brew-house, an indication of the importance of beer in the domestic economy. This was fully-fitted with nearly £50 worth of fixed boilers and

Engraving from *Universal Magazine*, 1747–8, of a small brew-house, illustrating the copper above its furnace (A), pump (B), mash tun (D) and cooling tray (H).

coolers, plus coopered equipment and a large number of glass bottles. The last were a real expression of luxury. Bottled ale and beer went back to the late sixteenth century and was especially popular in country houses in the summer. The main beer store was in the cellars where there were fifty casks (some holding 54 gallons, called hogsheads and some 36, called barrels), small open coopered tubs and funnels for filling casks and a large amount (486 gallons) of strong 'March Beer'.

The 1758 inventory gives a much fuller idea of a gentleman's brew-house, newly built in 1720 and fitted with all that was needed to supply a large household with its regular staple drink. A large, airy room two storeys high, it would have been fitted with louvres in the unglazed windows and probably a ventilating lantern in the roof. Brewing at this time was a labour-intensive process. The furnaces were set almost at shoulder height and were stoked by hand. The brewer had not even a hand-pump to help move the hot wort, ale or beer around the brew-house, but had to lift it in heavy oak coopered buckets, hundreds of gallons of boiling liquid for each mash. He had coopered ladles and funnels to pour the beer into barrels, and a hanger with chains by which two men could carry a barrel suspended between them. He had two 'gaging sticks' for checking the amount of wort against the capacity of his pans, but the only artificial light was provided by one iron candlestick.[41]

The eighteenth-century brew-house at Charlecote Park, Warwickshire, showing the two coppers, mash tun (*left*) and cooling tray (*right*). The brew-house at Dunham would probably have looked very similar to this, as inventories show it had two coppers.

The brew-house of 1819 was probably only slightly changed. The boilers had been fitted with lead covers and gave a total capacity of 300 gallons. There were three fermenting tubs and better lifting equipment: a hand-pump and wooden chutes or 'spouts' for moving liquid around, and a windlass and blocks for lifting barrels. In the cellar were almost 4,000 gallons of beer or ale in cask, probably of varying ages and in various stages, some in secondary fermentation whilst sitting on the 69 yards of stillages. This may seem a lot of malt liquor but it is by no means extraordinary and even fairly modest. Inventories from other great households around this time give figures of 11,000 or 12,000 gallons in store.[42]

According to the 1758 inventory, next to the brew-house in the corner nearest the moat was a small bakehouse. Placing these two next to each other was by no means unusual and in many households the brewer doubled as the baker. The techniques share a common expertise with yeast, the fermenting beer supplying barm for raising the bread. The inventory did not include the ovens themselves, though a separate wooden oven-door was listed. The bakehouse was also supplied with a large oak storage chest for flour and rodent-proof hanging shelves for the finished bread. It was also home to a turtle tub, for Dunham bought live turtles on a fairly regular basis, presumably for making into soup. By 1829 the bakehouse was redundant, superseded by the brick oven in the scullery and the iron oven fitted elsewhere in the kitchen suite. The old bakehouse was 'fitted up for cleaning boots and Clothes' with a boiler and slopstone sink.

Stables

The two stable blocks formed the first part of the 2nd Earl's rebuilding programme of the 1720s. The family maintained a long-term interest in hunting, and spacious accommodation was provided both for riding and coach horses as well as, in the nineteenth-century, race horses. The accommodation may seem especially extravagant given the fact that after the 1750s the coach horses were at Dunham for only the second half of each year. Stabling was required, however, not just for the family's horses. Records of fodder consumption show that 'strangers' horses' belonging to guests and other visitors were present at Dunham for perhaps four months of the year (see Chapter Five). In addition, the senior male staff kept their own personal horses in the stables. We know, for example, that when John Arnatt, the house steward, died in 1799 he left two horses (see Chapter Seven). It is also possible that some of the stabling space was used for tying cows whilst milking, a useful convenience for the dairymaids. Unfortunately, the early inventories did not include the stabling in their lists.

Other functional buildings in the park

The home farm was built in its present form in the early 1820s as a classic model farm with separate accommodation for a gentleman farmer and several families of labourers. Beyond the farmyard was also built a range of workshops, including a new smithy. Unfortunately, the farm was never included in the inventories and the garden and the mill only in the later ones. The slaughterhouse occupies an unusually prominent position at Dunham because of the presence of the deer park. Built in the 1740s, strictly speaking it was a butchery rather than a slaughterhouse as the deer were killed in the park and brought to the slaughterhouse for skinning and jointing. Much of the venison was given away as presents to friends and presumably the joints were distributed from here, those destined for the Dunham table being carried down to the kitchen larders for hanging. Though in the nineteenth century the building was used merely as a summer-house, even in 1905 some of the old equipment was still there, its contents including a deer-carrier and a drying-rail for skins.[43] The winch for lifting carcasses is still in place today.

Other critical buildings such as the water-house were left out of the inventories, so we have little information except for the occasional mention of repairs. The water supply to Dunham was highly complex. Water came from Hale Moss through underground culverts which supplied a cistern built underneath the water-house (now called the pump-house). This cistern was enlarged in 1777.[44] It fed two hand-pumps

The water-pump in the mangle-room at Dunham Massey.

at first-floor level which supplied the ground floor of the house and another pump at second-floor level to supply the first floor of the house. One or two men must have been employed once or probably twice a day to pump the necessary supplies. This system was replaced in 1860 when the mill was converted into a saw-mill and a water-driven pump was installed for the Platt family, who tenanted the house.

The laundry seems to have had its own separate water supply, again hand-pumped in the mangle-room from a well, or an underground cistern fed either from a spring or with rainwater collected from the roof. The housemaids' closets in the house and the butler's pantry were also connected to a soft-water supply. Most great houses collected soft rainwater from the roof to use for personal washing, laundering and brewing. The harder ground water would be used for cooking, drinking and general use. All would have to be regularly hand-pumped. Some houses had a gauge to show how low the supply was.

External privies discharged into the moat. Strictly for family use, in 1814 the 5th Earl installed a water-closet in a small room at the bottom of the Crimson Staircase. The water was brought from a specially constructed cistern, which was fed by cast-iron pipes from one of the watercourses in the park and carefully buried and planted with evergreen shrubs. Discharge from inside went into a stream running under the house, controlled by a sluice gate.[45] The piping and woodwork construction were put out on contract to a Mr Bellhouses, who seemed to be well experienced in such matters. From start to finish the job took four months. The water-closet itself was fitted with carpet and a spring to the door and must have been judged a success, for at least one more was mentioned in 1823 as needing re-oiling and a new blind.[46] Indeed, at the Earl's suggestion, a water-closet had been set up in Bowdon church as early as 1813.[47]

* * *

During the generations between the 2nd Earl of Warrington and the 6th Earl of Stamford Dunham offered a level of accommodation which was expected of the contemporary country house. We can see how standards generally improved over time, often in subtle ways. Change came slowly, accelerated perhaps by the succession of a new earl and new enthusiasm. Besides the more glamorous preoccupation with building alterations and the refurbishment of the main rooms, the 6th Earl began his regime by paying great attention to mundane problems of ventilation and waterproofing. Damp floors to corridors were relaid, 'air grids' inserted to ventilate floor voids, spouting installed, roofs repaired, floors retiled and chimney throats restricted to cure smoking.[48] New technology was embraced, but conservatively. Water-closets were provided for the family but the 6th Earl's tentative ideas about the installation of stoves for what could have been some form of central heating seem not to have been pursued.[49] Fashion dictated some changes. The 1820s saw a dislike of wainscotting and walls covered with pictures, many of which were taken down. The family apartments saw a move to pastel colours such as the tea green used in the Map Room and the salmon pink used to distemper the passages and the water-closet. Except for the 'drab' privies, functional rooms remained whitewashed.[50]

A household of the size and wealth of Dunham must have provoked inner

Dunham Massey from the west, showing the stables and coach-houses.

tensions between servants and their luxurious surroundings. As one historian has written, household goods can be 'vehicles for complex meanings, writ admittedly small, but no less powerfully felt through daily usage'.[51] A servant household was one stage removed from a personal household. Goods were utensils or commodities, not private possessions. Yet there were ways in which this relationship could be highly complex, for tools can be endowed with functional and emotional significance. The chef would have his favourite saucepan, the head laundry-maid her special set of irons, a footman a favoured lamp. Through the Dunham inventories some pieces moved from space to space over time but were obviously valued by different people, perhaps for different reasons. Thus a watchman's clock or a Windsor armchair seem to have a life of their own. By keeping regular inventories and marking with initials, dates, batch numbers and insignia, servants became the custodians of the possessive instinct of the owner. The housekeeper might become truly irate if the housemaid incorrectly adjusted the blinds which protected her employer's furniture from the harmful rays of the sun. These were attitudes that tended to strengthen the sense of common purpose which was such an integral part of the life of the successful servant household.

CHAPTER THREE

'Residents and travellers'

The Servant Household 1819-22

The bricks and mortar of the previous chapter set the scene but they tell us relatively little about how the house was actually run and who was involved. In order to make this task manageable, this chapter focuses more sharply on a single period, around the time of the death of the 5th Earl in 1819 and the few years immediately following, when the house was operating at its peak. It is not possible to be specific about the numbers of people to be catered for at this time. At the beginning of 1819, the Earl's children were all grown up with their own establishments, but as the whole point of Dunham was to provide a focus for country hospitality there would have been a variable number of both family members and friends staying at any one time.[52]

Unusually for Dunham, several lists of salaries and other payments have survived for the years 1819 to 1820. One of these is a list of wages due on 25 December 1819, compiled by Hugo Worthington, the land agent and senior manager of the whole of the Cheshire estates.[53] (Box 5, p.58) This gives a first insight into the organisation of the staff in that it distinguishes between those servants who were resident at Dunham Massey all year round and those who were 'travelling servants', moving between Dunham, Enville and London with the family. The wages in this list were due for the previous six months only, as at this time salaried servants were paid twice a year instead of the older tradition of once a year. In a few cases staff had been in post for less than six months. The resident servants numbered twenty-one, that is fifteen men and six women, whose total wage bill came to £354 11s for approximately six months. All of the six women were indoor servants: the housekeeper, one housemaid, two still-room maids, a kitchen-maid and a dairymaid. Of the fifteen men, only four were indoor servants: the house steward, the porter, brewer and usher. The rest were outdoor servants: the land steward or farm bailiff, the head gardener, two gamekeepers at Dunham and five out-gamekeepers, a groom and a stable-boy.

Working from his office in Altrincham, Worthington directed the domestic functions and all farming, mining and timber enterprises on the estate through various senior servants. Thus the home farm at Dunham was in the control of the land steward, John Davenport, who earned £200 a year. Davenport was a long-standing employee but newly promoted to be in overall charge not only of the farm but also the gardens, gamekeepers and miller. Under him worked Joseph Pickin, the head gardener, and Daniel Shaw, the Dunham head gamekeeper, usually called the park-keeper.

5

Full-time servants working at Dunham Massey, 1819
Wages due for the second six months of the year

Permanently resident

EGR 11/2/8/60

1819

Wages paid by Hugo Worthington to the Earl of Stamford and Warrington's Servants resident at Dunham Massey due 25 December 1819 —

Men Servants

	£ s d
John Poole, House Steward (from 6 Augt) at £90 p ann.	35 . 3 . 6
John Davenport, Land Steward	100 . 0 . 0
Joseph Pickin, Gardener	26 . 5 . 0
Daniel Moore Shaw, Parkkeeper	21 . 0 . 0
John Thorpe, Under-Keeper	10 . 10 . 0
John Cutler, Brewer	17 . 10 . 0
George Smith Groom	15 . 0 . 0
Thomas Davies, Porter	15 . 0 . 0
Thomas Barratt Usher of the Hall	5 . 0 . 0
Charles Brown, Stable-Boy	8 . 8 . 0
Reginald Penny (Out-Gamekeepers)	10 . 10 . 0
John Royle (Out-Gamekeepers)	10 . 10 . 0
John Galley (Out-Gamekeepers)	10 . 10 . 0
Jonathan Higinbottom (Out-Gamekeepers)	23 . 9 . 0
John Harrop (Out-Gamekeepers)	4 . 4 . 0

Women Servants

Hannah Prinsep, Housekeeper	17 . 10 . 0
Elizabeth Byrom (dead)	2 . 10 . 0
Alice Evans, 2d Housemaid, from 17 July at £12	5 . 5 . 0
Lydia Morton, Stillroom-maid	7 . 0 . 0
Jane Lingard, assistant to Do from 5 Augt at £8 8 0	3 . 6 . 6
Martha Norman, Dairy-maid	6 . 0 . 0
Ex. HW.	£ 354 : 11 : 0

Travelling between Dunham Massey, Enville and other houses

EGR 11/2/8/61

1819

Wages paid by Hugo Worthington to the Earl of Stamford and Warrington's travelling Servants due 25 December 1819.

Men Servants

	£ s d
Samuel Church Valet	36 . 15 . 0
Philip Osgood, Butler (from 25 July at £73 10 0)	30 . 12 . 6
William Iseard, Cooke (including allowance for Caps, Aprons &c)	39 . 7 . 6
David Seammen, Coachman	21 . 11 . 6
Do in lieu of Oil Brushes Mops &c for ½ a year	4 . 4 . 0
Thomas Shallcross, under Coachman	12 . 12 . 0
Edward Galland, Postillion	7 . 7 . 0
William Jones, Footman	12 . 12 . 0
William Jorry, Do (from 25 July)	10 . 10 . 0
John Wood Do Do	10 . 10 . 0
James Perkins, 1st under-Butler	12 . 12 . 0
Thomas Beckley 2nd Do (from 24 July)	10 . 10 . 0
William Chaliner, Stewards-room-man	9 . 9 . 0
John Lamb Groom	9 . 19 . 6
John Robinson Do	9 . 19 . 6

Women Servants

Catharine Ainsworth 1st Housemaid	7 . 0 . 0
Elizabeth Pritchard 3rd Do	5 . 10 . 0
Catharine Greswell 4th Do (from 25 Augt at £11)	3 . 13 . 6
Hannah Bennett 1st Laundry-maid (from 7 Augt at £16)	6 . 3 . 0
Alice Read 2nd Do 3 months at £11 and 3 months at £14	6 . 5 . 0
Margaret Millington 3rd Do (from 1 July at £12)	5 . 5 . 0
Jane Fellows 4th Do (from 1 Augt at £11)	3 . 17 . 6
Mary Bassett 1st Kitchen-maid £16	6 . 0 . 0
Edna Wood 2nd Do (in future £12)	5 . 0 . 0
Martha Bradbury 4th Do (in future £10)	4 . 0 . 0
Ex. HW	£ 291 . 5 . 6

Accountable also to Worthington was the house steward, John Poole, who earned £90 a year, substantially less than Davenport and newly in post having taken employment with the Stamfords in August of 1819. Poole managed all the indoor house staff, directly in the case of the male servants. The most senior of these was John Cutler, the brewer, followed by Thomas Davies, the porter (the main door-keeper), George Smith, the head groom, and finally Thomas Barratt, the usher (controller of the servants' hall).

Poole supervised the female servants through the housekeeper, Hannah Princep. She was paid an annual salary of £35, which made her directly comparable with the brewer. Comparisons in wages across gender, however, are unrealistic. The days of equal pay for women were far off and it was usual at this time to pay women roughly half the wages of men for similar responsibility. Given this fact, the Dunham housekeeper was fairly well paid by women's standards. The next senior woman to Mrs Princep was Lydia Morton, the still-room maid, who had control of an assistant, Jane Lingard. Martha Norman, the dairymaid, and Alice Evans, the housemaid, were equal in salary. The only resident kitchen-maid, Elizabeth Byron, died in 1819, so her salary record is incomplete.

Although the travelling servants were more numerous than the residents (fourteen men and ten women) their total wage bill came to less: £291 5s 6d for the half year. This was because there were more low-paid women and fewer highly paid men than in the resident household. The latter, after all, was responsible for the entire running of the house and park in the absence of the family. The travelling servants tended to be specialist personal servants, middle-ranked managers and lower-level manual workers.

At the top of this peripatetic household was a triumvirate made up of the cook, William Iseard, on a salary of £78 15s, the valet, Samuel Church, and the butler, Philip Osgood, both of whom were paid £73 10s a year. Of these, only the butler was in charge of a substantial male staff, which consisted of two under-butlers and three footmen. The outdoor travelling servants were headed by the head coachman, David Seammen, assisted by under-coachman Thomas Shawcross, a postilion (who drove the carriage horses by riding the lead horse, not from the carriage as did the coachmen) and two grooms.

Most of the indoor female servants belonged to the travelling household. These included the 1st housemaid, Catharine Ainsworth, and the 3rd and 4th housemaids Elizabeth Pritcherd and Catharine Gresswell. The resident Dunham housemaid slotted into the hierarchy as 2nd housemaid. Of the kitchen-maids, the resident Dunham maid ranked as 3rd, under Mary Bassett and Edna Wood and above Martha Bradbury. All four laundry-maids were travelling. The two lady's maids were not included in this list as their salary appears in the personal accounts of the Earl.

These travelling servants worked with the Dunham Massey household only for approximately six months of the year. The rest of the time they lived mainly at Enville but also went to London and Leicestershire, where the family had other houses and where they had to work alongside a completely different but much smaller set of resident servants. The resident Enville household was larger than Dunham's, totalling thirty-three in all, including keepers and other outdoor servants.[54] This brings the total number of full-time servants employed by the Greys at their two houses in Cheshire and Staffordshire to seventy-eight: more than the combined Staffordshire and London servants of the Duke of Sutherland, one of the wealthiest aristocrats in the country, a few years later.[55] The Sutherland figure of sixty-eight, however, did not include carriage staff, so the comparison is slightly misleading. Yet it is true to say that the Grey household was an extensive one by any standards.

Throughout the eighteenth and nineteenth centuries, domestic servants as a group were notoriously mobile, moving from job to job sometimes within a matter of months or even weeks. It is, for example, rare to find the same servant in the same post in consecutive decennial censuses. Country-house service was more stable than other sectors of the industry, but even here the comfortable ideal of the ancient family servant who had been faithful for decades was more mythology than reality. So, how stable was this household?

The December 1819 wage lists give a total of forty-five individuals in post and represent the household of the 6th Earl of Stamford, who had recently inherited from his father who died in May 1819. Several other lists of servants have survived from that summer, dating from shortly after the 5th Earl's death. These consist firstly of a list of payments of 'mourning money' dated May, secondly a six-monthly wage list dated June, and thirdly a record of those servants who received a legacy under the old Earl's will, dated July.[56] This is not, of course, an ideal time to draw conclusions about the general stability of the household, since the death of the master inevitably caused disruption. Staff turnover would be high, as the new master brought in new servants and sacked or pensioned off the old. Nevertheless, these records provide a useful illustration of the upheavals that followed such an event. Unfortunately, the lists do not record the same things, and it is difficult to be sure who was still in post at any given date. The mourning account, for example, appears to list all women servants including some casuals (twenty-one women in all), but only the senior menservants (seven men). These menservants received £15 each, four senior women servants received 13gns and the rest of the women servants 7gns. The absence of the junior menservants is probably explained by the fact that the payments were to offset the cost of providing themselves with full mourning dress for six months. Since the junior menservants such as footmen would have worn house livery, they needed only armbands and ribbons provided by the household, not a full set of clothes, and so were not included in the list.

The legacy list (totalling thirty-five recipients) may be misleading too, for some were old servants who had already left. The six-monthly wage list also appears to be incomplete, including only sixteen people, all resident servants. When we merge these three lists we arrive at a total of forty-four people, only one short of the household kept by the 6th Earl. Even allowing for the odd person who left, it seems that the size of the household probably changed little.

If this was true, did the staff change between the regimes of the 5th and the 6th Earls? Of the original forty-four, only twenty stayed to serve the 6th Earl. Less than half of the 6th Earl's household had served his father, and twenty-five new servants were taken on. This probably reflects the age of the old Earl's household, many of whom retired on his death. More important than mere numbers, however, was the fact that amongst the incomers were key members of the management. The new house steward, valet, butler, head coachman and head keeper were all in positions to make changes in routine if such were needed. The only touch of continuity at senior level was provided by the cook, William Iseard, and the old housekeeper, Hannah Princep. At a lower level, three new footmen and two under-butlers could have brought a fresh look to household hospitality, particularly as fashions in food presentation and service at table were changing at this time. On the female side, the new employees included two housemaids and a complete laundry staff. Despite the presence of the twenty who stayed, the new master had indeed set up a new household regime.

Were the twenty who stayed on with the 6th Earl settled servants with long service with the 5th Earl? The only record which helps us here is a wage list dated 1817.[57] This shows that of the twenty, twelve had been in service with the family two years previously. Of these twelve, all but two were resident servants at Dunham, showing perhaps that those who lived permanently at Dunham had a settled life, most had families and were thus less inclined to move around between jobs than the more mobile travelling servants. Into this category we can place the land steward, the head gardener, the brewer, the porter and the head groom. The housekeeper, the dairy-maid, the still-room maid and an assistant maid formed a stable little group inside the house and must have all got on well together. The usher had been in post some time. This was a responsible job but not a highly paid one, involving the serving of staff meals, control of food and drink allowances to the servants and generally looking after the servants' hall. It was often occupied by an elderly, semi-retired butler or by a youngster on his way up the ladder. Of the travelling servants only the head housemaid and the steward's room man, another low-paid trainee position, stayed on from 1817 to the 6th Earl's establishment.

Both the 6th Earl and his main agent, Hugo Worthington, must have believed in incentives, for most of the twenty servants who stayed on in 1819 to serve the 6th Earl were given wage rises. Twelve definitely received a substantial increase in their salary at the changeover of the master, four may have done and four carried on at the original rate. One of these last four had not been in post very long, but another was the old usher who carried on at the same wage he had received in 1817. The average increase among the indoor staff was over twenty-seven per cent, but some of the outdoor staff received even more. The farm bailiff, whose responsibilities grew substantially, had a three-fold wage rise. Sixteen of the twenty (including the usher) received a legacy from the old Earl of an extra year's pay (at the old rate). The new servants also had an incentive, for it seems to have been usual practice to set them on for a trial period. After several months of satisfactory service, many were given a rise of one or more pounds to their basic salary.

How stable was this new household of December 1819? A record of wages paid at Enville in December 1820 shows that of the travelling servants most of them were still in post; only a groom, a kitchen-maid and a housemaid had left.[58] The coachman, a groom and a housemaid had been given either a rise or promotion. Unfortunately a complete list of resident servants has not survived for subsequent years, but of those who are mentioned in the accounts of 1822, only two had changed since 1820: Hannah Princep had been housekeeper for some years and retired with ill health to be replaced by Anne Calder, and the still-room maid Lydia Morton left to get married. Most of the other key staff, amongst them the house steward, butler, gardener and head groom, remained. Whether this stability was long-lasting is impossible to say as we simply do not have the data. Domestic service was a mobile occupation; even country-house servants frequently moved from house to house, on the lookout for promotion, better wages, better living conditions, more congenial companions and marriage partners. This last factor, of course, encouraged male staff stability but accelerated female staff turnover as the case of Daniel Shaw, the park-keeper, shows. In March of 1822 he married Lydia Morton in Bowdon church.[59] It was Daniel's second marriage, and afterwards he returned to work and remained in his job for the rest of his working life. He was a local man anyway, so was likely to be less mobile than servants recruited from further afield. In 1822, however, it was extremely unusual for a female living-in servant to carry on working full-time after she was married, so his wife Lydia left.

The frequency with which servants changed jobs varied according to whether they were indoor or outdoor servants and whether their home was nearby. Of the list of indoor servants living in the house at Dunham in the 1820s, few bear local names. This contrasts markedly with the outdoor staff working at the farm, in the park or in the gardens, where the vast majority of both men and women bear such names. Many of these, the Pearsons, Gibbons and Holts for example, were well-known, long-established local families who had employment and service connections with the Booth family which stretched back over centuries. Certainly, a quick perusal of eighteenth-century payments for casual labour shows many of the same surnames appearing a hundred years earlier. Some indoor servants recruited from further afield might well stay with the family for decades, becoming more settled as they got older and better paid, but these were the exception rather than the rule. Young servants especially had to move regularly to gain experience and promotion, in particular where there was a slow turnover in the top positions.

The wage structure within the December 1819 household seems to have been a complicated one. Although some attempt had been made to use graded levels across the whole household, this had been confused by *ad hoc* promotions and individual circumstances. The hierarchical pattern can still be seen in the women's wages. Each of the housemaid, kitchen and laundry sections had four maids, numbered one to four. In all three the bottom grade was £10 or £11, but the top grade varied. In the kitchen and laundry it was £16, but the head housemaid and the still-room maid received £2 less, probably because they both worked very closely with the housekeeper, whereas the kitchen- and laundry-maids had more responsibility. The dairymaid, though working more on her own, had no staff to supervise and therefore received only £12.

The same hierarchical pattern can be seen in the grading of most of the men. There is clearly some effort at standardised grades, at 20 and 24gns, for example. Many of the men worked on their own, or in pairs where one was in charge of the other. The butler had two under-butlers, however, who were graded like the women. Amongst the grooms and footmen the hierarchical system was used only partially: one senior post was graded higher but the others were graded equally. This presumably relates to the nature of the work and the way it was structured. Most servants were given individual jobs that indicated their status; for example, the 1st housemaid never cleaned grates and the 4th housemaid cleaned only the servants' quarters. Each job was done at a specific time and by a specific person. Grooms' and footmen's work was different, for one of them had to be on call all the time the family was around. They therefore needed a rota system and this tended to encourage a more even wage structure. In adopting this system, Dunham was conforming to usual practice; many other household wage lists show that footmen were normally paid the same as each other despite often being called 1st, 2nd and 3rd footman.[60] The aristocratic Victorian household is often described as totally hierarchical, and this is true when

The housekeeper in her storeroom. Title page to A. Cobbett, *The English Housekeeper*, 1851.

hierarchy aided the smooth running of the household; but where it did not, other systems were used.

Salary structure may be complex, but other considerations make it difficult to calculate real remuneration. The existence of the legacy list in itself shows that servants received the occasional one-off reward, but more regular allowances were also paid. The December 1819 record, for example, indicates that the cook's salary included an allowance for caps and aprons, whereas the coachman received an extra amount of 8gns a year on top of his salary for the purchase of oil, brushes, mops and boots.[61] Footmen and other liveried servants such as coachmen and gamekeepers were entitled to at least one suit of clothes a year. The Greys' footmen and coachmen wore blue uniforms, the gamekeepers were in green and the race jockeys in black and gold. All dress liveries were decorated with gold and silver lace. Though made to measure for the individual, the uniforms remained the property of the family and had to be handed back at the end of service. When a new footman started, he usually served a probationary month or so wearing a second-hand uniform before the household incurred the cost of a new suit. The most expensive dress uniforms, worn only on special occasions, would be stored in a livery cupboard and checked in and

6

Bills for the purchase of servants' livery at Dunham Massey, 1821–2

EnvArch 1/8/1

June 1821, for working and dress livery.

Rt Honble The Earl of Stamford and Warrington

1821 June — To Peter Thompson and Son

				£	s	d
	9 Livery Dress Suits as usual	10-14-	+	96	6	-
+	14 Worsted Lace Coats and Waistcoats	5-15-6	+	80	17	-
+	14 Pairs of Blue Plush Breeches	2-5-0	+	31	10	-
+	10 Blue Livery Frocks	3-7-6	+	33	15	-
	28 Striped Livery Waistcoats	1-4-	+	33	12	
	7 Pairs of Blue Plush Breeches	2-5	+	15	15	-
	13 Pairs of Pattent Cord Breeches	2-5	+	29	5	-
	2 Postilions Jackets Silver Lace	6-10	+	13		
×	6 Livery Great Coats	4-7-6	+	26	5	-
	A Working Frock and Waistcoat for Gibbs		+	3	9	6
	2 Boxes.			1	10	-
				£365	4	6

1822, for repairing and altering working livery and for making new working clothes.

1822	The Earl of Stamford and Warrington To John Johnson	£	s	d
	For Work done for your servants	£	s	d
January 8	To macking George Smith frock	0	5	6
July 5	To Do Do Do Do	0	5	6
	To Repering Do liverys	0	2	6
12	To macking Charles Brown 2 stabel Weastcoats	0	8	0
	To Do Do Do frock	0	5	6
	To Repering Do liverys	0	2	6
august 5	To Devit Lemons frock stabel weastcoat hoveralls	0	12	6
	To Repearing Do liveres	0	2	6
	To macking Thomas Skallcros 2 stabel weastcoat	0	8	0
	To Do Do frock and hoveralls	0	8	6
	To Repering Do liverys	0	6	0
	To macking Edward Gatland 2 stabel weastcoats	0	8	0
	To Do Do frock and hoveralls	0	8	0
	To altring Do Strip Riding Jacit	0	2	6
	To Repering Do liverys	0	4	6
	To macking John Robbison 2 stabel weastcoats	0	8	0
	To Do Do Shuting Jacit and Getters Velvet	0	12	0
	To Repering Do liverys	0	4	0
	To Do for John Lamb	0	5	6
	To Do James Hepson	0	1	6
	To macking John Devis frock and weastcoat	0	9	6
	To altring and Repering Do liverys	0	5	0
	To macking James Perkins frock and weastcoat	0	9	6
	To Repering Do liverys	0	2	0
	To macking Thomas Berkleys frock and weastcoat	0	9	6
	To Repering Do liverys	0	1	6
	×	7	18	0

out by the steward or butler. The difference in cost between everyday wear and dress livery can be seen from bill extracts (Box 6, opposite).

Servants in the nineteenth century were ambivalent about livery. The practice dated from medieval times when male servants acted as small personal armies, and as such livery carried status. Deliberately archaic in form, nineteenth-century livery was modelled on the flamboyant fashion of eighteenth-century gentlemen. Servants were provided with magnificent clothing of a far higher standard than they could ever hope to own themselves, but generally it was intensely disliked, a stigma of servitude which was thankfully thrown off when they were promoted to higher levels of service.

The division of the household into resident and travelling servants caused complications, for both had their hidden perquisites and advantages. The travelling servants had all the experience of the London season, visits to other country houses and most probably foreign trips, all of which would present opportunities for the accumulation of tips and travelling expenses, as well as offering an exciting life. It could also present a genuine chance of education and betterment, as shown by a footman in the household of the Duke of Sutherland who took the opportunity of a prolonged stay in London to learn French.[62] On the other hand, travelling servants had less personal freedom than residents, who were left for long periods on board wages, under the eye of a senior servant. To some extent they enjoyed the best of both worlds. When the family left the house, those servants who remained had more control over their food. They often ate in small groups, perhaps even cooking their own food, as shown by the purchase of a dutch oven for use in the servants' hall in 1833.[63] Cooking in groups was often not wholely successful, however. One footman recorded the system in use at Eden Hall, near Penrith.[64] Here the first footman catered for the menservants, by which was meant he bought a yard of salt belly pork which lasted all week. In another house the oddman did the cooking for the men, but because he had no time to prepare the vegetables, the first footman was supposed to help out.[65] As he was usually tied up with other duties, more often than not the men sat down to an unsatisfactory meal of meat and bread. Amongst the residents at Dunham was one kitchen-maid, so she probably cooked for the others, perhaps using the grates in the servants' hall or the still room rather than the kitchen. The real advantage of board wages was of course that they were paid in cash weekly and, with careful budgeting, a fair proportion could be saved. This would accumulate if the family were away for long periods and might sometimes even double the servants' remuneration.

Another problem for servants on board wages was how to cope with their washing. All the laundry-maids were in the travelling household, busy coping with the family at Enville or elsewhere. Whilst they were on board wages, other residents were therefore entitled to 'washing money' to offset the cost of having their laundry done elsewhere. Obviously, an energetic maid who was happy to do her own washing, and maybe even other people's, could earn a few shillings in this way. It is likely that many households on board wages became entrepreneurial. In the Sutherlands' household at Trentham, the brewer/baker was given permission not only to go to other houses in the area to help with brewing, but also to buy in his own supply of

Dunham has few surviving pictures of servants. This rare photograph, taken in 1913, is of the laundry-maids at Ham House, Surrey.

flour and use the house bakehouse to make bread to sell to other servants and even outside the house.[66] At Dunham, the problem of laundry was solved by employing a casual washwoman from the village.

How were servants recruited onto the Dunham staff? In a family of twin households, one obvious way was to draw from the other household, and clearly this happened fairly frequently. Davenport, the land steward at Dunham, for example, sent his son to work at Enville, and in 1828 a servant called Robert Sketchley went to Enville after two years service at Dunham.[67] The 1851 census records recruitment from other family estates, too, for the park-keeper, Stephen Adams, was born in Leicestershire on the Greys' Bradgate estate and had moved to Dunham three to five years previously. Beyond this, the most favoured and most successful means of recruitment was by word of mouth and personal contact, often from servant to servant. Personal approach by would-be servants to the land agent, Worthington, seems to have been fairly common and is reported in the agent's correspondence to the Earl on several occasions. A good example comes in a letter dated 1799, when Worthington reported to the Earl at Enville that he had received a visit by a man named William Gatland:[68]

The male servants at Petworth House in Sussex in 1880. The house steward, not in livery, is in the back row, second from left; the chef is in the middle row, flanked by the lodge keepers.

Gardeners and estate craftsmen at Standen, West Sussex, *c.*1905. The estate bailiff, Charles Wood is standing on the left with his son, Ernest, next to him.

> One William Gatland has called here and wishes to serve your Lordship in the capacity of postilion. He says that he has been told that your Lordship's postilion is to leave and that he is well known to your Lordship's coachman. Gatland says that he is aged 19 years and that he has served Mr. Tatton at Withenshaw as postilion near two years. He seems a very nice good looking, small sized Boy indeed, but further I do not know him.

This case highlights another favoured way of finding staff, by handing posts on within a family. Twenty years later, in 1819, the postilion was an Edward Gatland, obviously a relation of William, possibly his son. The Worthingtons themselves handed down the agency of the family estates for several generations, John Davenport's son following in his father's footsteps at Enville. Similarly, Timothy Brownell handed on the post of estate carpenter to his son.

7

'A respectable and genteel looking servant'

EnvArch G2/2/2/13

Extract from a letter from John Trevanion, Mount Street, to the 6th Earl of Stamford at Dunham Massey, 17 July 1819

My dear Lord Stamford,
… After my letter had gone to the post yesterday I saw Philip Osgood, as Butler; form at Newberry in Berkshire, 5ft 10½ inches high, 36 years of age, lived six years with the late Mr. Wyndham M.P. for Glamorganshire, as Valet and afterwards Butler, five years with Sir Saml. Hood as Butler & six years and three months with L' Carhampton, who parted with him upon making an alteration in his Family in consequence of Lady C's health, upon the whole I think him a more likely servant to suit you then Bray [?], and he may be easily put off as being a Scotchman as I told him I feard that would be an objection, at all events I shall keep your answer from him, till you send me your wish's; Osgood is a married man but his wife (whom I yesterday saw) appears a most respectable woman and is settled in a very good business as Ladies Dress Maker in Davies St. They have two children at school, he had 70gs per annum with L' Carhampton, and of what he has always heard of your Family is most particularly anxious to live in it, as he wishes to get into a place where he is likely to remain …

Extracts from a letter from John Trevanion, Mount Street, to the 6th Earl of Stamford at Dunham Massey, 21 July 1819

My dear Lord Stamford,
… I have engaged Philip Osgood at 70gs per annum for you without any perquisites, if his character answers … he has just sent me the enclosed as a specimen of his hand writing which I think very tolerable …

Philip Osgood is rather marked with the small pox and a little freckled but is in my opinion certainly a respectable & genteel looking servant.

Extract from a letter from Lord Carhampton at Painshill to Lord Stamford at Dunham Massey, 29 July 1819

… Lady Carhampton's severe illness prevented us from seeing company, the services of Osgood could therefore be dispensed with. I had no other reason for finishing with him. He is capable in every respect of the situation of Butler and Groom of the Chamber …

These methods probably did not work so well with senior female staff, though junior staff might still be recruited by word of mouth from local rural families. As late as the 1930s a junior housemaid at Dunham was found her place by patronage; a friend who knew the girl's family back on the Cholmondeley estates had a word with Lady Stamford. Experienced professional staff would be more difficult to find and no doubt recourse would be made to respectable agencies in London who specialised in domestic service. Certainly when the 9th Earl came to set up a new household in the early twentieth century he used professional servant agencies.

8

Letter from John Poole in Macclesfield to the Earl of Stamford at Dunham Massey, 26 July 1819

EnvArch G2/2/2/13

ans 30 July

Macclesfield July 26

My Lord

I am honoured with your Lordships Letter of yesterday enclosing an abstract of the Duties to be perform'd by the House-Steward at Dunham, to which I willingly accede — In answer to your Lordships enquiries therein contained, I beg leave to state I am 32 Years of Age, Married but no family, a Native of Shropshire, and a Protestant of the Established Church, and have lived for the last 13 Years in Cheshire & Shropshire in the service of different Gentlemen — Should my being Married be any impediment, I beg to state it is my Wifes intention to go to service or to live with her friends — In regard to Terms I shall leave that entirely to your Lordship, to give what has been usually given in the Situation before — waiting your Lordships further commands

I remain

Your Lordships

Most obed^t

Humble Servt

Jno Poole

Saving Bank

Park Green

In the early nineteenth century things were more gentlemanly. In 1819 the newly inherited 6th Earl relied on someone called John Trevanion to find replacements for the old Earl's pensioned-off servants. He wrote to the Earl, in fairly familiar but business-like terms, reporting on interviews with applicants from agencies in London and following up character references with previous employers. From his general tone (he called a servant's experience 'form') and comments about dogs and horses (he asked the Earl if one of his keepers could break in a promising young setter), it seems he was a sporting friend. His death was recorded in the Torry journal for 1825.[69] It was Trevanion who recruited Philip Osgood, the new butler, but the Earl seems to have dealt directly with the new house steward for Dunham, John Poole (Box 7, opposite and Box 8, above).

* * *

Indoor servants not only worked at Dunham; it was their home too. Both Poole and Osgood were married men who were prepared to be separated from their wives for much of their working lives, though Osgood set up house with his wife in 1827. What sort of accommodation was provided in the house?

When the new kitchen court had been built back in the 1720s, bedrooms for living-in servants and labourers were provided on the first floor and above the brewhouse and stables, in the mill, the farm and the garden. The earliest record of their contents dates from 1758, at which time the quality of accommodation, the degree of privacy and the comfort of the furnishings varied considerably according to the sex and status of the individual. As time went by the variability tended to lessen, or at least to become less obvious. In 1758, however, the contrasts were marked.

In 1758, senior male members of staff were comfortable. The cook's room, for example, was furnished with a bed hung with 'green Kidderminster stuff', his window curtains were in a blue and white striped material, and there was an oak table, a washstand and chairs, a shelf and wall-pegs for his clothes. In contrast, at this date the butler was still a fairly lowly servant and his room reflected this. He had a simple low-level bed with a green camlet cover and red window curtains, one oak table and three chairs. It is not clear from the inventory where the footmen slept, though this may have been above the porter's and steward's rooms. The housemaids' room was less luxurious but still comfortable by the standards of the age, though not, perhaps, by ours. They shared three to a room, each with their own bed, which was 'half-headed', not four-poster. They had a fireplace, one table and one mirror between them and shelves and pegs for their clothes. They did have some privacy from each other as their closet-stool was tucked away in a closet off the bedroom. For their education they were provided with a large quarto-sized Bible. Over the coach stables, life was tougher. A manservant's bedroom here was furnished very sparsely with a low bed, two chests, two old tables, some chairs and a stool. The grooms' room was similarly furnished, but was also as much a workplace as a bedroom, housing a wooden horse for tack, a mortar and pestle for making medicines for the horses, and a corn chest. Other accommodation for the outdoor servants included a bedroom for the hinds (farm labourers), the garden labourers and two mill workers in the higher and the lower mill; the rooms also included rudimentary cooking equipment, for they were not included in the fellowship of the servants' hall.

By 1819, furnishings were perceptibly more comfortable for the lower servants. Three of the four footmen slept in one room, each in a single four-poster bed with mattresses and feather beds. There were four large trunks for their personal belongings, a clothes cupboard, some drawers and chairs, a desk and some stools. The 1st footman had a bedroom to himself, furnished similarly but with a few extra touches of comfort: he had a better-quality feather bed, a piece of carpet on the floor, a toilet jug and bowls and a mirror. One of the kitchen-maids also had a room to herself, fitted with a four-poster bedstead and a flock mattress with a good feather bed on top, three blankets and a coverlet. There were also a couple of tables and chairs, a cupboard and a toilet bowl and jug. The housemaids were in a dormitory of four

RIGHT: Servants' washstand at Dunham Massey, painted in the house-style, yellow.

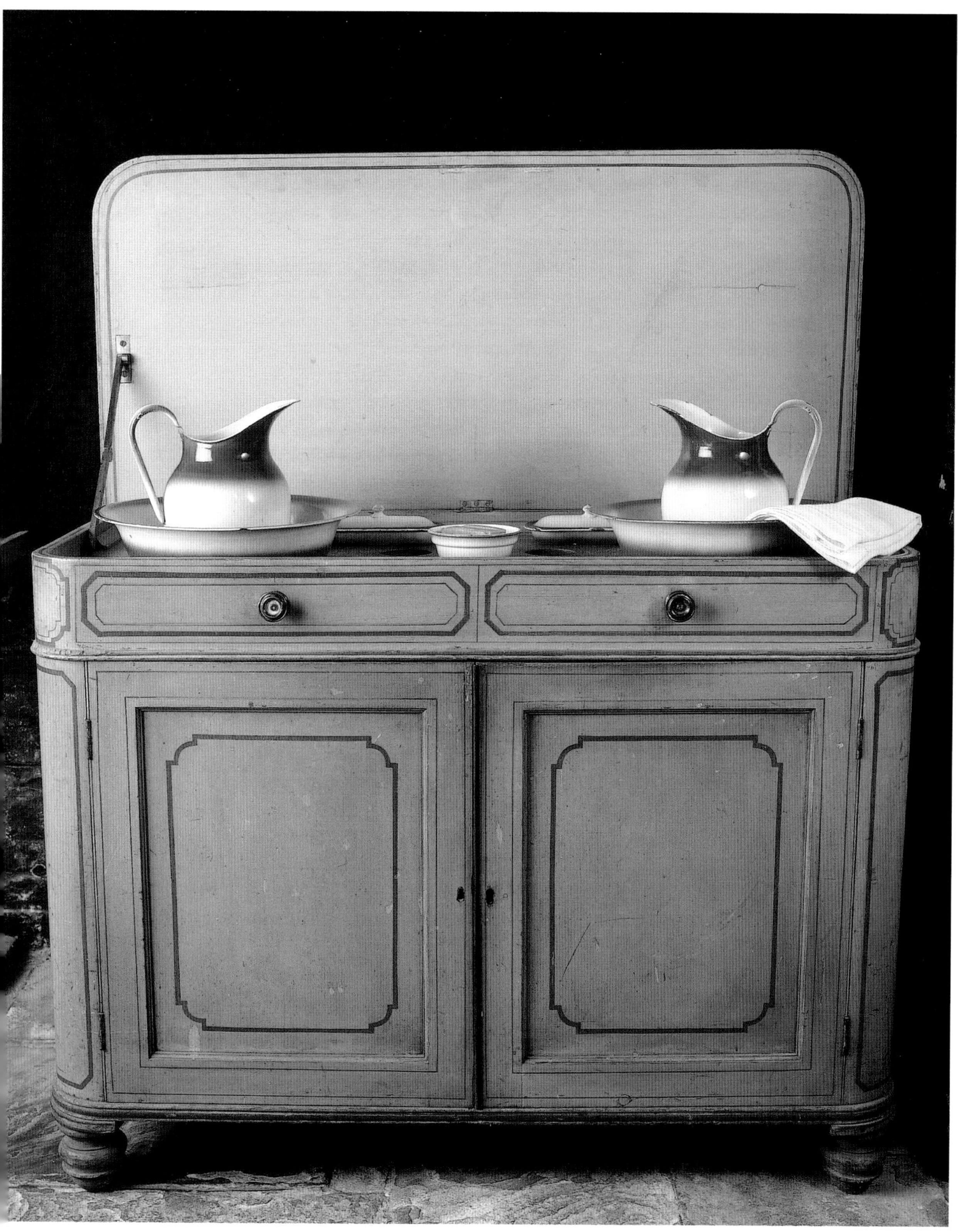

but each had a separate four-poster bed with mattress and feather beds, and each had a chair, a chest of drawers and a piece of carpet by the bed. They shared one pier dressing-glass and a small wall-mirror. The still-room maid was of slightly higher status, for she had room of her own and her bed had three mattresses under the feather bed. She also had a carpet as well as a rug and a small desk as well as a chair, dressing-glass and toilet set.

Several features marked the status of servants and their position within the hierarchy. One was whether they had their own rooms or were expected to share. Another was the amount and quality of bedding. Before the Victorian period, beds were fitted with solid plank bottoms on which were laid mattresses or palliasses. These were home-made of striped ticking stuffed with tight bundles of straw or horsehair, flock or wool according to wealth. Wool mattresses were definitely indicators of status. The family beds at Dunham were often fitted with three mattresses on top of each other – the lowest a straw palliasse, next a mattress of thick curled hair, then a top mattress of carded wool. On top of the mattresses were laid feather beds. In 1905 Lady Stamford's bed was like this, plus a bolster, four pillows, three Witney blankets and a white counterpane. Poorer people slept straight on a single mattress and it is a mark of the relatively high position of the Dunham indoor servants that they all had feather beds on top of the mattress. It is interesting that before the late nineteenth century, however, grooms were given straw rather than flock or hair mattresses. This may well have been for reasons of hygiene rather than just status, as straw palliasses were easily burnt and replaced annually. Feather beds were valuable and carefully inventoried by weight of feathers, usually around 70 to 80lb, and by quality of feathers, between 1s and 2s per lb. Clearly, feather beds were an important feature of country-house life and cleaning and maintaining them was a major chore.

Dressing and toilet facilities were also provided according to status and sex. In the 1758 inventory, each of the dressing rooms of the family members was furnished with a washstand and toilet set, with shelves, pegs, a linen press or cupboard for clothes storage. Wardrobes were not mentioned until 1819, but by the 1820s the best family rooms were equipped with mahogany wardrobes 'on the New Principle'.[70] Senior servants seem to have had good oak or mahogany furniture, which in later inventories was sometimes described as 'antique', but lower servants' furniture was old, ill-matched or made of cheaper wood and painted. In the later nineteenth century, however, we can see a definite Dunham style emerging, typified by the washstands that have survived in some number, painted yellow.

The quality of the chamberware was another obvious marker of wealth and status. Back in 1758 the cook had no waterjug or washing-basin permanently in his room. Later servants' bedrooms were supplied with these, but sets were often incomplete, damaged or unmatched. The servants never had more than seven pieces to a set, but Lady Stamford's set consisted of eighteen pieces of chintz-patterned china, chosen no doubt to match the bed-hangings, curtains and upholstery which were of chintz cambric. Other chamber sets for family use were usually white Queensware or blue Davenport, with one French set in the Rose Dressing Room.

Until 1814, when the Earl installed a water-closet for family use, the household functioned like most others by a combination of closet-stools (what later came to be

RIGHT: Servant's bedrooms were functional if spartan, as shown by this late nineteenth-century example from Llanerchaeron, South Wales.

called commodes) and outdoor privies. Each family dressing room had a closet-stool and pan, as also did the bedrooms of the female servants, but not the menservants. Later in the nineteenth century, closet-stools went out of fashion and were replaced by chamber-pots for night use. Presumably these were emptied down the privies, though some urine was saved for making lye and other cleaning purposes. There were at least two standards of outdoor privies, for in 1827 the flagged floor to the 'best privys' was raised, though where these were is uncertain. The servants' outdoor privies were in the garden behind the wash-house, with separate facilities for men and women. In 1823 these were painted a drab colour with oak-finished doors but later this was changed to dark chocolate. For ventilation there were wire lattices, and for privacy print curtains. Someone had problems in 1833, for the holes in the seats had to be cut larger.[71]

* * *

A household of forty-five individuals was not particularly extravagant by country-house standards in the nineteenth century. In the absence of systematic records of wages it is impossible to say whether this size of household was representative of other periods at Dunham, but given the general consistency over time in many other respects, it probably was, allowing as we must for variations in family size and ages. What does seem extravagant to modern eyes is the fact that half of these people were employed to look after a house which for six months of each year was empty but for themselves. The level of care which such a staff could give to the fabric of the building and its contents should give pause for thought, especially for modern administrators. To obtain some idea of why such a staff was needed, and what tasks they were engaged upon, we need to look at the day-to-day records of the manager in charge, the steward.

CHAPTER FOUR

'Sundry small sums to Poor People'

The Work of the House Steward

The aim of the following three chapters is to look at the work of the household at Dunham Massey within a single year, 1822. The previous chapter introduced us to the three players critical to the management of the household economy at Dunham in the early 1820s: John Poole, the house steward; Anne Calder, the housekeeper; and John Davenport, the land steward, previously the farm steward. All three worked under the land agent, Hugo Worthington. Davenport had been in post since 1801, Poole was appointed in the autumn of 1819 and Mrs Calder sometime between 1819 and 1822. The key role as far as the house was concerned was Poole's. He controlled the house staff, kept the household records and supervised Mrs Calder, who managed the female staff on his behalf. She kept her own records and supplied Poole with written copies of them. This was probably a straightforward relationship since both had clear-cut responsibilities, at least on paper, and both were permanently resident at Dunham so would be used to working with each other. Poole indeed proved to be one of the longest-serving house stewards the Greys ever had, remaining in post until 1834. Mrs Calder appears to have been replaced by Mrs Iveson by 1825.

Poole's relationship with Davenport appears to have been good, despite the fact that one was a newcomer and one an old hand. Historically, however, the farm and house stewards had been at odds. At issue was the question of who was responsible for the maintenance of the park, and the difficulty went back some years. Between 1800 and 1813 the job had been given to the house steward, then Robert Foot, a faithful and reliable servant of the 5th Earl who was happy with this situation. Davenport was not, however. On Foot's death in 1813, he lobbied Hugo Worthington to ask the Earl to place him in charge of the park as he felt he could do the job more efficiently and at less cost than any newly appointed house steward. Worthington wrote to the Earl at Enville recommending the suggestion as a means of preventing 'any small misunderstanding as to what matters belong to the care of the House Steward, and what to the Farming Steward'.[72] A shakily written reply came from the Earl, then aged seventy-six and irascible. Clearly irritated by the request, he referred to Mr Davenport's repeated applications on the matter and his own repeated answers in the negative:

> I have always found it difficult to get a person for House Steward unless he had some other employment than in the House, and that is my reason for giving him the care of the Park.... It will be very easy to settle the business belonging to each if they are disposed to be accommodating to each other. The parting with Upper Servants and making new regulations in my Family are not agreeable at my time of life.

The 5th Earl certainly had a point, for in the ten years prior to his arrangement with Foot there had been four house stewards. Foot was highly valued by the Earl, for in March 1813, when 'a very great disagreement' occurred between Foot and the housekeeper Mrs Princep, the Earl was clearly more concerned that he might lose the services of the steward than those of the housekeeper, whose health in any case was 'precarious'. When Foot's successor, John Parkhurst, was eventually appointed in 1813, he took up the role of manager of the park in line with the Earl's instructions. He remained in post for six years, leaving at the death of the old Earl in 1819, when Poole was appointed. The new Earl clearly had no qualms about changing the old order, for by 1822 Davenport was running both farm and park and indeed was responsible for the accounts of the head gardener and the miller as well as the stables.

Poole appears to have been happy to restrict his responsibilities to the house. In 1822 this was far from being a sinecure, for he not only had to supervise the normal servant household and cope with a six-month stay by the family and their guests but he also had the additional stress of a major upheaval in the house caused by the 6th Earl's programme of building improvements. There were workmen all over the place, dust everywhere, stonemasons and carpenters keeping up a continual hammering, scaffolding causing security problems, consignments of goods and equipment to be checked, a clerk of works to be accommodated, bills to be paid: all whilst trying to keep the normal routine of the household running smoothly. In addition, his own room had recently been replastered and was now being painted. Poole kept a separate ledger, a building account book, which recorded the expenditure incurred by the architect, John Shaw, and which finally reached a total of £6,480.[73] This record gives at least a glimpse of the complexities of such a project and how they impinged on the household.

The accounts began in December 1821 and continued until February 1823. Items were usually unspecific as to site, but it is clear that work started early in 1822 with the purchase of scaffold planks, poles and ropes. Throughout 1822 there were regular payments to tradesmen: carpenters, blacksmiths, plumbers, sawyers, bricklayers, marble masons and marble-polishers, glaziers, bell-hangers and turners. By December 1822 the work had shifted to plasterers, painters, picture-gilders and cleaners, carvers, repairers of china and paper-hangers.

The alterations were completed using a mixture of local tradesmen and imported craftsmen (Box 9, p.78). Local labour, whether employed directly by the estate or through contractors in the area, played a far from negligible role in the work, though locals tended to be less specialised than the workmen brought up from London. In addition to their wages, all the men were entitled to beer money, and the London

The entrance to the Great Hall of Dunham Massey, seen from across the inner court. This was the site of the corridor built in 1822 and later demolished.

men were entitled to travelling expenses to and from Dunham. Since these were listed individually they give a little more detail than the wage payments, which were simply lumped together. Twelve carpenters were paid travelling expenses from London at the beginning of the job in January 1822 and at the end of the job return travelling expenses were paid over a period of three or four months as individual carpenters were laid off and went home. Marble-polishers were still arriving in April

9

Labour costs of alterations to Dunham Massey by John Shaw, 1822

EGR 7/19/1

	£	s	d
Staff from London			
James Berry, clerk of works	91	9	0
Carpenters and marble masons	802	2	4
TOTAL	893	11	4
Dunham estate labour			
John Hope, bricklayer	437	14	1
Dan Parsons, blacksmith	70	19	10
Timothy Brownell, joiner	197	4	4
TOTAL	705	18	3
Local contract labour			
John Pearson, glazier and plumber, Altrincham	357	6	1
Joseph Davies, stonemason, Millington	474	14	9
Thomas Carter, slater, Altrincham	21	19	10
Zanetti & Agnew, gilders and framers, Manchester	505	9	0
William Johnson, turner, Altrincham	3	3	6
Reynolds & Gregory, upholsterers, Manchester	98	8	4
William Gilgrass, plasterer	4	8	0
Man taking care of scaffold ropes		2	6
TOTAL	1,465	12	0
Unknown provenance but probably not local			
William Thomas, plasterer	1148	7	1
William Featherstone, painter	764	10	7
Heap, marble mason	18	14	8
Peter Clure [?] bell-hanger	96	3	0
Dupper, Slodden & Co., paper-hangers	1	7	0
John Thomas, carpenter	2	16	0
TOTAL	2,031	18	4
Total beer money paid	31	2	10
Total travel expenses paid	115	6	3
Total carriage bills	245	13	11
GRAND TOTAL	5,489	2	11

and left in July. The rate for a single journey to London seems to have risen over the year from £2 15s to £3 10s. James Berry, the clerk of works, made two trips home to London, one in June and one at the end of the job in August, when various other expenses were paid to him such as postage and a £20 gratuity from the Earl. He also made trips to Manchester and Liverpool (one in the company of John Poole), perhaps to check out suppliers. Beer money was paid at a rate of 2s a week. The total sum paid out indicates 311 man-weeks' work. The London glazier stayed for five days, two paper-hangers from Manchester five weeks, but by far the largest sum of beer money (£23) was paid out to William Thomas and his men, the plasterers.

The carriers' bills cover mainly long-distance carriage of equipment and high-value goods. The craftsmen from London, for example, did not carry their tools and patterns with them but sent them separately in tool chests at a cost of almost £30. The painters also sent a basket of equipment. Carriage of the scagliola columns for the new dining room (what is now the Saloon) cost £54, and new furniture bought in London cost over £100 to send to Dunham by T. & M. Pickfords. This was not without mishap, for two years later Pickfords refunded an amount of £30 for damage to china which had to be repaired by Zanetti and Agnew, a firm of framers and carvers in Manchester.[74]

Timber scaffold poles, planks and ropes were bought locally. Health and safety issues do at least appear in the accounts, though they were not rated very highly, given the sum of 2s 6d paid to a man for regularly checking the scaffolding. Approximately 30,000 bricks were bought through three local suppliers, and items such as nails were delivered from Warrington. The estate was not able to supply all of the large quantity of lime for mortar needed and had to buy in £22 worth. Alterations to the roof required the hire of four large tarpaulins for six weeks, costing £1. Danzig oak for boarding came via Liverpool up the Bridgewater Canal.

It is likely that most of the onus of bill payment for the building project was borne by James Berry, the clerk of works. John Poole, however, received all incoming cash deposits from Hugo Worthington with which to pay the bills and he kept the overall record. The amount of cash going through his hands for this part of his work was substantial (the cash coming in varied from £200 to £1,000 a time), yet in terms of numbers of bills it was probably less demanding than his routine work of running the household.

For the routine household payments, Poole kept two running ledgers, the cash book and the account book, which are both key to making sense of the housekeeping system.[75] The two ledgers are totally separate and have different functions. The rest of this chapter is largely based on the cash book, whilst the account book throws more light on the housekeeper's work and therefore forms the basis of Chapter Five. Cash books have survived for only limited periods in the nineteenth century and none at all from the eighteenth; thus comparison with earlier house stewards' records is not possible.

The cash book recorded purchases made by John Poole himself. It was organised in the usual way, with incoming finance shown on the left-hand page, usually by way of cash amounts given by the land agent, Hugo Worthington, while on the right-hand page were the daily records of Poole's outgoings. The year is divided into quarterly accounting periods when the books were balanced: at the end of March, June, September and December. Cash book entries were usually single-line. For further detail we need to refer back to the original record, the bundles of vouchers which are the actual paper bills sent in by the tradesmen and signed off by the steward.[76] Both cash book and account book were checked, signed and dated by the Earl, invariably on the Tuesday of each following week, when the steward must have

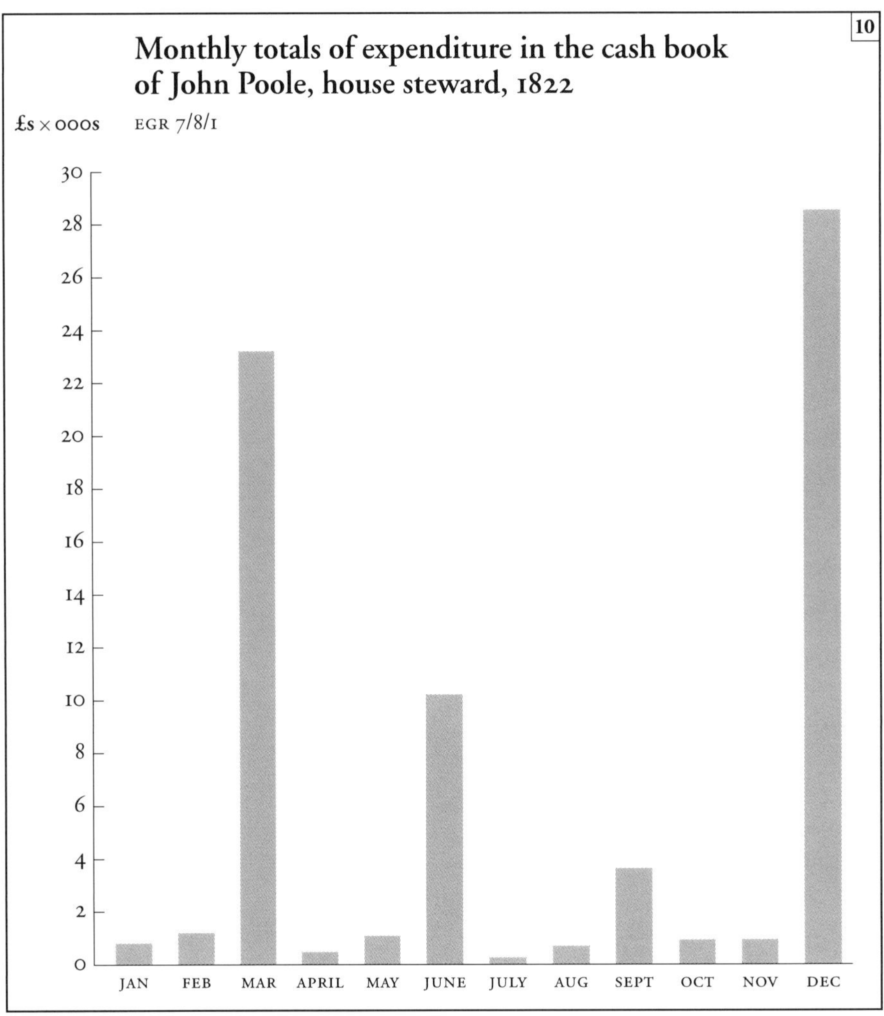

presented himself and his records in the Earl's business room. In some cases pencil notes in the margin show that someone, probably the Earl himself, checked Poole's arithmetic and rarely found it wanting. For his clerical work Poole bought pens, but the Earl bought pencils through his personal accounts.

Poole had a regular annual routine for the payment of bills (Box 10, above). A few were settled quarterly in December, March, June and September. These were mainly the smaller creditors, usually modest-scale businessmen such as the taxidermist and the turner, who could not afford to allow their clients to accumulate credit. More tradesmen were paid twice yearly, in June and December; among them were the maltster, whose bills would have accumulated to a huge amount otherwise. Well over half the accounts, however, were paid in annual bills at Christmas. These included most of the large and medium bills and also many of the smallest. Some of them were regular suppliers who allowed bills to accumulate, but others were one-off single bills for jobs done earlier in the year. In a few instances small amounts were allowed to accumulate for years. Payment and record-keeping must have kept the house steward and to a lesser extent the housekeeper extremely busy at the end of

December. After the 25th the tradesmen's bills began to flood in, sent by post or presented in person. This came to a head on 31 December, when the cash book recorded sixty bills paid, totalling over £890. Almost a third of the steward's annual housekeeping bills by value were paid on this single day. Annual settling, of course, favoured the house at the expense of the suppliers, but presumably the latter were happy to comply in return for the status bestowed on their business. They must have been established businessmen, able to support loans or with sufficient cash flow from other customers to enable them to pay their workmen throughout the year. As a system it had the benefit of regulating the amount of cash kept in the house over long periods.

Quarterly deposits of cash were received by Poole from Hugo Worthington in June, September, October and December, all in round sums, the smallest £200, the largest £660. In December, four issues of cash were made within four days to cover the annual payments to tradesmen and to leave a balance with which to start the new year; thus, at the beginning of January 1822, Poole had £352 cash in hand to bring over from the previous December. As he was still cash in hand at the end of the first quarterly accounting period on 25 March 1822, no more cash was needed. The reserve was not topped up until June, when there was a deficit owing to him of £19 16s. He was then issued with a further £200, but by the end of September he was again owed a balance, this time of over £48. The substantial input during December, however, again left him with a balance in hand, of over £450, which would hopefully last until June. In addition to the main cash deposits from Worthington, two smaller cash inputs were received to offset payments made by Poole against the racing and furniture accounts. This means that a total of over £3,090 in cash went through John Poole's hands during 1822, probably kept in a box in the house safe. On two occasions he was out of pocket, presumably having to stand this from his own personal resources.

It is important to remember here that we are dealing only with the house steward's out-payments, not those of other senior servants or, indeed, with the personal expenditure of the Grey family. Poole's own expenditure within the cash book for 1822 can be simply categorised (Box 11, below). By far the largest sums paid out by

11

Expenditure in the cash book of John Poole, house steward at Dunham Massey, 1822

EGR 7/8/1

Trade and craftsmen	£1,667	18s	0d
Charity	£329	17s	7d
Medical treatments	£197	16s	8d
Travel and post	£157	12s	9d
Racing	£103	15s	
Casual labour	£98	12s	1d
Rates	£1	5s	4d
Total expenditure for 1822	**£2,556**	**17s**	**5d**

the house steward were made to cover trade and craftsmen's bills, paid out to over sixty creditors. Fifty per cent of these were small accounts of under £10, presented by a wide variety of firms and individuals. All but one of the rest were medium-sized, between £10 and £99. These included a local baker who supplied salt to the household, a bookbinder, a chandler providing candles and soap, a tailor, plumber, two millers and a brazier. Only one account came to over £100: the maltster, John Barratt, was easily the largest supplier at £913 13s 7d.

The goods supplied and the services rendered covered a wide range. Whilst the upheaval involved in the major building works was taking place, the new Earl set up an extensive programme of building maintenance, directly under Poole's supervision. The estate carpenter, Timothy Brownell, was paid for sawing new floorboards and for seventy-nine days' joinery work costed at 3s 4d a day. The estate bricklayer, John Hope, billed three days cutting airholes into the east front to provide ventilation into the structural voids and half a day's work for himself and a labourer in setting a substantial number of new chimneypots. Problems with copper boilers in the wash-house and brew-house were addressed by John Hope with the help of Samuel Clarke, a coppersmith from Manchester. A contract plasterer, William Gilgrass, was employed to replaster the stable loft and whitewash the servants' quarters, while a local locksmith cleaned house door-locks and made new keys. An important job was the fitting of new iron downspouts and piping to the stable block and kitchen court, though this was later replaced by copper spouting.

John Pearson, a contract glazier and plumber from Lymm, must have been a familiar figure around the house. His family and the labourers they employed offered a versatile and useful service. Besides fitting the windows in the new courtyard corridor and north front, Pearson replaced cracked window-panes and fitted new sashes in Lord Grey's Room, the Yellow Damask Room and the Maroon Room. He repaired lead piping in the kitchen and replaced small areas of quarry-tiled floors in the servants' hall, porter's lodge, stables, brew-house and dairy. He also supplied a new ball-and-lever mechanism for the Earl's water-closet off the staircase, and his men cleared the house drainpipes of leaves. One of his family in Altrincham was a professional painter who painted three washstands, made six new labels for the calling-bells, relettered seven old ones, and painted a new coat of arms for the Earl of Warrington in the parish church. One of the Pearsons' labourers spent four days painting wire flower-stands and two others two days each painting the coach-house doors a chocolate colour. They provided various amounts of paint (prussian blue for the coachman), solder (for the brewing copper), rosin, putty, turpentine, and dry white lead and black lead for the housemaids. Pearson even mended pewter and silver.

A skilled tradesman expected around 3s 6d a day for his time. This was the rate charged by William Gilgrass, who was the plasterer and colour-washer used routinely by the house, though the carpenter charged 2d a day less and some of Pearson's skilled men earned 3d more. Gilgrass charged 2s 8d a day for a partially skilled labourer and 1s for a completely unskilled man. It seems to have been usual for the contract craftsmen to charge not only for their time but also for travel expenses and beer allowance. Burford, the supplier of iron spouting, charged £3 for travel and both Gilgrass and Pearson charged a daily beer 'lowence' of 4d per day per head. All

12

Transcript of a bill for linen, from John Satterfield, 1822

EGR 7/12/8/29

John Satterfield, Manchester, Linen Drapers to their Majesties

			£	s	d
Feb 19	Dying a quantity of buff calico		3	9	0
	Paid for glazing sundry pieces of furniture & Buff calico		2	13	0
	29 yds buff calico		4	1	9
	Glazing			1	3
March 15	Paid for glazing sundry pieces of furniture		19	6	
May 18	" " " & linen		1	18	0
July 2	6 under blankets	@ 16s	4	16	0
	2 pair 12/4 blankets	@ 63s	6	6	0
	1 " 13/4 "	@ 70s	3	10	0
	1 " 14/4 "	@ 88s	4	8	0
July 6	8 half yds 6/4 flannel	@ 6s 6d	2	15	3
July 13	71 yds furniture dimity		17	5	7
	2 12/4 Marseilles quilt	@ 27s	2	14	0
	2 14/4 " "	@ 46s	4	10	0
July 19	54 yds Merone ferret	@ 2 half d	11	3	
July 20	7 yds striped silk dam.	@ 9s 6d	3	6	6
July 31	24 yds crimson cord	@ 9 half d	19	0	
Sept 4	1 cub quilt	@ 10s 6d		10	6
Dec 17	78 yds brown Holland	@ 11 half d	3	14	9
Dec 23	26 yds " "	@ "	1	4	11
TOTAL			**54**	**16**	**6**

were paid without demur, even though Poole's account book shows that the household had already issued its own beer to Gilgrass's men working in the house.

Many new items were bought, both luxuries and routine goods. For new fillings for bed mattresses Poole ordered from a local supplier 33lb of best white 'stoved' feathers (ie cooked and sterilised in an oven) at 1s 3d per pound. He later bought a further 50lb from an upholsterer and feather warehouse in Manchester. John Johnson, a local tailor, supplied men to work extensively in the house, making and fitting curtains, bedlinen and 'furniture' (ie drapes for four-poster beds), possibly for the Maroon Room. His bill for £11 13s covered 148 days at 1s 6d a day and twenty-five days of an apprentice at 1s 2d. The textiles on which they worked were obtained from John Satterfield, a cotton, linen and wool merchant from Manchester, who had to have some pieces specially dyed and glazed to suit (Box 12, above).

Glassware was bought: tumblers, decanters, champagne flutes, wine glasses and water bottles, many of them made 'to pattern'. A bill from the silversmith's includes the repair of a coffee-pot and the provision of new silver trays for the footmen. The bookbinder supplied thirty-five volumes of works by Richardson, Gilpin and Beaumont and Fletcher. He re-bound other books and spent several days rearranging the

Bill from William Vickers to John Poole, house steward, for new coppers and re-tinning, October–December 1822

13

EGR 7/12/8/2

Manchester Decr 1…

Rt Honble Earl of Stamford

Warrington

1822 To Wm Vickers

Date	Item	£ s d
Jany 12	2 Copper Sauce Pans 16..14 at 2/8	2.5.0
" "	Large Hand Bell	.. 12 6
Feby 16	Tinning Sauce Pan	.. 3 ..
" "	Repairing Water Boiler &c	.. 5 6
" "	Tinning Boiler	.. 5 6
" "	a 1 Inch Bibb Cock for Do Screw bolt	.. 8 ..
Mar 20	2 Glue Kettles	1 12 ..
" 23	5 Block Tin Dish Covers 16/11/10/6/6.6/6	2 10 ..
" "	1 Carrot & 1 Turnip Scoop	.. 4 6
Apl 2	12 Tin Paint Cans 1/3	.. 15 ..
" 17	Tinning large Pot with 2 Handles	.. 6 6
" "	" 2 large Soup Pans & Covers	.. 13 6
" "	" 1 Small Soup Pan	.. 4 ..
" "	" 4 Fish Kettles	1 10 ..
" "	" 3 Drainers	.. 14 ..
" "	" 3 Round Soup Pans	1 1 ..
" "	" 6 Oval Do	1 6 ..
" "	" 4 Drainers	.. 10 9
" "	" 3 Lip Sauce Pans	.. 6 6
" "	" 3 Dishes & 2 Basons	.. 14 6
" "	" 3 Frying Pans	.. 6 ..
" "	" 11 Stew Pans & 15 Covers	1 1 ..
" "	" 4 Round Dishes	.. 10 ..
" "	" 3 Oval Dishes	.. 8 ..
" "	" 1 Coffee Pot 2/9 New hinge 1/9	.. 4 6
" "	" 2 large Soup Pans & Covers	.. 13 6
" "	" 38 Stew Pans	5 8 ..
" "	" 17 Skimmers	.. 17 ..
" "	" 20 Spoons, 4 Ladles & 10 Iron Table Spoons	.. 17 ..
" "	" 5 Ale Cans	.. 9 ..
" "	" 2 Copper Bake Plates	.. 6 ..
" "	" 1 Large Sauce Pan	.. 6 ..
" "	New Bottom to Stew Pan	.. 12 ..
" "	" Patch to Dish	.. 2 6
" 20	Tinning 34 Stew Pans & 33 Covers	6 8 6
" "	" 1 Large Sauce Pan & Cover	.. 6 ..
" "	" 2 Square Bake Plates 2/	.. 4 ..
" 30	" Jelly Moulds	1 1 0
May 14	a Bottling Cock	.. 3 9
	Carrd forwards £	36 11 6

Date	Item	£ s d
1822	Brot forwards	36 11 6
May 27	1 Dozn Iron Table Spoons	.. 2 ..
June 18	new Small Screw to Garden Engine for Elbow Screw	.. 6 ..
"	Repairing Branch &c Fixing screw on	.. 3 ..
July 18	1 Large Pan & Cover	2 14 ..
" "	1 Middle Size Do	1 17 ..
" "	1 next Do	1 5 ..
" 23	2 Large Painted Dust Cans & Covers	.. 16 ..
" 27	2 Japanned Do	.. 16 ..
Augt 7	Pair of Copper Scales & Beam	.. 13 6
" 12	a Nest of Apothecaries Wts from 1/2 lb to 1/2 Qr of an ounce	.. 12 ..
" 19	Cleaning & Repg Copper Tea Kettle	.. 2 6
" 30	Copper Patch for Stew Pan & Tinning	.. 3 6
Sep 3	Tinning large Sauce Pan	.. 2 6
" 7	1 lb Brass Weight	.. 2 6
" "	Tinning Sauce Pan	.. 2 ..
" 28	" Large Pan & Cover	.. 5 ..
Octr 2	6 Tin Shaving Cans 1/3, 6 Bottoms for Do	.. 7 6
" 5	6 Coal Cans 10/	3 .. ..
Decr 17	Tinning 1 Large Stew Pan & Cover	.. 6 ..
" "	" 1 Do 5/ & 1 Do 4/	.. 9 ..
" "	" 1 Do without Cover	.. 2 6
" "	" 1 Small Do & Cover	.. 3 ..
" "	" 3 Small Do Do	.. 7 6
" "	" 4 Do without Covers	.. 4 6
" "	" 5 Stew Pan Covers	.. 7 6
		52 1 6

whole Library, for which he was paid 12gns. The taxidermist sent regular bills for mounting birds: a peacock, a black grouse, a pair of quails, a bald coot, a tern and a swan. A local turner made two stands for displaying gold cups, won by his Lordship's racehorses. Matting was bought to cover precious carpets and leather to bind their edges. The cushions in his Lordship's pew in Bowdon church were repaired, and Zanetti and Agnew regilded a table and cleaned mirrors and picture-glass in the house. Local men overhauled the clocks and tuned the piano (at 1gn a time).

William Vickers, a Manchester brazier, not only supplied new equipment for the kitchen and domestic offices but also patched and relined existing copper saucepans and stewpans (Box 13, opposite). Copper pans could poison food if the thin internal layer of tin were damaged; so since pans were cleaned by scraping with fingernails, salt, sand or lemon skins, sending them away to be relined was not only an important job but a never-ending one, requiring some degree of organisation on the part of both kitchen staff and tinsmith. Vickers' workshop was in Manchester and in April and late December, when the family were away from Dunham, successive consignments of pans were packed up in hampers and sent by a local boat carrier, to be returned a few days later. Smaller tinware items were provided by a more local tinman who also offered a repair service. Items such as oil-cans and tundishes (funnels), which today would be thrown away as being at the end of their working life, were carefully sent away to be repaired.

Bills from both estate and contract craftsmen illustrate the degree of work involved in routine maintenance. As we saw from Chapter Two, the blacksmith, Daniel Parsons, cleaned and oiled the kitchen smoke-jack several times a month besides carrying out repairs to a trivet, spits and skewers. He repaired the oven in the pastry and a lock in the porter's lodge and made two heaters for box smoothing iron. In the brew-house the bricklayer and brazier worked on one of the boilers and regular visits were made by the contract cooper, John Walton, who repaired barrel staves, replaced iron hoops (charged by the pound weight) and supplied new barrels and a new hop-sieve. Walton also supplied smaller hair sieves for the cook and the housekeeper and replaced sieve bottoms for them. The housekeeper asked for a riddle for sorting feathers for mattresses and the cook needed two new ice tubs and wooden spoons. The dairymaid ordered a ladling pail, a 'maidening tub' and maiden (a wooden stand), and someone (possibly the laundress) ordered two new 'betwalls' (beetles).

The annual bill from Edward Bolton, a local ironmonger, amounts to a prodigious list of small-scale supplies totalling £67 7s 11d. The most expensive item was the purchase of twelve stove pots and twenty-four bottoms (£4 15s 4d) for the charcoal stoves in the kitchen. The rest of the items were usually less than £1: hundreds of drawer and cupboard locks and handles, escutcheon plates and keys, nails and tacks of various sorts, turn-buttons, cup hooks, castors, hinges and cranks for the bell system. Bolton also cleaned and repaired locks in the domestic offices, the locksmith being responsible for door locks in the higher-status family and public rooms.

Other bills were for domestic consumables. Barratt the maltster's bill was largely for malt and hops, with a smaller amount for sundries such as brandy, gin and vinegar, corks, ivory black, brown and cap paper and oils. The annual salt bill came to over £67 for a total of 84 bushels in four quarterly deliveries, and £37 was spent on stationery supplies: fifteen reams of paper and thirteen bottles of ink. No fewer than 450 'best pens' were needed to keep the household functioning. Poole was also responsible for maintaining light in the house; he bought the cotton wicks and 22 gallons of best spermaceti oil (derived from whales and very expensive) for the lamps in the family apartments, as well as 135 dozen best-quality 'Kensington' candles ordered from a chandler in Paddington, who also supplied over 7cwt of 'best white soap'. He also bought thirty bags of sawdust for sprinkling on the kitchen floor to soak up spills, packing-cord for parcels, blacking for polishing boots (a total of 119 bottles for the year), new 'common stag cutlery' for the servants, a couple of kitchen knives for the cook, new brass taps for the brewer, new nets and fishing hooks for the keepers and mousetraps for the house. A firm run by two sisters, Sarah and Mary Dean, who lived on the estate, supplied the domestic textiles needed by the servants to operate the house. Conveniently close, they received no less than seventy-seven orders during the year for fabrics like sheeting and bed lace, ticking, diaper cloth, towelling, dowlas linen, blanketing, window-blind linen, canvas, green baize, scarlet binding, thread and various ribbons and tapes. Some of these were for the outdoor servants: tape for the keepers and brewer, and linen and flannel for the grooms.

It might be thought that such a deluge of goods and services represents a backlog of work accumulated over many years during which the old Earl had allowed the house to tick over, running itself into a genteel state of decay. There is probably some truth in this, but Poole's overall expenditure for 1822 was not exceptional. The requirements of upkeep were continual, especially in such a complex social and technical environment as a large-scale country house. Although new items were bought, much of the expense was in routine maintenance and the repair or replacement of parts of existing equipment. There was no large-scale modernisation of technology as there was to be at the beginning of the next century, when the effects of a long period of statis had to be addressed.

* * *

As the list on p.89 (Box 14) shows, charitable giving was much less important in terms of value than paying for goods and services. The expenditure is of a different order, illustrating as clearly as anything can do the great gulf between the social priorities of the privileged family and its neighbours. Yet most country houses saw charity towards the local poor as part of their traditional function of responsible care, as well as a means of binding themselves to neighbours and in times of trouble earning peaceful submission. Some charitable costs came out of the personal expenditure of the family, but others appear in the household accounts and were an important part of the steward's administrative work. At Dunham these were complex, organised through various channels and taking various forms. Many payments were accounted through Poole's cash book, but smaller amounts were put through other accounts such as those kept by the housekeeper, the farm and the mill. Payments were also made through the Earl's personal accounts for annual subscriptions to a wide variety of Cheshire and Manchester charities, including the Asylum for Deaf and Dumb Children, the General Dispensary for the Relief of Poor Married

Women, the Royal Universal Dispensary for Children, and the Society for the Support of Young Tradesmen.[77]

At a small-scale level the household was authorised to give sums, usually a shilling, to the travelling poor, that is, people in need who presented themselves at the house. Many larger country houses wishing to discourage undesirables from loitering around the grounds delegated this job to a salaried lodge-keeper, but since most of the lodges at Dunham were occupied by estate workmen, donations were dispensed at the back door of the house by the steward or housekeeper. Recipients were usually described as simply 'a poor man' but occasionally more detail is given: 'an Irish family', 'a poor man from Sunderland', and, more exotically, 'two poor German sailors'.

On fourteen occasions during the year, more specific applications were made to the house steward by local estate tenants who petitioned for assistance in times of trouble; for example, an old man asked for help when his daughter died, another when his cow died. These were always named and usually given £1 or less; they were never accounted as being donations to the poor, which would have been unseemly for his Lordship's tenants. Poole was also responsible for paying a series of annual donations to nine parishes, 2 to 6gns each and totalling £39 18s, probably the parish poor rate. The estate also tried to find employment of sorts for the poor of Bowdon. This took the form of weeding the causeway path between Bollington and the house, paid at a regular amount of £1 a month.

Donations of food and drink were made by the estate to the poor. The total value of these in 1822 amounted to around £60 and were made by Poole himself or through Mrs Calder or directly by the farm. The cellar book records four bottles of port given to the poor, valued at 19s. One and three-quarter pounds of tea and 14lb of brown sugar were bought by Mrs Calder specifically for the poor, paid for in one annual bill of 13gns. That barley was given to the poor is shown by an entry in the mill accounts for grinding 52 bushels at a cost of £3 18s 9d.[78] The barley itself appears in the farm grain book, and was issued every week at a rate of four measures a week.[79] Elsewhere in the accounts barley is valued at 4s a measure, which would give an annual value of £41 12s, plus the milling costs. This tradition had been established back in 1691 under the terms of the will of Dame Elizabeth Booth, the second wife of the 1st Baron Delamer, by which a yearly allowance of £5 was dedicated to the poor of Bowdon, to be given in the form of bread 'on every Sunday forever'. This was distributed every week in the church immediately after morning prayers, to twenty-four poor, aged parishioners.[80] The records of 1822 do not make it clear whether the dole was still given in the form of bread or simply as barley flour.

In addition to these weekly doles, on some specific occasions barley bread was made and distributed to all comers, especially the children of Bowdon. Alfred Ingham, a local historian writing in 1879, remembered the distribution of the Dunham 'barley hump' with great affection and 'the tenderest memories'. The bread was, he recalled, 'a few inches square, good and wholesome, hard nearly as a board, but not proof against the assaults of a vigorous appetite… . It was first come, first served. The boys were ranged on one side, and the girls on the other, and … a barrow filled with these "humps" was wheeled, and a piece given to each child.'[81] These distributions were similar in kind to the birthday issues of Dunham ale, which was also recalled by the same writer as being highly potent.

Further charitable support was given through the apothecary, Nathaniel Broadbent of Altrincham, who was reimbursed a sum of £78 2s for attendance and medicines for the poor.[82] Unfortunately, Broadbent's bills were unspecific, but we can get some idea of the ailments he was dealing with if we refer to a similar set of bills paid by the household of the Earl of Bradford at Weston-under-Lizard in Staffordshire at around the same time.[83] At Weston, the most commonly used treatments were laxatives, diuretics and emetics of various types. This reflects current thinking about 'morbid matters' hidden inside the body which had to be let out. Blood-letting, by scarifying with a sharp blade or cupping with a heated glass to draw the blood to the surface, was used for the same purpose, but for the poor at Weston blistering was more common because it was cheaper and required less skill to apply; some sort of acid or strong alkaline ointment was used to raise a weeping blister through which matter could escape. Cooling balms made of beeswax and olive oil to soothe the skin after blistering were common in the Weston bills. Many other treatments were for physical injuries such as broken wrists or badly cut fingers. Very common, too, were feverish illnesses and bad chests, the latter perhaps reflecting the presence amongst the poor of an aged population. Probably the poor at Dunham received similar treatments to these, but there must have been many more of them than at Weston for the bills are large by comparison: £78 for the year paid by the Earl of Stamford compared to £14 by the Earl of Bradford. Indeed, the 6th Earl's generosity in this respect was noted by his son-in-law and remembered decades later by a local writer.[84]

Poole's cash book shows several regular payments for schooling. In the absence of national funded education, charitable schools supported by local aristocratic houses were one of a few options for people of poorer means in the 1820s. The household at Dunham supported six such schools in nearby villages at a total cost of £29 10s 6d for the year. Bills were paid, for example, from John and Sarah Neild, stipulating the teaching of nine children in reading, writing and sewing. Eight of the nine were girls and cost £1 each a year. The boy was taught reading and writing only.

One of the schools for which Poole made salary, clothing and bedding payments in 1822 was the Little Heath School. This was funded by an endowed charity dating back to 1757 when a local man named Thomas Walton died, leaving securities and cash worth £15,000, of which £1,000 was left for local charitable purposes.[85] Walton had been house steward at Dunham in the 1740s but was also a landowner with interests in the salt industry. Because of his connection with Dunham, the 2nd Earl of Warrington and members of the Grey family were appointed as executors of his will. The money was used to provide a building and regular income for the Little Heath Charity School. Building work was carried out in the 1760s and Mary, Countess of Stamford, the daughter of the 2nd Earl of Warrington, was nominated the first sole visitor of the school, with rights to appoint and dismiss staff, to admit and discharge pupils and to set rules. At times the Stamford land agents were treasurers of the charitable trust which ran the school. Its original objectives were modest: to provide lessons in reading, writing and knitting (the latter for the girls only) and to enable pupils to recite the catechism by heart and take part in morning and evening prayers. The school survived into the twentieth century, to be administered eventually by the local education authority. Thomas Walton's charity also funded the Seamon's Moss School, in Oldfield's Brow, Dunham Massey. This was a school for boys aged over eight years, resident in Dunham Massey, Bowdon or Altrincham and already able to read. Pupils normally left at age fourteen, apart from exceptionally gifted boys who were prepared for university. Again Mary, Countess of Stamford was appointed visitor, with powers over the staff and pupils and the appointment of governors.

The largest single category of Poole's charitable accounts was the clothing and bedding donations (Box 14, below). As active executor, Mary, Countess of Stamford had control of the Walton Charitable funds, and any surplus left over from the main educational charities was channelled to her other interests, mainly the Bedding for the Poor Charity. Over a period of sixty or seventy years, from the 1770s to the 1840s, considerable sums both from the Walton Charity and the Grey family resources went towards this extraordinary charity, which became a large-scale and well organised operation.

The charity's aim was to alleviate some of the worst circumstances of poverty by providing bedding and clothing to the poor in the townships of Altrincham, Dunham Massey, Bowdon and Bollington. Originally, bedding was distributed to deserving cases in all the parishes once a year with an extra donation at Christmas. After 1805 this was changed to alternate years in different parishes. What was extraordinary was the fact that systematic annual surveys were made and registers kept. Potential recipients were inspected to assess both their needs (whether they needed sheets, blankets, quilts or chaff beds) and their worth (whether they were deserving of help and whether they or their spouses were local). The surveys recorded names, numbers in the family, numbers of beds and the state of their bedding, whether they

14

Donations for charitable purposes made through the cash book of John Poole, house steward at Dunham Massey, 1822

EGR 7/8/1

Doorstep giving	£1	18s	6d
Petitions	£9	14s	2d
Parish rates	£39	18s	
Schooling	£29	10s	6d
Bedding and clothing	£138	9s	7d
Tea	£13	13s	
Wine		19s	
Barley	£45	10s	9d
Medicines	£78	2s	
Work	£12		
TOTAL	**£369**	**15s**	**6d**

had coverlets or rugs, blankets and sheets, bed mattresses and whether they were kept clean.[86] In 1786, for example, almost 200 households were inspected in six townships, with a further 190 over the next couple of years. The Altrincham register for 1822 lists 158 named individuals receiving sixty pairs of blankets and sixty pairs of sheets. In the tough times of 1818 the recipients included working tradesmen such as a weaver, butcher, turner, shoemaker as well as a soldier, gardener and cotton-spinner. Many were widows living on their own or left with large families.

Such inspections were indicative of the extent to which the ordinary population was prepared to accept, perhaps even welcome, the attentions of the wealthier members of the community into an area as intimate as this. In the 1786 survey, the tone of the comments shows that beds were physically inspected and occasional judgement made on individuals. Of Samuel Pixton's bed, in which three people slept, it was noted: 'Nothing upon it but what they borrow. A worthless husband but deserving wife.' That there was a need for the charity is clear. The widow Grace Brundret had two children and all three slept in one bed. They 'had neither bed nor bedstead, lie upon the floor upon some old rags and only one blanket and one sheet to cover them'. In a separate house nearby, Robert Brundret had a family of seven, sleeping in two beds: 'Upon one nothing but old rags. Upon the other a quilt and an old blanket.' In yet another branch of the same family a young girl had been left orphaned to cope with her three younger siblings: 'Upon one a quilt, a piece of a rug by way of a blanket and one sheet. Upon the other nothing at all. NB. Very clean and has particular merit. Her father and mother are both dead and left 3 small children besides herself and she has ever since taken care of them without troubling the Town.' There is a special poignancy about one entry relating to tailor John Johnson, which might well be describing the home of the father or grandfather of that John Johnson, tailor, who in 1822 worked on the furnishings in the house at Dunham and was also contracted to make warm clothing for the poor.

The house inspections were probably made by parish officials, but the Stamford household was involved in co-ordinating the response. The land agent's wife categorised recipients, copies of the reports were sent to the Earl for his inspection and much of the practical administration of the charity, the purchase and distribution of the bedding, for example, was carried out by the house steward at Dunham. Poole's cash book for 1822 records a total purchase of £81 17s from the household's main supplier of domestic fabrics, the Misses Dean, for blankets, sheets and bed quilts for the charity. Sheeting was bought by the yard and had to be made up by hand, probably by the Dunham housemaids during their afternoon sewing sessions.

Poole's accounts also show regular amounts being paid towards the making of shoes and warm clothing for the poor, amongst them boys attending Carrington School, but warm coats were also made for adults. These payments were probably recharged to Lord Warrington's Charity, a trust set up under the terms of the 2nd Earl of Warrington's will in 1758 to provide apprenticeships, schooling and clothing for poor children and for clothing and relief for the aged and infirm poor of Bowdon. The money endowed amounted to £5000, yielding an annual dividend of £168.

* * *

Summary of apothecary's bill, October–December 1822

15

EGR 7/12/8/8

	£	s	d
For the House: Antimonial wine, a bottle of castor oil, 4oz gum arabic, 8oz spirits of lavender, 4oz salts of tartar, phials		14	11
For Mrs Hawkes [Lady's maid?]: 4 visits, pills, linctus, plasters, emetic	2	0	0
John Thorpe [gamekeeper]: 2 visits, blisters, cerate, castor oil	1	14	5
William Footman: 15 visits, opening abcess, cerate, lotions, ointments	4	3	6
Anne Housemaid: 1 visit, 2 blistering plasters, ointment	1	3	6
Mrs Calder [housekeeper]: 2 visits, mixtures, pills, drops	1	0	6
Mr. Church [valet]: ointment, mixture		14	6
Mr. Davenport [land steward]: 3 visits, mixtures, liniment, electuary	2	1	0
Thos. Beckley [under-butler]: plaster, leeches		14	0
D. Shaw [gamekeeper]: arsenic, mixture		5	6
Mrs. Jones [lodge-keeper]: pills		2	6
John Cutler [brewer]: pills, mixture, leeches	1	2	6
Ann Laundrymaid: mixture, plaster		11	0
Mary Davenport [laundry-maid]: leeches, plaster, blister, cerate		17	0
John Lamb [groom]: mixture, plaster		5	0
Thomas Shawcross [under-coachman]: oxalic acid		3	0
John Davies [porter]: 1 visit, oil of vitriol, plasters		11	6
Mr Osgood [butler]: pills, powders, lip ointment		4	0
Lady Jane Grey: 2 visits, draughts		12	6
TOTAL	19	0	4

The list on p.81 (Box 11) shows that the third largest category of Poole's expenditure was £197, spent on medications and treatments for the household members and here we see an interesting and perhaps unexpected pattern. Of the £197, fifty-four per cent went to the same apothecary used for the poor, Nathaniel Broadbent, this time mainly on the servants. A further twenty seven per cent went to veterinary bills for the horses, with under eighteen per cent on medical bills for the family, though of course other medical expenses would have been incurred in Enville, though none appears in the London accounts.

Most of the servants were treated by the apothecary when they needed medical attention. Broadbent's bills were presented quarterly and for the period January–March 1822 the bill came to over £7 and included fourteen visits to named servants. In the last quarter of the year, the three months up to December, Broadbent's bill was well over twice this amount and included thirty visits, an increase largely due to the addition of the travelling servants (Box 15, above). As with the poor, illnesses and treatments alike are left unspecific. Items are usually listed simply as embrocations, mixtures and pills, aperients, emetics, electuaries (medicine bound with honey) and a collyrium (eye ointment). On several occasions the apothecary supplied blistering-plasters and leeches. The patients included a wide spectrum of the household, from the housekeeper, land steward and butler to a housemaid, two laundry-maids and two keepers. The most expensive and intractable problem was an abscess on one of the footmen. Other treatments were no doubt occasioned by accidents. Torry's journal reminds us generally throughout this period that even the relatively cosseted world of the estate was dangerous. It records occasions when one man was badly hurt by a barrel of ale rolling off a cart, the miller fell into the mill pool, carts were upset or collided with pigs, and numerous people fell from horses, including Daniel Shaw the park-keeper and David Seammen the head coachman.[87] Treatment was given open-handedly. A later writer recalled the generosity of the 6th

16

Bill from William Cooper to John Poole, house steward, for doctoring the riding and carriage horses, October–December 1822

EGR 7/12/8/81

The Right Hon.ble the Earl of Stamford

1822 To W. Cooper Dr

March 14th Bay Mare Visit and Six Febrifuge Draughts. 1. 2. 6
20, Visit, & Six, Febrifuge Pectoral Draughts — 1. 2. 6
27, Visit & Six, Draughts Repeated — 1. 2. 6
31, Visit. & Six Draughts Repeated — 1. 2. 6
Aug 5th, Dressing's Application's to Quick Silver Feet to Nov.r 28th — 3. 3. 0
Visit — 7th Visit — 1. 1. 0
7, Smith, Visit & Expences to Removeing Quicksilver Shoes, & One Bard Shoe — 10. 6
Two Brown Coach Horses, 12 Expectoral Draughts 1. 4. 0
12, Visit — Bay Horse Three Vermifuge Ball's — 16. 6
Cathartic Ball — 2. 6
16, Visit, Two Br.n Coach H.s Twelve Draughts Rep.d 1. 14. 6
Bay Mare, 1 Nights Hay & 5 feeds of Corn, & Shoeing — 8 —
20, Bay Mare 2 Nights Hay & 7 feed of Corn — 6. 6
21, Visit. — 26, Visit, — 1. 1. 0
£14. 17. 6

Earl in this respect: 'any workman on his estate who was unwell had only to report himself at the hall, and he would receive a paper authorising him to be absent from work and to receive the attendance of Dr. Broadbent'.[88] Neither was treatment limited to permanent employees, for Poole's accounts also include items for several members of the building teams temporarily working on John Shaw's project, including James Berry, the clerk of works who had problems with his ears and eyes, and two of the joiners, one of whom was blistered and bled. Broadbent's bills included items for general use within the household, such as phials of sal volatile and bottles of castor oil. He also supplied substances for purposes other than medication. The park-keeper bought arsenic, probably for vermin control, and the under-coachman bought oxalic acid, a stringent cleaning substance, as well as physics of various sorts for horses.

A few of Broadbent's bills related to medications for the family, but the usual attendant for family members was Mr Peter Holland of Knutsford, who was paid £35 16s for treatment over a three-month period. The bill covered a total of forty-nine visits to the house, each charged at 7s 6d, a much higher rate than Broadbent's. Again individuals were named but the treatments left indeterminate; they are itemised usually as mixtures, emulsions, juleps (sweet drinks) or pills, but one patient, Miss Everest, was regularly blistered. Twenty-four of the visits were made to Lady Jane Grey and the same to Miss Everest. The only servant to have been treated by both apothecaries was Mrs Calder, who was visited by Holland twice.

Veterinary bills incurred by the grooms and the coachman made up a substantial proportion of the total medical expenses. The yearly bill from the horse doctor William Cooper amounted to £54 19s and covered thirty-seven attendances and treatment for saddle, coach and draught horses (Box 16, opposite). Many were for work on the Earl's horse, Quicksilver, especially cleaning and replacing shoes. Sometimes this was done by Cooper, sometimes by a smith who appeared to work for him. One of the brood mares, a bay, was given a number of treatments, including sedatives, bleeding and laxatives. It would seem she was also taken into Cooper's care at his surgery for he billed for several days' hay and corn plus one night's attendance on her. Other prescriptions for expectorants and diuretics were made for members of the Earl's team of brown coach horses.

* * *

Dunham may have been a provincial household but it was highly sophisticated in its requirements. Like most country houses, it relied heavily upon 'messages' – letters, notes and parcels from a wide variety of sources using whatever methods were around at the time. Family members and servants were often away from home and the aristocratic network of friends and family relied on the postal and carrier services, as did distant suppliers and tradesmen servicing the great house.

Deliveries of parcels, baskets or boxes were a common feature of household life. Acceptance and payment was part of the house steward's job, and a rough estimate shows that a parcel delivery, which might be of several boxes or baskets at a time, took place on two out of every three days. Deliveries were clearly concentrated into the summer and autumn months when the family and their friends were in residence at Dunham. Most deliveries cost between 1s and 5s, the total cost during the year amounting to over £74.

Some of the parcels were delivered locally from Altrincham and Knutsford. A delivery to or from Knutsford cost 3d one-way, so a single bill of £1 could cover up to eighty occasions. By far the most frequent point of long-distance dispatch was London (forty-six deliveries) followed by Manchester (twenty-nine), Warrington (twelve) and Liverpool (eleven). Usually the cash book does not record the contents of parcels but on the rare occasions when it does, they are mainly luxury foodstuffs of some kind. There were regular deliveries of biscuits from Liverpool, boxes of tea, coffee, porter and cheeses from London and baskets of game from Muker and Askrigg on the Pennines and also from the family's Leicestershire estate at Bradgate. Two deliveries were of hunted hares from Ashton-under-Lyne and two of turtles. Several deliveries from Warrington were not of foodstuffs but goods such as nails and boxes of soap. Enville sent a box of birds to be mounted by the taxidermist in Altrincham. There were also numerous parcels from family members in London, probably expensive foodstuffs for store. Occasionally the cash book records the payment of carriage on larger items bought by the family in London or Warwickshire, such as a new dining-table and carpets, but these are offset in the cash books by income from the furniture account, part of the Earl's personal expenses.

The dependence on foodstuffs arriving by parcel delivery was by no means new in 1822. Records from the 1760s show that deliveries to Dunham were not as numerous as they were to be in the 1820s but nevertheless fairly frequent.[89] As in 1822, many parcels were food items, including a barrel of anchovies, a bottle of oil, a chest of oranges, a hamper of grocery, pots of lampreys and a hogshead of rum. One parcel, however, contained a gun case, another some stockings and two were of expensive wax candles from London. Boxes were also made up to be sent to Enville, including a hamper of Dunham pears, a box carefully packed with 560 tiny fir trees, and a cage with seven live ducks. Elsewhere, the use of public carrier services to deliver highly expensive and perishable foodstuffs from London to the country is documented as early as the 1580s in the archives of the Shuttleworth family of Bolton and the Purefoys of Buckinghamshire.[90] In these cases, the carrier became an extension of the household system, not only delivering the goods but ordering them, paying the bills and arranging for repairs to be carried out.

In 1822 delivery to Dunham was by private parcel services connecting with both public and private carriers. Many were paid for at the door on delivery, but a few regular carriers were paid by annual bill at Christmas. Messrs Pickfords' annual bill of over £55 amounted to almost seventy-five per cent of the total amount spent on carriers. Pickfords delivered most of the long-distance goods from London, which arrived in sixty-one separate consignments on their boat service to their wharf on the Bridgewater Canal in Manchester. The household also used the Bridgewater Canal Company itself for twenty-seven consignments over the year, bringing casks of china and pottery from Liverpool, spirits and wine and many unspecified boxes and crates.

The most important local carrier was a woman named Mary Allen. Over the year, Allen's boat carrier service handled 177 different consignments, usually of several parcels, boxes, hampers, casks, crates or bundles at a time, and seems to have been the regular service used to and from Manchester, including collecting Pickfords' deliveries from their wharf. Most consignments are unspecific as to contents, but her bill itemises some: barrels of vinegar, boxes of cheeses, nine fire-grates, seven coal boxes, bundles of carpeting and matting, eighteen chimneypots, eight slop pails, large parcels of sheet music, a hamper of soda water and a bag of feathers (this last was Poole's order from the feather warehouse in Manchester). During October and November alone, Allen made twelve deliveries of barrels of oysters. Her boats also carried goods from Dunham to Manchester, including a large copper boiler which was repaired and returned a week later and all the copper kitchen utensils sent for re-tinning or re-hammering.

In 1822 the public letter post was still using a system of payment at the point of delivery according to weight and the distance travelled. A record was made, therefore, of payments for the receipt of letters, usually by John Poole but also by George Smith, the head groom. Poole's bills amounted to £5 6s in the year. Given that the cost of delivery of a single-page letter from London to Manchester was around 1s, this covered only about a hundred letters in the year. It was also possible, however, for the sender to pre-pay for delivery, and Poole's cash book records the purchase of books of franks to the value of £4 10s, for use when sending post out.

Postilions and a groom at a posting stage in *Gretna Green* by J. F. Herring, 1846.

Networks of communication were clearly of great importance to the working of the house, and any disruption or change to the existing system created serious problems. One such argument had arisen in 1800, when a new mail coach service was established between Birmingham and Manchester.[91] The old post coach service had a branch leaving at Stone in Staffordshire to connect to Lancaster and Liverpool. This branch ran through Knutsford and on to Warrington.[92] The post for Dunham was offloaded at the Knutsford receiving office and transferred to a local horse-mail delivery service which operated to Manchester, calling at Dunham and Altrincham. This old service was discontinued in 1800, and the replacement coach went to Manchester by a shorter route, leaving Dunham and Altrincham without the direct service from Knutsford. Since most of Dunham's mail came from the south, a diversion through Manchester must have seemed extremely irritating. After representations from the Earl, the Post Office offered a slower foot delivery service from Knutsford to Altrincham, calling at Dunham, but charging an extra penny per letter.[93] Further irate correspondence ensued, with the Postmaster General accusing Isaac Worthington (the Earl's land agent) of organising the opposition to the penny rate within Altrincham. The penny service was withdrawn and replaced by a daily boat postal service between Manchester and Altrincham, using the Bridgewater Canal, though the Earl still received his own delivery of southern mail direct from Knutsford at his own expense. The boat service seemed to work adequately until 1811, when it was withdrawn following a violent robbery of the mail boat. After this, the post was brought from Manchester by road messenger to Altrincham, thence to Dunham, which often resulted in late delivery at the house and continual complaints by the family. This was the service which was in place in 1822.

The public mail service was acknowledged generally to be expensive and not always convenient.[94] Many people opted instead to use private or public carrier services, or indeed any sort of *ad hoc* personal connections. Dunham was no exception, for the household clearly used private foot messengers on many occasions. Sums of 3s paid to a messenger sent to Manchester occur several times, but most are related to the Earl's racing activities. He seems to have kept in touch with race results from both Worcester and Warwick races by paying for messengers, costing 3s a time. Speed, of course, cost dearly. To send an urgent message on horseback to Knutsford Races cost 7s, the return by foot messenger of Lord Grey's coat, left at the races, a mere 1s 8d.

Many of the servants themselves were highly mobile in their day-to-day work, and both full-time and casual staff were entitled to travelling expenses when working away from the estate. When individual servants needed to travel they usually used the slow but sure public carrier services, allowing themselves several days, the cost offset by agreed travel expenses. Some, however, used the faster post horse system. Charles Brown, for example, a stable-boy who travelled with his Lordship's horses, accumulated £3 11s 4d expenses over the season for bating (feeding the horses), turnpike tolls and hire of post horses on return journeys. A man called Samuel Harrison seems to have been a sort of private carrier-cum-armed guard paid to provide a game-carrier service to the estate. In 1822 he took his Lordship's horses and hunting dogs to Muker in Swaledale, from where he arranged delivery to Dunham of consignments of grouse. The expenses of the round trip, which took seven days, totalled £9 3s 5d. Harrison was also sent to Langholm in Scotland to fetch grouse, at a cost of £9 13s 6d, including coach fare, board and a special tip of £1 'for bringing the Birds safe', no doubt richly deserved considering the desirability of the goods in his care and the length and danger of his journey.

Other servants made shorter but more routine trips. John Poole himself made nine visits to Manchester in the year for business purposes, probably to visit the bank and tradesmen. For each trip he claimed 5s expenses. Other people's servants, too, were rewarded for bringing gifts; tips of 10s 6d and 5s were given to Mr Egerton's and Mr Lees's keeper for bringing venison. The estate wagoner, Thomas Burgess, was paid meal expenses whenever he worked away from home with the wagon teams, which were re-charged to whichever department, house or farm, he was working for at the time.

Of course, Dunham was only one of the Greys' houses and moving the household between estates was by no means cheap. Such removals were recorded in the personal accounts of the family rather than by the steward. The 6th Earl's accounts, for example, contain a record of the move from Dunham Massey to Enville on 4 December 1822 (Box 17, below).[95] Using post horses, the family and nine servants were moved in a single day at a cost of £15 6s 6d. This system used the same carriages for the

17

The expenses of travelling by post coach from Dunham Massey to Enville, 4 December 1822

EnvArch 1/8/1

		£	s	d
Altrincham	horses		15	0
	boys and ostler		7	0
Knutsford	horses	1	5	0
	boys and ostler		7	0
Brereton Green	horses	1	15	0
	boys and ostler		8	0
Newcastle	horses	1	2	6
	boys and ostler		7	0
Stone	horses	1	12	6
	boys and ostler		8	0
Penkridge	horses	1	5	0
	boys and ostler		7	0
Wolverhampton	horses	1	5	0
	boys and ostler		8	0
Turnpikes		1	2	6
Greasing			2	0
9 servants expenses		2	5	0
Waiters etc			5	0
TOTAL		**15**	**6**	**6**

18

The expenses of travelling by post coach from Enville to London, 1 May 1822

EnvArch 1/8/1

Samuel Church was his Lordship's valet

1822 The Earl of Stamford & Warrington
May 1st To Samuel Church for Post Horses from Enville to London

		£ s d
6 Horses to Dudley	Miles 10	1.. 17.. 6
Post Boys & Ostler		0.. 19.. 6
Birmingham		1.. 17.. 6
Post Boys & Ostler		0.. 19.. 6
Stone Bridge		1.. 17.. 6
Post Boys & Ostler		0.. 19.. 6
Coventry		1.. 10.. 0
Post Boys & Ostler		0.. 19.. 6
Dun Church		2.. 1.. 3
Post Boys & Ostler		0.. 19.. 6
Daventry		1.. 10.. 0
Post Boys & Ostler		0.. 19.. 6
Towcester	8 Horses	3.. 0.. 0
Post Boys & Ostler		0.. 18.. 0
Stoney Stratford		1.. 10.. 0
Post Boys & Ostler		0.. 19.. 6
2 Brickhill		1.. 19.. 9
Post Boys & Ostler		0.. 12.. 0
Dunstable		1.. 17.. 6
Post Boys & Ostler		0.. 19.. 6
St Albans		2.. 8.. 9
Post Boys & Ostler		0.. 19.. 6
Barnet		1.. 17.. 6
Post Boys & Ostler		0.. 19.. 6
London		2.. 5.. 0
Post Boys & Ostler		0.. 19.. 6
Turnpikes		3.. 9.. 9
Greasing & Ostler at Stratford		0.. 5.. 0
Greasing on the Road		0.. 2.. 0
		~~37.. 15.. 6~~
		38. 15. 6

May the 1	Bill at Dun Church	1.. 12.. 6
	Waiter & Chambermaid	0.. 5.. 0
2	Bill at Stoney Stratford	2.. 9.. 2
	Waiter & Chambermaid	0.. 15.. 0
	Boots	0.. 1.. 6
	Waiter on the Road	0.. 2.. 0
		£ 4.. 19.. 2
	Posting Bill	37.. 15.. 6
		£ 42.. 14.. 8
	Cash in Hand	50.. 0.. 0
	Due to your Lordship	7.. 5.. 4

Settled the Contents
May 2 38. 15. 6
4 [Saml?] Church
43. 14. 8

50. 0. 0
43. 14. 8
6. 5. 4

whole journey, but separate teams of horses were hired for seven stages, the cost varying according to distance between stages. Each stage required the hire of fresh horses to the next stage, plus post boys to return the horses to their home inn, ostlers to feed, water and rub the horses down and grease for the carriage axles. At each post inn the passengers probably took a short break, with perhaps a meal at Newcastle (The Castle Hotel) or Stone (The Crown). Waiters serving drinks and food had to be paid, as also the travel allowances for the servants and the turnpike tolls.

Sometimes servants made the journey to Enville on their own, using family carriages and family coach horses. This was cheaper but slower than using post horses, as the same horses travelled the whole journey and had to be regularly 'bated' (rested, fed and watered) at inns at Penkridge or Wolverhampton and Brereton Green, with an overnight stay at The Crown in Stone.

At the end of April 1822 the 6th Earl moved his household from Enville to London for the Season. On 29 April seventeen of the travelling servants set out using both systems of travel. The head coachman, David Seammen, kept the account of the journey for the eleven servants who used the families' private carriages and horses. Setting off early in the morning (6 or 6·30 was the usual time) the party stopped for breakfast in Birmingham then continued until the overnight stop in Coventry. Breakfast next day was taken in Daventry, the next night stop at Stratford, followed by breakfast at Dunstable with a final overnight stop at St Albans. Eleven servant breakfasts cost around £1 4s, overnight stays between £2 and £3 plus 10s for chambermaids at the inns. The total bill for the eleven servants was just over 13gns. The butler, Philip Osgood, was in charge of another party of six servants which set off from Enville on the same day, using the faster post horse network with one of the family carriages. Between Enville and London there were thirteen stages for changes of horses, with one overnight stop. At two of the stages repairs were needed to the carriage, costing 13s. The total cost of this journey for six servants was £28 13s 6d. The Earl and his valet Samuel Church followed on 1 May, again posting, a journey costing just under £50 (Box 18, opposite). So the total move cost over £90.

Such large-scale journeys were not only expensive but took a good deal of organising. Presumably, overnight accommodation and post horses had to be booked by letter at every stop on the way. The coachman may have done this but more probably the steward himself. The extensive baggage needed for a family stay of several months would have proved a problem in the restricted space of the carriages, so bulky items were packed up well before and dispatched using Pickfords' canal service. Before the canals, public road carrier services would be used, which might take three or four days to London. This meant that for days, even weeks before a move, the household must have been in a state of restrained upheaval, involving personal body servants and others of the travelling household but co-ordinated by the resident steward and the housekeeper.

* * *

Throughout 1822 Poole's cash book recorded routine expenses totalling £103 15s 3d paid to George Smith, the head groom, and to his assistant, for the cost of the upkeep of racehorses. Payments were made six times in the year and, together with small sums paid for messengers from various racecourses, were offset in the accounts by balancing income from his Lordship's racing account, details of which appear in the personal records of the Earl.

Other items in the steward's cash book were for casual labour of various forms. These were both regular and one-off jobs, usually paid as day labour. One of the house steward's responsibilities was security of the premises and to this end he made several payments to 'sundry watchmen' for watching the house at night. There were eight watchmen in all, on a duty rota of two men each night, each paid 1s a night. They patrolled inside and out, changing places with each other every hour. Such measures were usual in houses of this size and wealth, repositories of substantial collections of gold and silver plate, particularly when situated on the edge of a rapidly expanding industrial urban area.[96] According to the records of the Sutherland household at Trentham, similarly sited on the edge of the Potteries in Staffordshire, the night watchmen were instructed to patrol the outside of the house in an irregular route, calling out the hours in such a voice as to be heard by people still awake but not to disturb those sleeping.[97] At Dunham additional security watchmen were also paid a total sum of £15 for one-off situations such as watching loaded wagons.

Other payments related to vermin control. Purchase of mousetraps shows that infestation was a regular occurrence in the house itself, but outdoors the problem was more serious, causing losses to game and feedstuffs. This is the explanation for Poole's purchase of 16s 6d worth of 'ratstails' from the miller, incentive payments for the destruction of vermin. One of the regular quarterly payments which came out of the house steward's budget was for 'vermin bills', paid to eight keepers in all, amounting to over £48 in the year. Half of this went to the two Dunham keepers, Daniel Shaw and John Thorpe, the rest to keepers on other estates. This must have made a substantial contribution to the annual remuneration of the two Dunham keepers, amounting to over £12 each a year. It also represents the destruction of a fair number of animals, not all of which would be considered vermin today, as the March bill shows (Box 19, opposite). Similar incentive payments were made through the head gardener for the destruction of wasps. In this respect, the Dunham estate was following widespread local practice, for Alfred Ingham, writing in 1879, described retrospectively the system of payments per head of vermin used by local farmers: 'Small boys of the place received a large amount in the way of head money'. Farmers, so he recalled, looked on birds as enemies, an attitude probably related to the importance of arable crops and vegetable-growing before the 1880s, when much of the estate was converted to intensive dairying.[98]

Poole was also responsible for various casual jobs around both the house and the parish church. A sum of 3s 6d was paid in April for 'cleaning the privies seven times', a task which was not considered suitable for housemaids. Four regular payments of 19s 6d every thirteen weeks (ie. 1s 6d a week) were made to Betty Podmore for cleaning in Bowdon church, and at Christmas payments were made to a woman for cleaning all the pews in the parish church at Altrincham. Peter Fletcher, licensee of a local inn, was paid £2 8s 9d for supplying coals to heat the Altrincham pews, presumably using some sort of portable braziers. The seasonal ritual of family and

Payments for vermin made by John Poole, house steward, March 1822

EGR 7/12/5/16-19

Paid to D.M. Shaw and John Thorpe

32 dogs and cats @ 1/- each	£1	12s	0d
5 polecats @ 1/-		5s	0d
2 owls @ 1/-		2s	0d
16 weasels and stoats @ 7d		9s	4d
2 hairs [sic] @ 7d		1s	2d
106 crows and magpies @ 3d	£1	6s	6d
39 starlings @ 2d		6s	6d
40 rats @ ½d		5s	0d
TOTAL	**£4**	**7s**	**6d**

Settled Daniel M. Shaw

Paid to James Shaw

35 dogs and cats @ 1/- each	£1	15s	0d
3 weasels @ 7d		1s	9d
20 crows and magpies @ 3d		5s	0d
20 starlings @ 2d		3s	4d
TOTAL	**£2**	**5s**	**1d**

Settled Daniel M. Shaw

Paid to John Gatley

20 dogs and cats @ 1/- each	£1		
4 hawks @ 7d		2s	4d
24 crows and magpies @ 3d		6s	0d
15 starlings @ 2d		2s	6d
TOTAL	**£1**	**10s**	**10d**

Settled Daniel M. Shaw

Paid to John Royles

18 dogs and cats @ 1/-		18s	0d
2 hawks @ 7d		1s	2d
5 crows and magpies @ 3d		1s	3d
TOTAL	**£1**	**0s**	**5d**

Settled Daniel M. Shaw

country-house life impinged on the house steward's accounting system in other ways too, for he made payments to carol singers, to musicians employed to play at the dinner party celebrating Lord Stamford's birthday and to parish bell-ringers ringing in May Morning.

Poole's responsibility was for the overall management of the house, and this was by no means a negligible job, even without the added stresses of a major building project in its midst. Yet we can see that many of his personal duties took him beyond the confines of the house, both physically and psychologically, for he needed to keep in touch with outside people to supply the services he required. In this respect the 5th Earl's instincts were correct. A good steward could not restrict his vision to the internal routine of the house, but of necessity had to concern himself with the outside world. For the fine domestic detail indoors he needed the assistance of a housekeeper.

CHAPTER FIVE

'A butcher's bill for veal'

The Skills of the Housekeeper

In 1822 the head of the household was the house steward, John Poole, but much of the day-to-day internal organisation was delegated to Mrs Anne Calder, the housekeeper. She was responsible for supervising both the permanent Dunham female servants and the travelling female servants during their half-year residence at Dunham. In total, therefore, her staff consisted of four housemaids, four laundrymaids, one dairymaid and two still-room maids, who acted as her personal assistants. She also supervised a variable number of lady's maids.

The work of the kitchen- and scullery-maids was supervised by the cook, William Iseard, although Mrs Calder was responsible for their overall employment. In many country houses the male cook was called 'chef', but this does not seem to have been the case at Dunham where they were called cooks, even though until the twentieth century they were male. The relationship between Mrs Calder and Iseard must have been a slightly awkward one, at least potentially. Iseard was paid over twice the housekeeper's wage and she was not responsible either for or to him. Yet the two must have had to liaise closely about guests, menus and stores, for Mrs Calder purchased the provisions, paid the food bills and kept the accounts. She also paid bills for casual help in the kitchen and supervised the making of butter in the dairy. For at least some of 1822 she was not well, for she was attended several times by both Broadbent and Holland.

Much of her daily routine of supervising housemaids' work, checking bedrooms were correctly serviced and linen stores issued, went unnoticed in the household record. Given an efficient housekeeper, it went unnoticed too by the family, for a mark of the well-run household was its unobtrusiveness. What does survive is the record of Mrs Calder's purchases, recorded within the steward's account book. This was written up by John Poole from summary accounts and vouchers (bills from tradesmen) handed to him by Mrs Calder, presumably on a weekly basis. Only a few of these last exist, though the account books are present.[99] These form the basis of this chapter, which focuses on the year 1822. Since the equivalent account books have survived from the eighteenth century, it is possible to draw some comparison with an earlier period as a check on how fashions in food supply changed, and this has been incorporated in some of the tables and in a short section towards the end, using especially the account book from 1743–4, the first volume of the series.[100]

It is important to remember that the account book is a complicated record kept

Descriptions of the housekeeper's rooms at Dunham show they were well furnished and reasonably comfortable. This tallies with a depiction of the housekeeper's room at Aynhoe Park, Northamptonshire, painted in December 1846 by Lili Cartwright.

by the house steward to summarise other servants' payments and outgoings from stock of various sorts. Within the account book, each week is given a page and each page is divided into five sections:

1. Housekeeper's expenditure
2. Supplies from the dairy
3. Amount of food used during the week
4. Issue of grain and meat from the farm
5. Issue of drink and candles by the butler

The first three of these were the responsibility of the housekeeper. The fourth was sent in by the farm steward and the fifth was kept by the butler, or, in his absence, by the steward himself. These sent in their weekly record on a single piece of paper and the steward then painstakingly copied them down in his account book.

It helps if we realise that the household account book derives from an older form of record, kept by most wealthy households, which tracked domestic consumption

20

Bill from John Barratt to Anne Calder, housekeeper, for brushes and mops for Dunham Massey, 1822

EGR 7/12/13/3

Altrincham

Mrs Calder

For The Right Honble Earl of Stamford & Warrington

1822 Bt. of John Barratt

Feby 1	24 Mop heads	20d	2. 0. 0
6	12 Brooms	5/4	3. 4. 0
June 1	12 Furniture Brushes	2/	1. 4. 0
	24 Bannister Brushes	20d	2. 0. 0
	12 Dust Brushes	18d	. 18.
	12 Hearth Brushes	4/	2. 8. 0
	12 Clamp Brushes	4/	2. 8. 0
	24 Scouring Brushes	2/8	3. 4. 0
	12 Scouring Brushes	18d	. 18.
	6 Carpet Brushes	7/	2. 2. 0
	12 Stove Brushes	20d	1. 0. 0
	24 Brooms	5/4	6. 8. 0
	24 Brooms	3/8	4. 8. 0
	24 Mopheads	20d	2. 0. 0
July 1	12 Furniture Brushes	2/	1. 4. 0
	6 Stove Brushes	18d	. 9.
Aug 1	6 Oile Brushes	4d	. 2.
	6 Black lead Brushes	2/	. 12.
	24 Mop heads	20d	2. 0. 0
Sept 1	24 Mop heads	20d	2. 0. 0
Octr 1	3 Clamp Brushes	5/	. 15.
			£41. 4. 0

in terms of amounts but not values. The record was restricted to foodstuffs, with the single addition of candles, and by the eighteenth century had evolved into what were usually then called 'house books'. The layout followed the five-fold system listed above, which seems to have been in fairly standard use. Dunham's account book tracked four separate accounting centres: the housekeeper's stores, the dairy, the farm and the cellars. Some costs of casual labour and purchases were added, as well as values of supplies issued. A single exception is that of household-made beer and ale

21

Sample page from John Poole's housekeeping account book, March 9th to 16th, 1822

EGR 7/1/12

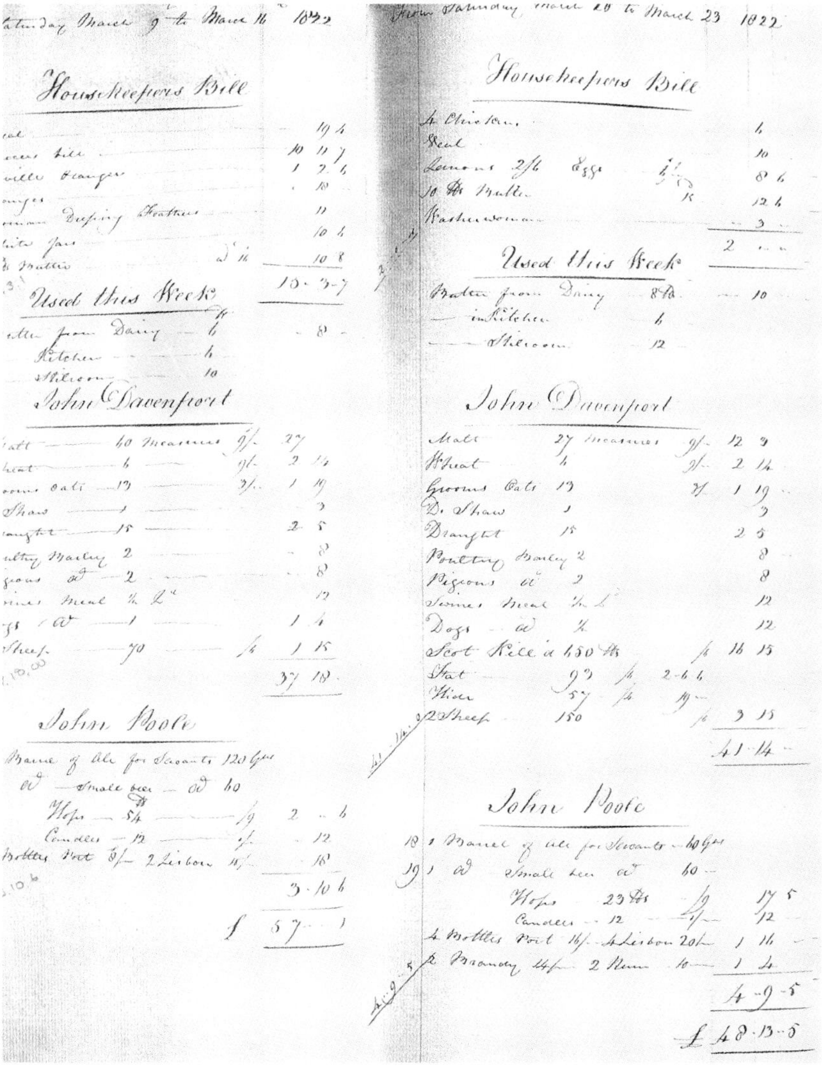

which was never given a value, though raw materials used (malt and hops) were. All of this makes the account book a complex record, especially when it comes to trying to assess what proportion of the food consumed was purchased from outside and what proportion was home-produced.

We need to bear in mind that some of the values ascribed to home-produced foodstuffs in the account book may be token rather than realistic, a book-keeping exercise in theoretical internal accounting. This was a feature of household recording by no means unusual even in medieval houses.[101] Some values, for example, did not fluctuate during the year: the price of meat in 1822 was fixed always at 6d per pound,

Copper colander, part of any well-fitted kitchen's *batterie de cuisine.*

with no seasonal variability, regardless of whether it be from an old cow, a sheep, a lamb or very high-quality Scotch cattle. Some of the other values used by the farm steward, however, do vary seasonally: the price of malt and grains goes up and down with the time of year, probably because these were mainly bought in and were therefore open to the vagaries of the commercial world. Some home-produced foodstuffs do seem to have been actually paid for and amounts are therefore accurate. At the end of 1822, for example, the housekeeper entered an exactly calculated sum of money (£31 10s 7d) as 'Mr Davenport's bill for poultry'.

Compared to Poole's, Mrs Calder's bills were smaller and fewer and usually paid weekly, or at least shortly after the delivery. Some regular account-holders, however, were paid at the end of the year: the grocer, the fish man and the farm bill for poultry, for example. In a routine which was similar to the steward's, the housekeeper was given cash payments direct from Worthington. These were received in July, August, October and two in December. At the end of December 1822 she had cash in hand of over £242, enough to last until summer again. The total cash going through her hands was around £1,242. Presumably she too kept cash sums in the house safe.

In 1822 Anne Calder had responsibility for the payment of wages to a number of day labourers in the house. Whereas Poole paid mainly outdoor people, such as

The kitchen and staff at Minley Manor, Hawley, Hampshire in the 1890s. The kitchen is set out ready to start work: the table shows a classic layout – tablecloth, work boards, seasoning boxes down the middle and cooking cutlery either side.

church cleaners and allowances to gamekeepers, Mrs Calder's domain was the day-to-day internal working of the house, heavily dependent on female labour. She spent £16 17s, for example, on extra house-cleaning during the year. The standard rate for casual cleaning was 1s a day, giving her 337 days. Most of this extra cleaning was done by four unnamed regular women, working seventy-three days each. A fifth woman, Betty Bancroft, was paid 1s a day for a total of twenty-one days, for keeping the stable mess-room clean. Yet others were paid smaller one-off amounts as 'charwomen'. Although this was all day labour (the wages were reckoned by the day), the sums were recorded in the cash book in different ways. One-off sums for periodic jobs such as scouring pewter were paid immediately, but regulars were paid only once a year: Betty Bancroft was paid in December for her twenty-one days and the four regulars in July for their seventy-three days. So either the regular day labourers were made to wait for their wages as if they were salaried, or the housekeeper paid the wages each week but delayed making the record, which, given the general care in keeping records, seems unlikely. There were clearly disadvantages in working at the big house!

Some day labourers were used by Mrs Calder for jobs other than house-cleaning. Since the four full-time laundry-maids were all on the travelling servant list, the resident household at Dunham had to employ casual local labour to do the washing. This was again paid at 1s a day and amounted to forty-six days work for the six months up to July. During this period one washerwoman was paid weekly or fortnightly in sums of 2s or 3s a time; a second woman was paid the same rate but her money was accumulated into less regular amounts. So perhaps the day labourers could ask for their money regularly or could opt to accumulate it as a form of saving. When the family came to Dunham and the full-time laundry-maids took over, payments to casual washerwomen did not cease as might be expected. Presumably the amount of washing was such that extra help with heavy washing was needed. The total annual bill for day labour in the laundry represented eighty-three days' work.

Extra help in the kitchen was needed on fewer occasions, as amongst the resident servants was one of the kitchen-maids who cooked for the others. Even so, extra help was paid for thirty-six days' work, all in the board-wage period. This may have been for assistance in cleaning rather than cooking, as one amount paid in early July coincided with purchases of sand for scouring the floor and tables; the kitchen may well have been gearing up for the return of the cook.

Some of the jobs which Mrs Calder put out to day labour were unpleasant and full-time staff were probably reluctant to undertake them. One job which kitchen- and scullery-maids hated because it was hard on the hands and very time-consuming was 'picking' (plucking) poultry and game. Given the number of birds used in the kitchen, this was a routine chore and two women were paid 1s a day to do it as needed. The feathers were used by the household; two sums representing a total of almost six weeks' work were paid for dressing feathers for use in beds and pillows. This would consist of sorting and sieving, washing and drying feathers in bags in the oven. These were in addition to the feathers bought by the steward, which were probably better quality.

Other amounts were paid to needlewomen, amounting to a total of £4 3s, which took the form of payments to two women, Mrs Shaw and Mary Barratt, with no indication as to the nature and amount of work done. It was probably repair to the household linen, or even making up sheets for the bedding charity.

Amongst the regular visitors to the house were a man and boys to sweep the chimneys. With hundreds of flues, many in almost continual use, keeping chimneys in good order was a constant worry. Some very large households even employed their own salaried sweep, but Dunham preferred to pay them as and when needed. This amounted to three payments in the year, totalling £4 5s, of which 7s was paid to 'the boys', the rest to the sweep. One bill specifies the sweeping of thirty-nine chimneys, so we can work out that the going rate for sweeping a chimney was just over 1s each. The kitchen flues were swept three times in the year, which is not very frequent by country-house standards, but this was in addition to the blacksmith's regular ministrations to the smoke-jack.

Cleaning required the purchase not only of time but also materials and these were paid for from the housekeeper's accounts. As much as any other record, the bill for brushes supplied by John Barratt illustrates the size of the Dunham household (Box 20, p.104). In clear contrast to the modern-day situation, in the early nineteenth century materials were a good deal more expensive than labour. So although the housekeeper's total casual labour bill of just over £34 was enough to buy her 691 working days, it was less than the bill for the annual supply of 16 firkins of household soap (£40) or brushes (£41).

*   *   *

22

Total consumption of food, ranked by value, 1822 and 1743

EGR 7/1/12 and 7/1/1

1822

Item	£	s	d
1. Meat total	£1,270	1s	6d
Beef	£838	17s	9d
Sheep	£293	15s	4d
Pigmeat	£70	3s	
Poultry	£49		
Game	£19	14s	3d
2. Beer total	£715	6s	
Malt	£664	18s	
Hops	£54	8s	5d
3. Wine	£548	2s	
4. Cereals total	£457	1s	
Horses' oats	£236	11s	
Wheat	£216	10s	
Milling bills	£23	8s	3d
5. Groceries	£371	5s	3d
6. Dairy	£274	9s	6d
7. Fish	£155	15s	11d
8. Fruit & veg	£25	17s	7d
9. Miscellaneous	£6	18s	6d
TOTAL	**£3,511**	**5s**	**3d**

1743

Item	£	s	d
1. Meat	£304	2	9
2. Cereals	£220	0	6
3. Dairy	£91	11	6
4. Beer etc	£77	12	8
5. Wine	£45	15	11
6. Groceries	£33	13	4
7. Fruit and Veg	£22	16	7
8. Fish	£12	7	8
TOTAL	**£808**	**0**	**11**

Note: the values should not be used as direct comparisons as no modification has been made for inflation between 1743–4 and 1822. The purpose of the listing is to rank items in relative importance.

Payment for day labour and cleaning, however, made up only a small part of Mrs Calder's responsibilities, for most of the cash which went through her hands was for the purchase of foodstuffs. Mrs Calder seems to have kept the records for almost all the bought-in groceries (Box 21, p.105), game, fish, dairy produce and general provisions, whilst the land steward kept the record of supplies from the farm, the meat and grains supplied to the house and other departments. The cost of the supply of food to the household, exclusive of fruit and vegetables, totalled over £3,500 for the year 1822.

The list (Box 22, above) categorises food types by value, showing that the most valuable single category was meat, made up mainly of beef, followed by sheep meat (mutton rather than lamb), and smaller amounts by value of pork, poultry and game. Beef on its own was the single highest-value food item. Next in value came the raw materials for the brewing of the Dunham beer and ale, lending credence to the legend that England was built on beef and beer. Malt and hops were more expensive than the total bill for wines for the house, the next category down. Although, pint for pint, the cost of wines was obviously greater than that of beer, the sheer quantity of the latter meant it was more valuable in total. Cereals rank after meat, beer and wine. Over half the cost of these was represented by oats for the riding and carriage horses, an item of larger value than wheat for the household flour. After cereals came the grocery bill, including a major item for the purchase of salt. Then followed the dairy produce, the fish bills and such small quantities of fruit and vegetables as were bought in. Since no record was kept in 1822 of the amount or value of garden produce supplied to the house from the kitchen gardens, this item is necessarily incomplete. One interesting entry within a number of miscellaneous foodstuffs was the regular purchase of muffins, which seem to have been a favourite at breakfast.

What proportion of these foodstuffs was provided by the estate itself? It is only possible to be certain about some items. As the list opposite (Box 23) shows, almost all the meat was supplied by the estate. In fact, all the beef was self-provided, the eighteen per cent of cattle meat which was purchased being veal. Indeed, adequate supplies of meat from immature stock posed a long-term problem for the farm, which had to supplement home supplies by regular purchases from outside. Unlike today, the taste for veal must have been well established, even amongst servants, to go to so much trouble.

The farming enterprise at Dunham seems to have been much more focused on meat production than on dairying, which was limited to butter production. We simply do not know about the supply of milk in 1822 as there is no record of it, but almost certainly it would have been provided by the dairy. There seems to have been no cheese made at Dunham at this date, when over ten and a half hundredweight of Cheshire, Wiltshire and Stilton cheeses were bought in from two cheesemongers in Manchester and London, through Poole's cash book.[102] Cream, too, was entirely bought in, presumably because butter-making took precedence. Even so, home-made butter accounted for only fourteen per cent of the annual consumption, the rest being bought in.

The housekeeper also paid bills for game birds, usually a few shillings or even pence at a time. The origin of these is not recorded, but occasional payments were made for delivery, which indicates they came from a source further afield than the immediate Dunham estate; for most items, however, delivery was free. If the major source of these was local, from Carrington Moss for example, a system of internal accounting was in place which required payments to be made. It is likely that some deliveries at least were from Leicestershire, as in the 1830s and 1840s there are records of consignments of game being brought from the Greys' family estates at Bradgate. As we have seen, grouse came from Muker in Swaledale and Langholm in Scotland. Some managed game-products, such as grouse and venison, were in over-supply, in so far as the family was able to make gifts of both to their relatives and friends. In 1837 the Dunham housekeeper recorded a total of 120 brace of grouse, twenty-nine of which were given away.[103] There is evidence from 1826 that the estate gave away thirty-nine venison half-carcasses and other joints as a means of cementing relationships with friends and gentlemen of the area as far afield as Chester, and as a means of establishing the family's pre-eminence at local events such as the

Proportions of foodstuffs consumed at Dunham Massey which were provided by the Home Farm and Dairy, 1822 and 1743–4

By value unless otherwise stated.

EGR 7/1/1 and 7/1/12

1822		1743–4	
Chickens	90% by amount	Beef	99%
Turkeys	97·8% by amount	Veal	22%
Ducks, pigeons, geese	100% by amount	Pork	97%
		Mutton	100%
Beef	82·54%	Lamb	87%
Fat pork	100%	Chickens	0%
Porkit	100%	Fowls	30%
Sheep	100%	Turkeys	100% (with stock in hand)
Milk	no record	Ducks	0%
Cream	0%	Geese	62%
Butter	14·21%	Pigeons	100% (with stock in hand)
Cheese	0%	Partridges	100% (with stock in hand)
Eggs	only bought amounts recorded	Game	no record
Fish	only bought amounts recorded	Venison	100%
Game	only bought amounts recorded	Milk	100%
Fruit	only bought amounts recorded	Cream	no record
Vegetables	only bought amounts recorded	Butter	12%
Wheat flour	100% estimated	Cheese	100%
Groceries	0%	Eggs	5·5%
		Vegetables	84%
		Cereals	100%
		Groceries	0%
		Fish	no record
		Ale and beer	100%
		Wine	15%

Note: assessment of the degree of self-provisioning can become very confusing. In 1743–4 one third of the geese were bought from outside, but were purchased live for fattening at home and were not in fact used until much later. So would it be valid to say all the geese came from home supplies? Ducks and chickens had a fast turnover, being slaughtered regularly in small batches and eaten quickly. For this reason, for the purposes of the table above they have been categorised as being bought in. This is an arbitrary distinction and in reality the situation in 1743–4 may have been little different from that of 1822, though in the table they appear at opposite ends of the spectrum.

Altrincham mayor's feast day, the Tarporley Hunt dinner and Knutsford Race Week, during which they gave venison to three of the town inns.[104] Only four carcasses were delivered to the house.

The extent to which the estate provided the rest of the food for the household in 1822 is unknown, because only the amounts bought in are recorded. Mrs Calder listed bills for fish and shellfish, but the Dunham moat provided large quantities of trout (250 brace in 1823) and the personal records of the 6th Earl for 1822 show

24

Fruit and vegetables for a week: extract from vegetable book, Enville gardens, 1866–70

EnvArch G/1/8/2/1

1–7 August 1866

Vegetables and Salads

Potatoes for kitchen	12½ pecks*
Potatoes for dairy	4 pecks
Potatoes for stables	1½ pecks
Broad beans	3 pecks
French beans	1¾ pecks
Scarlet runners	1¼ pecks
Peas	2 pecks
Onions	8½ pecks
Carrots	½ peck
Cauliflowers	12
Turnips	8
Cabbages	7
Lettuces	28
Cucumbers	8
Mustard & cress	7 bundles
Parsley & herbs	6 bundles
Radishes	3 bundles

Fruit

Strawberries	7 lbs
Peaches for dessert	13
Peaches for kitchen	22
Nectarines	11
Melon	1
Grapes	½ lb
Apples for dessert	1 peck
Apples for kitchen	1 peck
Black currants for kitchen	1 lb
Red currants	3 lbs
Gooseberries for desert	3 dishes
Gooseberries for kitchen	1 dish

* 1 peck is ¼ of a bushel, a measure of volume not weight.

Note: supplies were sent from the gardens seven days a week throughout the year.

that, in addition, unknown quantities of fish were sent from Enville to Dunham Massey.[105] It is reasonable to assume that most of the vegetables were provided by the kitchen garden at Dunham. In the absence of a scale by which to measure the Dunham garden enterprise, it may help to refer to the earliest vegetable book kept at Enville (Box 24, above). Even so, a surprising number of fruit and vegetable purchases recorded in 1822 show that the house was by no means totally self-sufficient in this respect. Mrs Calder spent over £15 on lemons, almost £4 on oranges, 30s on mushrooms, 4s on apples, 10s on plums and £1 12s on cowslips, presumably for making into wine. She also bought from outside 30lb of honey and 10lb of honeycomb.

The value of wheat flour recorded as supplied by the farm to the house indicates that the estate was probably largely self-sufficient in this, though small amounts of more specialist flours were supplied by Heywood's of Manchester.[106] Unfortunately, the housekeeper's grocery bills from John Barratt have not survived for 1822, but they have from the 1830s, when the same firm was supplying a variety of imported spices

25

Fruit and vegetables sent to London: extract from vegetable book, Enville gardens, 1866–70

EnvArch G/1/8/2/1

Packed for London, 25 May 1866

French Beans	200	Herbs	6 bundles
Asparagus	300	Radishes	2 bundles
Cabbages	1 doz.	Young onions	1 bundle
Broccoli	1 doz.	Cucumbers	6
Parsnips	1 doz.	New potatoes	1 punnett
Young carrots	4 doz	Gooseberries	1 punnett
Lettuces	1 doz.	Parsley	2 punnett
Spinach	2 pecks	Mustard & cress	2 punnetts
Onions	2 pecks	Beet roots	4
Mushrooms	¼ peck	Grapes	3½ lbs
Old carrots	¼ peck	Strawberries	2½ lbs
Rhubarb	1 bundle	Mixed flowers	2 boxes

(black and white pepper, ginger, nutmeg, mace, cinnamon, cloves and mustard), three qualities of sugar and other dry goods (currants, raisins, orange and lemon peel, almonds, rice, arrowroot and pearl barley).[107] Salt for general cooking purposes was bought separately, but Barratt supplied high-quality bay salt. He also provided general household consumables such as pack-thread and twine, and laundry consumables such as powder and stone blue and patent starch.

Over and above this general pattern of supply, Mrs Calder's weekly records illustrate seasonal patterns which are very pronounced, in some cases relating to the annual round of climate, food availability and farming practice. Supplies from wild and semi-wild sources were highly seasonal. Game birds and fish were available at specific times of the year, mainly late summer and autumn. Of the farmed food products, fat pork shows the climatic pattern most clearly, being slaughtered only during the winter months, probably for bacon. Porkets (young pig slaughtered to be eaten fresh not salted) were available in spring and autumn. At Dunham, pigs were normally fed on swill from the kitchen, but before slaughter, during the late summer and autumn, this was replaced or supplemented by meal to fatten the carcasses and to ameliorate flavour and colour.

The most important features of seasonal variability, however, related to social rather than to climatic influences, in particular the presence or absence of the family at Dunham Massey. Most country houses show clear patterns of annual residence, usually related to the London social season, with an absence from the country during late spring and summer. Dunham's routine was idiosyncratic in so far as the year was split into two: December to July spent at Enville, July to December at Dunham. This routine dated from the succession in 1758 of Lady Mary Booth and her husband, Harry Grey, 4th Earl of Stamford and owner of Enville. It became a tradition which dictated the whole household regime for a hundred years.

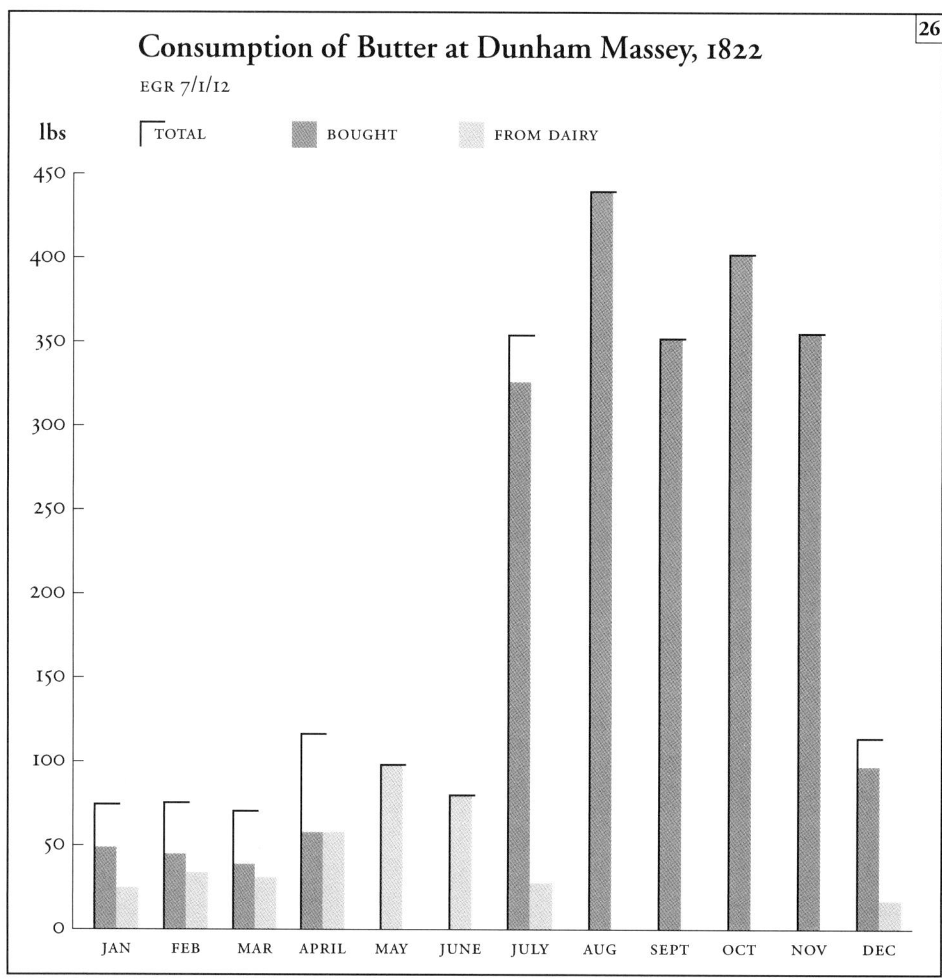

The supply of many foods fluctuated with this split in the year, but none more so than that of butter. Graph above (Box 26) shows that during the first half of the year up to the end of June, when the household consisted of around twenty servants, the consumption of butter was running fairly evenly at under 20lb a week. A pound a week each is perhaps not an extraordinary level of consumption given that bread and butter was the staple food for all the servant meals except dinner and that butter provided an important cooking fat. This level was interrupted once by a rise of an extra 10lb during the week from 23–30 March when the household entertained some guests. From the end of June until three weeks before the new year, consumption greatly increased, peaking at 140lb per week at the end of July and again in October. This pattern is clearly dictated by the presence of the family members, their guests and accompanying travelling servants – a variable household but probably numbering between fifty and seventy people.

A complication is that until March butter was supplied more or less half and half by the Dunham dairy and purchases from outside. From March to June almost all came from the house dairy. From July all through the summer, the supply was entirely bought in. This probably reflects the increased demand for milk when the

A dairymaid pouring milk into settling pans to separate the cream, illustration from *The Farm: a new account of rural toils and produce* by Jefferys Taylor, 1832.

family and guests were present, which meant that no butter could be made. Surrounded as they were by the rich dairy lands of Cheshire, buying in butter was probably no hardship. The consumption of eggs shows a similar family pattern and that of cream shows it even more markedly as it was only used during those months when the Greys were at Dunham.

Meat supplies also varied with the absence or presence of the family and here the variability was related not only to quantity but also to quality. Mutton was a staple everyday meat, and sheep were slaughtered and eaten throughout the year; veal was bought from a butcher all year round, and cows from the farm were killed fairly regularly each fortnight, all part of the basic meat diet for servants and household in general. The level of consumption increased substantially, however, from 100lb of mutton and 230lb of beef per week before July, to an average of 300lb of mutton and 425lb of beef per week in the second half of the year. This was further supplemented during the later period by higher-quality lambs and Scotch store cattle, the latter bought by the farm and fed on as a specialist beef supply, providing another 300lb a week. In an even more concentrated pattern, the domestic rearing of chickens was entirely aimed at the family's and guests' consumption, rather than servants', for the small numbers of chickens used in the first half of the year were all bought in, whilst after July all were home-produced. As would be expected, there was a noticeable rise in barley and meal used for fattening the poultry during the summer.

The need to reconcile the natural seasonality of food with the demands of a social family required a specialised farming system which included the use of a living larder, with animals slaughtered only when needed. This system was best illustrated by the Scotch cattle. Expense being no object, these were fattened on cereals for twelve months, but they were slaughtered individually, one a week during the

ABOVE: The butler's room at Dunham Massey, created *c.*1906, with extensive cupboards for linen, glass and china, and timber sinks for washing fragile objects.

LEFT: The salting room in the service basement at Tatton Park in Cheshire, showing the sort of equipment that would have been used at Dunham in the nineteenth century: a sturdy chopping slab, a pickling chest and overhead racks for hanging the joints of meat.

hospitality season. Food preservation from one season to another must also have played its part, but was probably less important than in households lower down the social scale. There are few direct records of food preservation at Dunham and we have to rely on indirect evidence such as the household's consumption of salt, which seems prodigious to modern eyes. In 1822 John Warburton made twenty-one deliveries of fine salt, each of 4 bushels, that is 84 bushels in the year at a cost of over £67. In the 1830s John Barratt supplied smaller quantities of saltpetre (26lb in all) and bay salt (14lb), all essential in the process of salting meat. Barratt also supplied 6lb of isinglass used in the preservation of eggs.[108] The housekeeper's records show purchases of earthenware containers such as white preserve jars, salting pans and other stoneware. She supplemented her own produce with bought preserved items, including buttered eggs and hams.

As might be expected, cereal consumption also shows a sharp rise during summer and autumn. The increase in amounts of wheat provided by the farm for the household was straightforward, but the consumption of oats shows a slightly more complex pattern, reflecting both the need for winter fodder to supplement or replace paddock grazing and the number and usage of riding and carriage horses present at Dunham, itself an indication of the presence of family and visitors. Thus issues to the family coachman are recorded only for the period July to early December, showing that the carriage horses were at Dunham only during this time. Issues of oats to 'strangers' horses' (belonging to guests or guests' servants) were almost non-existent

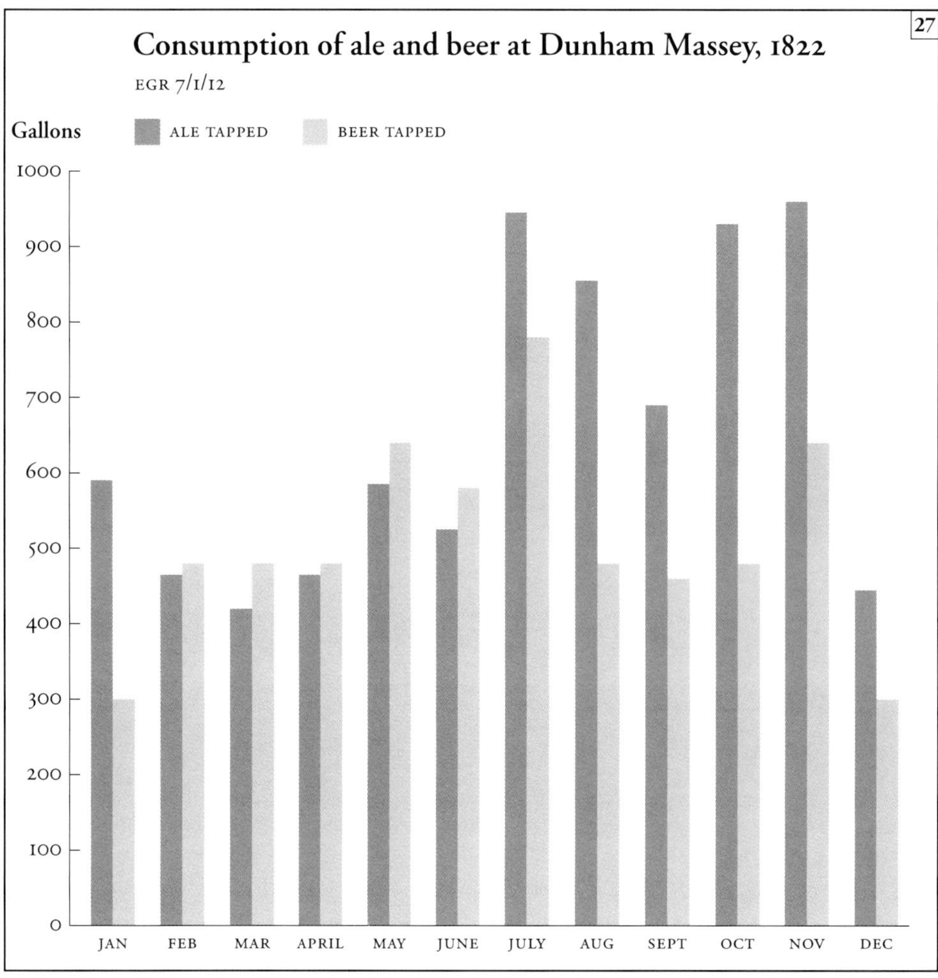

during most of the first half of the year, but then became a noticeable item between the end of July until November.

Do the same patterns of home production and seasonal variability apply to alcoholic drink? John Poole incorporated into his household account book the records kept by Philip Osgood, the butler, of the consumption of wines, spirits and hops (and thus of beer-making), ale and beer-drinking, and also the use of candles. The complication here is that for the first half of 1822 the butler was absent from Dunham Massey, working with the family at Enville and elsewhere. During this period the butler's supplies were issued and recorded by John Poole himself, who handed over to the butler on his return in July.

In 1822 all of the household's requirements of beer and ale were met by home production, there being no record of any purchases of beer, though 118 gallons of cider and £3 12s worth of soda water were bought.[109] The hugely important place which malt liquor occupied in the domestic economy of Dunham can be gauged by the value attached to its raw materials. The account book gives no value for ale and beer, but the total annual purchase of malt and hops amounted to over £660. This compares with £549 spent on wine. From the record of issues, it appears that brewing took place at Dunham Massey on a weekly basis, every week throughout 1822 except for one week beginning 16 November, when the brewer took his annual holiday. The pattern is fairly regular. The normal brew was of between 27 and 30 bushels of malt. Occasionally the brew would be much smaller (half the amount normally issued) and sometimes much larger (double the amount). The issues of hops coincide largely with this pattern. There seems to be little in the way of seasonal variability in brewing therefore, though we cannot estimate variations in strength and quality that might have resulted from changes in temperature or demand.[110]

The records of malt liquor consumption, however, are a different matter. Unlike the brewing records, these show that two strengths of liquor were made: ale (stronger, highly hopped) and beer (weaker, less hopped). Consumption of both follows a clear seasonal pattern (Box 27, opposite). The twenty or so resident servants were drinking one 60-gallon barrel of beer every week, that is on average 24 pints each a week. This would obviously vary with individuals, it being usual for men to be allowed twice the amount given to women. It would be drunk as a staple drink at every meal, including breakfast, though tea would certainly be offered as an alternative and would be preferred by many of the women. A dramatic rise in beer consumption began in May, a good two months earlier than the rise in general food consumption. Poole noted that this was due to the allowances required by workmen in the house, including the plasterers, for whom it would be a contractual addition to their wages. Beer had long been regarded as much a food as a drink, an essential element in the diet of hard-labouring people, and therefore to give workmen beer was to contribute to their productivity. Only in July was consumption related to the return of the travelling servants with the family.

Ale consumption follows a similar pattern, showing that the servant household drank not just the weaker table-beer. Ale-drinking was more closely controlled than beer and restricted to a pint or so (half the amount for women) after the servants' dinner, taken around midday. However, other people drank ale too. During the autumn hospitality season, ale consumption could rise to 300 or 350 gallons a week and this was not just due to the increase in numbers of servants, for Poole made a note of the issue of ale barrels to the family parlour and to tenants paying their rent on Leasing Day. A diary written by the 6th Earl's son-in-law in the 1840s records also the family custom of allowing 'an unlimited supply of beef and ale' to anyone arriving at the house on an errand, and the practice was still remembered fondly in the 1880s, long after its cessation.[111]

In addition to ale and beer, the servants' regular allocation included some wines, the record for 1822 clearly demonstrating the difference between the first and second halves of the year. The distinction is reflected firstly in the way the wine record was kept, and secondly in the amounts and types of wines consumed. During the winter and spring of 1822, Poole had charge of the keys to all the cellars, and his weekly record of withdrawals was incorporated into his household account book. In the third week of July, head butler Philip Osgood returned to Dunham with the family and took up his cellar book once again.[112] He first brought it up to date by adding Poole's totals and then carried on making an entry of all wines and spirits withdrawn, noting when these were special issues for special occasions.

28

Consumption of wine at Dunham Massey, 1822 and 1743–4

EGR 7/1/1 and 7/1/12

1822

Wine	NUMBER OF BOTTLES Jan–July	July–Dec	Total for year
Port	125	467	592
Lisbon	84	292	376
SR Port	82	284	366
Sherry	40	207	247
Madeira	32	96	128
Claret	16	93	109
Brandy	21	79	28
Champagne		76	76
E.I. Madeira		59	59
Rum	9	27	36
Barsac		24	24
Hock		15	15
Red Moselle		8	8
Sauterne		7	7
Burgundy		5	5
Moselle		5	5
Cyprus		4	4
Vin de Grave		3	3
Red Hermitage		2	2
Constantia		2	2
Sack		1	1
Malmsey		1	1
Frontiniac		1	1
TOTAL	410	1,758	2,168

1743–4

	PINTS
Red port	304
White port	258
Birch wine	100
Claret	58
Malmsey	49
Rhenish wine	38
Currant wine	34
Sack	19
Champagne	14
Clarry wine	11
French white wine	10
Frontiniac	9
Brandy	6
Burgundy	4

When we look at the patterns of wine consumption in 1822, we find that during the first half of the year around half the total number of bottles of wine and spirits drunk were port, ranked into two qualities (Box 28, above). Some was best-quality port issued to the family table, with occasional bottles of claret, madeira, sherry, brandy or rum. Note that here there is confirmation of the butter records, that some entertaining did take place in the house in the spring and that some members of the family must have stayed at Dunham for at least short periods during the first half of the year. The cellar book explains that issues were made when the architect John Shaw and family friend General Heron came to Dunham on specific occasions to hunt or to lunch or dine with his Lordship. In addition, the Earl made special visits for two annual social events in this period, during which large quantities of wine were consumed. One was a dinner held in March for the 'Master Tradesmen', apparently an annual affair, though not held at the same time each year. The other was

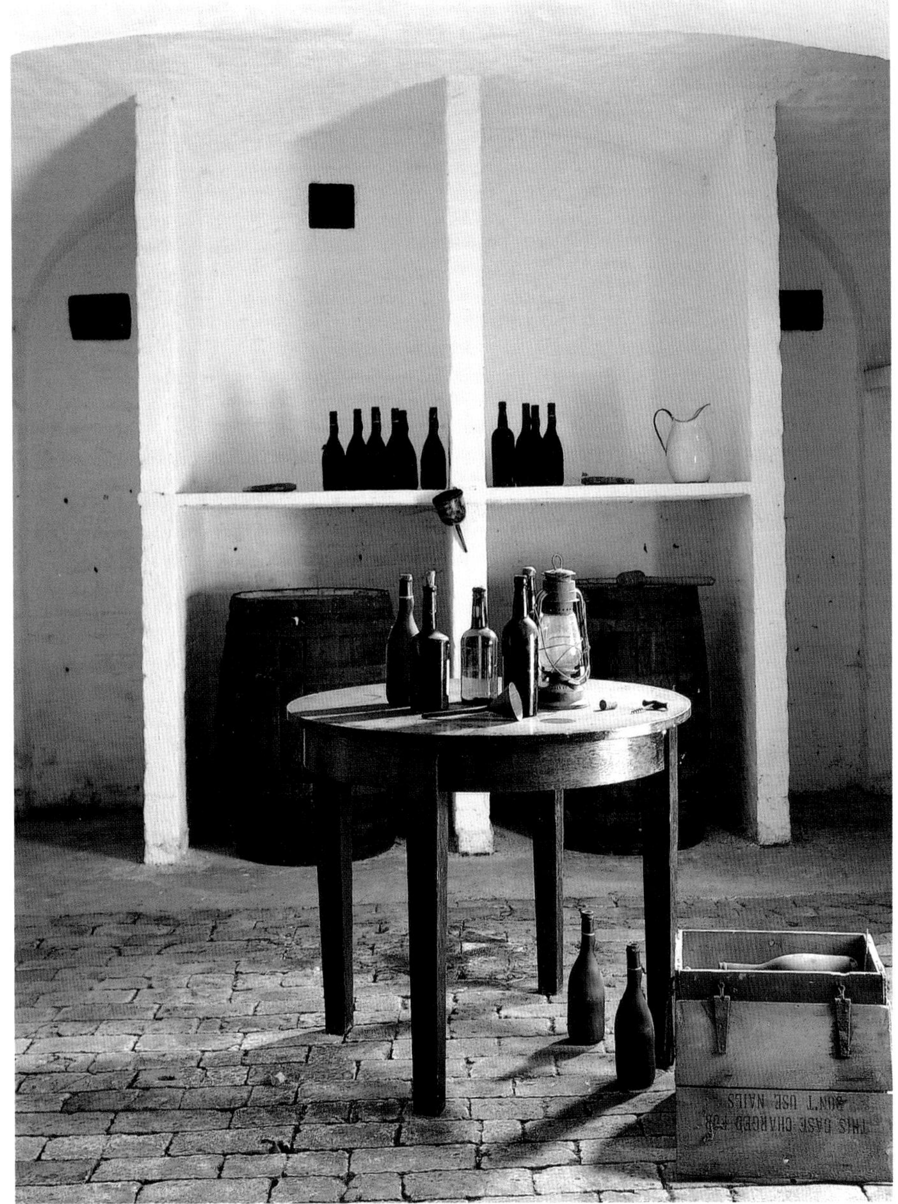

The wine cellars and their bins have survived at Dunham but are now used for general storage. The cellars at Tatton Park, Cheshire give an idea of what they looked like, though they are hardly well stocked by nineteenth-century standards.

a party in June attended by officers of the 28th Yeomanry. On one occasion, too, a bottle of sherry was put into his Lordship's carriage to be used as and when needed.

During the first half of the year, wine-drinking was by no means confined to such occasions. Each week, regular as clockwork, two bottles of second-quality port and two bottles of Lisbon wine were issued to the steward's room for consumption by the resident senior servants. This second-quality port was valued at 4s a bottle, the Lisbon at 5s, giving a weekly value of 18s. In addition, over this period two bottles of brandy went to the kitchen, no less than ten to the housekeeper's room, and to celebrate three family birthdays the servants were issued with two or more bottles of brandy, rum, Lisbon and port. On these occasions, too, a bottle of port was distributed amongst the poor. From 20 July to the first week in December 1822 this pattern changed. The family and their accompanying 'travelling' servants took up residence, guests arrived for house parties and the shooting, and the weekly value of the wine drunk becomes highly variable, rising to anything between £5 and £74. The cellar book gives us a glimpse into current tastes in wine as well as the social life of the household.

The routine of family wine consumption at meals shows that in 1822 the favourite dinner wine was Lisbon. Together with the two qualities of port, Portuguese wines made up over sixty per cent of all wines and spirits drunk at Dunham in 1822. This is a tradition which went back to the eighteenth century, when the fashion was established for drinking port rather than French claret, which had been the favoured drink in earlier centuries. The change to port was a fashion bolstered by the Treaty of Methuen, signed between England and Portugal in 1703, which reduced the duty on all Portuguese wines by a third, in return for access into the Portuguese market for British woollens.[113] Those who knew their wines still preferred French but they were difficult to obtain and thus did not figure largely even in the eighteenth-century records at Dunham; though claret was the third most favoured wine it was well behind port in levels of consumption. By 1822 there had appeared in the cellar books both a higher-quality vintage claret and a madeira, thanks to the change in bottle shape from the bulbous vessels of the first half of the eighteenth century to the cylindrical flask, which could be binned on its side, thus enabling the proper ageing of wines. In 1822, too, a greater variety of French and German wines were available in the cellars, even though they seem not to have been widely drunk.

During the second half of 1822, apart from family drinking at table, regular amounts of wine and spirits continued to be sent to the servants. The cook used eight bottles of sherry, eight of brandy, six of Lisbon, three madeira and two port. It is unclear whether this was for the cook's personal use or for cooking, though at least one sherry and one brandy were specifically issued for mincemeat. Thirty-three bottles of brandy and four of sherry went to the housekeeper's room, probably for a daily after-dinner drink by the senior servants and an occasional drink for tradesmen, and a bottle of brandy went to Poole, perhaps for his nightcap. As earlier in the year, extra sherry, brandy and rum were issued to the servants on two birthdays: the Earl's and that of his son-in-law, the Reverend James Law, the Vicar of Bowdon.[114] Similarly, at the quarterly Leasing Days generous quantities of alcohol were distributed. When his Lordship was at home, seventy-eight bottles of port and eighty-one of Lisbon were drunk on these occasions in addition to the barrel of beer. Likewise, family outings and picnics were lubricated; four bottles each of brandy and rum were drunk at Worcester Gold Cup Day and two bottles of sherry at Knutsford Races. Nine bottles of brandy and one of rum were issued on shoots, and twenty-two bottles of sherry were taken to the Knutsford Ball.

According to a wine bin book, which begins in 1819 and carries on until the 1840s, the main wine merchant used by the household at this time was Crosbie and Chetwode's of Liverpool, though a London merchant was used for the claret and champagne.[115] The family and steward's wine were of different qualities but supplied by the same merchant. There were two main wine cellars in use at this time; the larger was called the 'Claret Cellar' and contained the expensive wines, whilst the

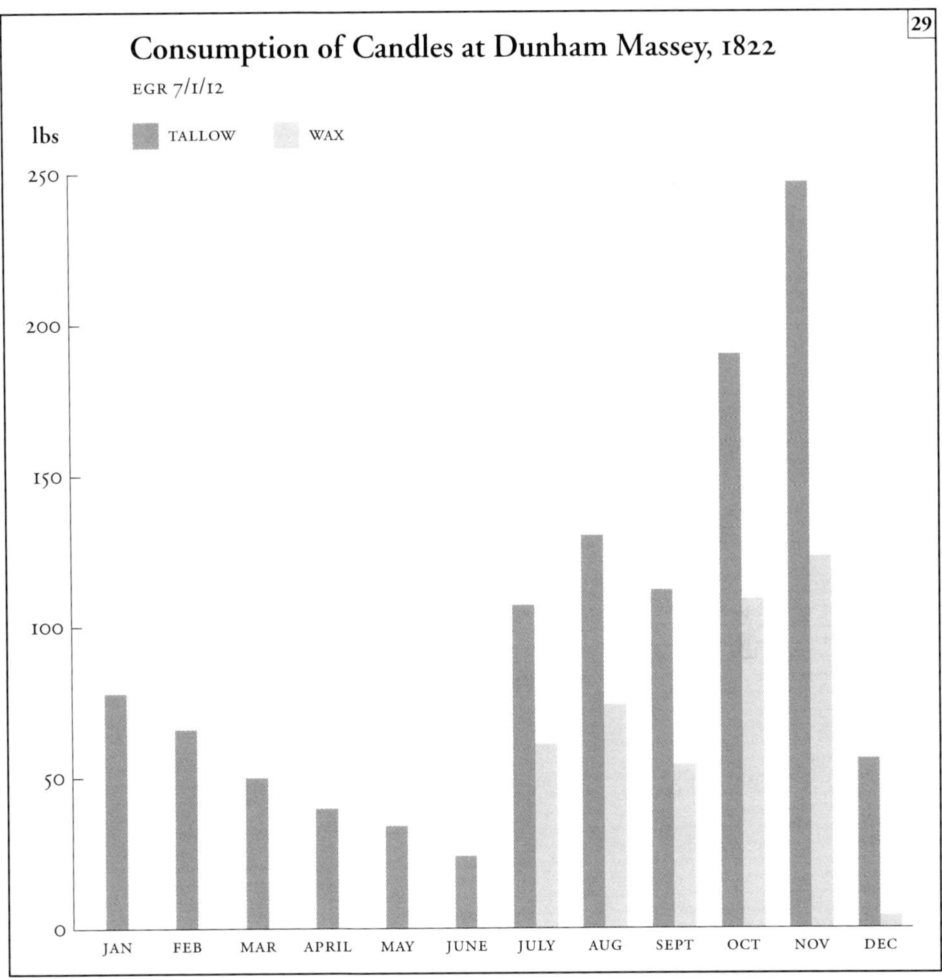

'Small Cellar' contained the port. As a reminder of the old days when wine was usually supplied in the cask, in the 1820s port was bought and paid for by the pipe (a large cask containing 108 gallons), though it was delivered from Crosbie's ready-bottled. Sherry was bought by the butt (also 108 gallons), again bottled. In 1743 all wines had been supplied in the cask, which is why the earlier consumption records were kept in terms of quarts and pints, not bottles.[116]

Back in the sixteenth and seventeenth centuries it was usual for household food consumption records to include one non-food item, candles, presumably because many were home-made as a by-product from kitchen fat. At Dunham the tradition of noting candle consumption along with the food continued until the nineteenth century, even though the practice of making candles at home had long since lapsed. Usefully, candles provide perhaps the clearest indicator of the seasonal presence of the family. In 1822, during the period when the family was absent from Dunham, the household bought supplies of tallow candles for servant use, at a winter and spring price of 1s per pound, reducing to 9d per pound in summer. Poole's account book records not only the seasonal consumption of such tallows (Box 29, above), tracking the number of servants in the household and the extent of daylight hours,

The best-quality wax candles were needed for chandeliers and candelabra in the family rooms. At Dunham, many of these have been electrified, but this spectacular chandelier at Arlington Court, Devon, is still fitted with candles and the light intensifying cut-glass prisms that helped save on the number of candles used.

but also the start in July of the use of good-quality wax candles, costing 4s per pound. This peaked in the week of 27 July as the chandeliers were filled ready for the season, to be followed thereafter by regular but smaller withdrawals as candles were replaced. Voucher records show that all the supplies were purchased.

* * *

It is clear that Dunham was a highly traditional household. Yet fashions in food and food supply did develop over time, so it is worth looking backwards in the household record to see if any changes can be detected. The first Dunham house book to survive dates from 1743–4, and the consistency between this and the account book of 1822 is amazing.[117] The system as kept by John Poole in 1822 was essentially identical to that kept by Thomas Walton, the house steward in 1743–4, both sharing the same weekly amalgam of housekeeper's expenditure, dairy supplies, items used during the week (recorded by the 1743 housekeeper, Mrs Kinaston), farm supplies (recorded by the farm steward, Thomas Hardey) and cellar supplies. Very few innovations in record-keeping were made over the period of eighty years and probably longer, a different picture from some households where successive house stewards altered the system. There were, however, a few minor changes which represented a deterioration in detailed accounting. For example, the 1822 ledger made no note of the foodstuffs sent from the kitchen garden, which was treated as an integral part of the household and which did not have to re-charge its costs. In the eighteenth century the head gardener was required to keep a record of the weekly total value of raw fruit and vegetables sent to the house; though short on detail, it does give us some idea of the value of garden produce within the balance of accounts. The 1743-4 house book also included venison carcasses culled from the park. Both items seem to have been dropped at around the turn of the century.

We can see from the first house book that the pre-eminent position of beef within the household diet went back a long time. In 1743-4, for example, the ranking order of meat was roughly the same as later (see p.109). Beef was provided by 'fat cows', fed and slaughtered throughout the year, though specifically Scotch cattle were not mentioned in the earlier account. Game was similarly important in 1743-4, though the record differs slightly in some respects. The woodcock season was similar, but the grouse were available earlier and pheasants were not mentioned at all. Some items appear in 1743 which do not appear in 1822, such as occasional purchases of larks, fieldfares and smaller wild birds, probably for consumption or possibly as vermin control.

Oats were similarly the most important animal feed cereal in 1743-4, though barley rather than wheat was the second cereal in general importance at the earlier date. Being short on gluten, barley made an indifferent-quality bread, so it is unlikely that it was used at Dunham as a household bread cereal; some of the barley consumption may represent dispensations to the poor, though it was also used extensively as animal feed. The pigeon flock, for example, was normally fed on barley to supplement their scratchings in stubble fields. The issues of barley sent for malting were enumerated separately. In 1743-4 there were also substantial issues of 'shullings' (barley husks), probably used for poultry-feed and dog-meal, and French wheat (the eighteenth-century name for buckwheat), used to fatten pigeons in winter and spring just before slaughter. Here we have, apparently, a pattern of a more varied use of grains in 1743-4 as compared with 1822.

In 1743-4, eighty-four per cent of fruit and vegetables were home grown (see p.110). This still left room for a surprising number of fruit and vegetable purchases, showing that the house was by no means self-sufficient. As in 1822, lemons were used to add sharpness to fat-rich cooking and were a major purchase; seven per cent of the total value of all fruit and vegetables, whether home-produced or bought, was contributed by lemons. Mrs Kinaston also bought apples, apricots and walnuts, revealing a deficiency in supply from the kitchen garden at Dunham. Two of Mrs Kinaston's purchases reflect more general developments, however. She bought a large quantity of poppies, indicating that as housekeeper she retained the old skills of distilling analgesics, a role which by 1822 had succumbed to the professional

The dovecote at the home farm, Dunham Massey, was being completed during 1822. The door is painted in the crimson estate livery colour.

ministrations of the apothecary. Again, a little less than seven per cent of the total value of all fruit and vegetables used in 1743–4 was made up of purchased potatoes, especially in the period from June to January. In the early eighteenth century, potatoes were still a fairly new vegetable and clearly the home farm had only a limited supply to offer. By 1822, potatoes had become a staple element in most people's diet, Cheshire had become an important regional provider and the farm had no problem in meeting the household's requirements.

A comparison of the accounts for 1743–4 and 1822 reveals one striking overall trend, that of the diminishing role of the Dunham dairy. In 1743–4 the dairymaid was responsible for the provision of milk, eggs and some butter, the amount of which was reduced because much of the milk supply went to the production of cheese. Mrs Kinaston received from the dairy a regular supply of four or five cheeses a week, supporting the evidence of the 1758 inventory, which listed a full complement of cheese-making equipment. The eighteenth-century dairy staff also had care of the pigeon and partridge flocks, the turkeys, geese, fowl, and even the carp in the ponds. Birds and carp were bought live in small numbers whenever available to add to the home-bred stock. The annual live stocktake made at Dunham on Lady Day 1744 (Box 30, below), makes it clear that the housekeeper, through her dairymaid, was responsible for the bird flocks. The pigeon house must therefore have been somewhere convenient to the house. In the early 1820s, after the building of the dovecote at the home farm, farm servants were responsible for the bird flocks and would bring the young birds up to the house slaughtered. The growth in popularity of shooting driven (as opposed to sitting) game birds in the early nineteenth century contributed to the general decline of domestic flocks such as partridge, though the fashion for pigeon flocks survived longer.

One item in Mrs Kinaston's expenditure in 1743–4 which at first sight appears out of focus with the rest of her work was her payment for vermin control. We have seen that this was a feature of the house steward's role in 1822, but in 1743–4 items for the 'purchase' of undesirable predators appear in the housekeeper's expenditure, in a rather haphazard mixture of food items and decidedly inedible vermin. These total £1 8s, most of which was for rats, paid for in June and January, probably at the presentation of rats' tails. Other items such as hawks, magpies and crows appear on odd occasions, mainly in the autumn. There is, of course, a logic to this: as the custodian of a living larder she was a sitting target for predators.

Seasonal variations in all these supplies show a much simpler pattern than in 1822.

30

Stock list from Dunham Massey, taken on March 25th, 1744

EGR 7/1/1

Mrs Kinaston [housekeeper] in stock for Breeding and Killing

13 Turkeys
7 Geese
1 Gander
49 Fowls
103 Partridges

Thomas Hardey [farm steward]

8 Saddle horses
2 Colts
6 Coach horses
9 Draught horses
2 Feeding cows
11 Milking cows
4 Barren cows
1 old cow to be sold
1 old cow for calves
2 bulls
29 Wethers
3 1-year-old calves
20 Ewes
14 Lambs
2 Boars
1 Sow
5 young swine
9 Pigs

In 1743–4 the household was that of the 2nd Earl of Warrington, resident at Dunham all the year round and paying only fleeting visits to London. Variability was therefore related to climate and animal life-cycles rather than family absence. The dairy, for example, could provide no butter at all between the middle of December and almost the end of April. Eggs were produced at home only during March and April and at other times had to be bought. The staple beef supply shows no seasonal variation at all. As at a later date, one cow was killed regularly every fortnight, meaning, of course, that the cows had to be fed over the winter, issues of oats for the cows being made between November and early April. Calves were killed only in the period from late April to early July but a regular purchase of veal maintained a steady supply all year round; likewise with sheep. Records of bird-feed reveal the way the different flocks were used to supplement each other throughout the whole year. In 1743–4 there is more information about the supply of sea fish, available in usefully staggered seasons. Issues of oats show that the family carriage horses seem to have been present for all but one week in April, and strangers' horses were present on and off throughout the year except during February and March. Present in 1743–4, but entirely absent later, was the record of oats fed to the pack of greyhounds during the autumn and winter; this may relate to the practice of hunting rabbits or even the park deer, which was then a fashionable pastime. In 1743–4 we do have direct evidence that potting meat and fish was an important process. The housekeeper's records of stocks used include several references to potted game; partridge, grouse and hare were sent down to the London house, and also potted lampreys and salmon. Lady Mary's recipe book also includes instructions for potting fish, cheese, hare, turkey, rabbit, tongue, beef and other meats (see p.130).

In 1822 only two strengths of beer were made, but in 1743 there had been a more varied choice available. Besides ale (probably at this time a medium-strength drink) and small beer (a weaker staple drink), the Dunham brewer of 1743–4 was making a March beer, his best-quality strong beer designed as an after-dinner drink for the servants and men of the family. We thus have a picture of a declining choice in domestically brewed beer, which is very much in accord with evidence from country houses elsewhere.[118] Despite its name, March beer at Dunham was made in April, the largest and strongest brews of the year. Being strong, March beer would keep well even over several seasons and the butler's consumption records show that people drank it throughout the year, with peaks highest in August and September. Brewing of ale and ordinary small beer was carried on all year once a fortnight and the consumption of both was highly consistent, at 36 gallons of ale and 54 gallons of small beer a week. Cider, on the other hand, was definitely a hot-weather drink for July and August.

Within the Dunham household in 1743 wine-drinking was generally less important than it became in 1822, though port was pre-eminent. It was ranked not into best and second best, but into red and white, this last being considered slightly vulgar. In the 1740s fifteen per cent of the wine consumed was home-made, most of it a birch-sap wine which appears to have been very popular all year round (see p.120). In 1743–4 the candle consumption records show a relationship only to daylight hours and there is no pattern associated with a prolonged absence by the family.

* * *

Do we have any record of the forms in which food items appeared on the table? Unfortunately, no menu book survives from the nineteenth century, but we do have Lady Mary Booth's two-volume recipe book dated 1730[119] (Box 31, p.130). Both volumes are beautifully neat, well organised into sections, with a third notebook for recipes for syrups, conserves and the drying of herbs and flowers. The books show a very rich and varied cuisine typical of the eighteenth century. Food was fairly simple but with exotic touches, rich in butter, cream, sugar and citrus fruits, especially lemon. Nutmeg, mace and anchovies were the common flavourings. Most of the soup recipes are straightforward, using ingredients like turnips, mushrooms, peas and onions and there are a couple of versions of 'solid' or 'cake' soup – based on calf's foot jelly, reduced to a solid lump, then cut into squares for keeping. The second volume contains recipes for meat pies and what are called 'made' meat dishes, that is, stewed or baked mutton, beef and veal, game dishes as well as sauces for roast meat. Only very occasionally are instructions for roasting given, this being so basic as not to require explanation, though a classic recipe for roast hens does include some information. There are numerous recipes for puddings, both sweet and savoury, as well as cold sweets such as fruit creams. Often there are several versions of puddings; for example, there are nine recipes for almond pudding, eight for orange, eight for oatmeal, and two for carrot. There are also several pages of table layouts.

Lady Mary Booth, Countess of Stamford, daughter of the 2nd Earl of Warrington, painted by an unknown artist, *c.*1765.

31

Recipes from Lady Mary Booth's collection, 1730

Volumes kept at Dunham Massey

Birch Wine

To every gallon of Birch Water* (first boyled 2 hours ...) put 2 pound of white sugar, boyle it so long as scum rises & take it off clean, then pour it into a Tub, let it stand & settle & when cold pour it from the grounds & to every 12 gallons put a pint of yeast & keep it close covered & when you think it has worked enough – run it into a Vessell first fum'd with brimstone, stop it close & ... drink it like White Wine, do not bottle it till Christmas ... This will keep 4 years

A Pye of a Breast of Veal

When you've blanch'd it, force it, with what force you please, & being well seasoned put it in a fine paste, or else cut it in pieces & so season it with pepper, salt & sweet herbs minced small, so make up your pie & when baked pour in a white sauce, made with yolks of eggs allayed with verjuice.†

English Stake Pie

Cut a neck, loin or breast of mutton into stakes, & season them with pepper, nutmeg & salt, then take a few sweet herbs & mince them small with an onion or two, & yolks of three or four hard eggs, then put the meat into the pye, with some capers, & strew these materials on it, then put in butter & bake it moderately for three hours, let the pye be raised round & pretty deep, so serve it to table with a cover on.

Pigeon Pye

Take your pigeons as soon as they are killed, & dress, clean & draw them, then season them with pepper, salt, beaten cloves & mace, then put into your pye some minced chibols,‡ & sweet herbs, then the pigeons & artichoke bottoms, chesnuts, yolks of hard eggs, very thin slices of lard, some colliflower indifferently well boyled, capers, oyster & mushrooms, lemon & butter, strew in some more seasoning then close and bake it & when 'tis baked pour in some verjuice, & sweet butters, thickened with yolks of eggs.

Apricock Jumballs§

Take your ripest Apricocks, pare them & cut the meat from the stone into a silver dish & with the back of a spoon make them as small as you can, then set them on the fire & let them boile till you perceive the stuff goes thick or rather goes stiff & keep continual stirring then let the fire slack under it & spread it in the dish & turn it continually till it grow as thick as a reasonable stiff paste, then make it into a round ball & let it lye & cool all night, next day take the whitest loaf sugar seived fine & knead it into the pulp till it be stiff, then role it & make jumballs & knots & lay them on a sheet of paper before the fire but at a good distance from it ... This you may do with other fruit.

Cream Caudle

Take 4 spoonfuls of Sack** & one of Beer, set it on the fire till it boyles, then put it into a pint of cream & a spoonful of sugar, stir it till it boyles, than take it off the fire & serve it. This is but enough for one mess.††

Roasted Turkey

Take a young turkey & make a pudding with a little cream, some crumbs of bread, a few currants, a little salt & mace beaten, put it into the craw of the turkey & so roast it. For the sauce take half a pint of white wine, some good gravy, a pint of oysters with their liquor, a little salt, mace, 4 anchovies, stew all a little, than put in a bit of butter. Dish up the turkey & pour on this.

Summary of instructions for roasting Hens

Parboil them first, drain, lard all over with strips of bacon, strew with a little flour, roast in front of the fire but do not baste. Put slices of toast in the dripping pan so that the hens drip on them. Then mince some bacon, add some beaten eggs and fry this mixture like a pancake. Serve the hens in a dish with the toast in the bottom, and the fried mixture cut up and sprinkled on top.

---

* Birch sap
† Juice of unripe grapes or crab apples
‡ Chives
§ A sweet or fruit-based biscuit shaped into knots etc.
** A sweet wine originally from the Canary Islands
†† Mess, one serving for two or three people

Some of these recipes were probably used for the servants' meals, but of this there is no direct record. The servants appear to have enjoyed a varied and plentiful diet, even during the first half of the year when they should have been on board wages. Some food items were absent at this time; they were not given luxuries such as chickens, fish or cream, but staples such as beef and beer continued even though the family was absent. These two items were the traditional mainstay of the servants' diet, so much so that many servants complained of the monotony. It was usual for a large joint of beef to be roasted each Sunday, thereafter to appear cold every day until consumed and replaced by yet another joint.

* * *

To sum up, we can see how the Dunham food-supply and consumption records can be used to sketch in the annual pattern of family occupation. They highlight firstly the regime of the 2nd Earl of Warrington, who lived quietly at Dunham all year, entertaining a few visitors every month except February and March, the traditional off-season for hospitality; and secondly the 6th Earl of Stamford, who divided the year between two houses, using Dunham as a venue for late-summer and autumn house parties based on shooting and horse-racing. This pattern of hospitality was such an unremitting element and required such a high degree of organisation that the housekeeper kept written guest lists.[120] In 1826 Dunham received a total of 153 house-guests, divided evenly into groups during the period between July and November. The only individuals who came more than once in a year were relatives. Others were members of the Cheshire county society, families such as the Cholmondeleys, the Egertons, the Leicesters, the Herons and the Langford Brookes, many of whom lived fairly near but who stayed for several nights. The sexes were evenly balanced; some were married couples, but at least half attended on their own and included members of the peerage, the clergy and many men of senior military rank. Class united them, however, for the 6th Earl was remembered as being 'a thorough aristocrat in respect of the company he kept, and only associated with county families. As was said ... by an old workman of his, "He didna dine with cotton lords".'[121] Most guests would bring their own footmen to wait on at dinner and the colourful suits of their livery must have made a fine sight.

Though clearly the degree to which Dunham was able to provide its own food supplies varied widely from item to item and month to month, there does appear to have been a substantial degree of home production. This must have had important implications for the system of livestock-rearing at home farm, especially when combined with the seasonal variability in food requirements during 1822. For this reason we now move out of the house to view home farm and the park, which played such a critical role in the household economy.

CHAPTER SIX

'Carrots for the deer'

A Land Steward at Work

Since the supply of both foodstuffs and services to the Dunham household was heavily dependent on the home farm, we need to trace the chain of management back to that point. If John Poole, the house steward, and a relative newcomer to Dunham, was the hub of the house management in 1822, John Davenport, farm steward since 1801, was the central figure in the management of farm, estate, gardens and park. Davenport's duties were widened after the death of the 5th Earl at the expense of the house steward's, but the two still seemed to overlap a little, especially as regards the stables, where veterinary bills for saddle and carriage horses appear in both their accounts. This is an unusual confusion, however, and it seems clear that under the overall control of the agent, Hugo Worthington, Davenport instigated, supervised and paid for all work done at home farm, the Dunham estate and the park. He had supervision of the accounts of the Dunham park-keeper Daniel Shaw, the head gardener, Joseph Pickin and the miller, Robert Booth, as well as co-ordinating the work of those members of staff who provided services across the whole range of departments, such as the blacksmith, Daniel Parsons, and the wagoner, Thomas Burgess. Some of these, like the carpenter, Timothy Brownell, in turn supervised their own workforce.

Davenport's promotion came at a time when the estate was investing in new premises in these departments. The home farm with its associated houses and workshops was still being finished in 1822. The Davenports, Thomas Burgess and his assistant, Joseph Grestley, all lived there, as did three other farm servants, two of whom were a married couple. These were all permanent staff on the residential salaried list. By contrast, most of the skilled and unskilled labourers working under them were paid weekly, with wages calculated on a day-labour basis. The monthly bill for the main farm workers totalled between £58 and £64 a month for twenty-nine men. It was a stable workforce, varying little from month to month and working all the year round. In addition, gangs of casual female labour were employed in the fields and park, doing work which was labour-intensive, requiring a low level of skill but a high level of back-breaking handwork. This too was fairly regular and the women were organised into teams of perhaps seven or ten, usually with one or more men working with them. They were paid day rates for a variety of jobs throughout the year.

Davenport also paid the regular quarterly contract bills from John Leigh the

RIGHT: The herd of fallow deer at Dunham is over two hundred strong. There have been deer at Dunham Massey since the fourteenth century and today they form a vital part of a complex and fragile ecostructure.

32

Account of the livestock at Dunham Massey at 1 January 1823

EGR 7/1/12

1 Sir Oliver
4 brood mares
7 colts and fillies
3 hacks
12 cart horses
1 helpers' old horse

13 milk cows
1 bull
15 fat cows
5 lean cows
9 fat Scots
20 lean Scots

45 fat sheep
133 lean sheep
29 ewes
2 rams

10 fat pigs
6 porkets
12 store pigs
4 breeding sows
3 boars

John Davenport, Bailiff

LEFT: The eighteenth-century slaughterhouse at Dunham Massey. This is a rare surviving example of a building in which deer carcasses were hung after they were culled.

wheelwright, John Warmishaw the saddler, John Walton the cooper and Cooper the horse doctor. He dealt with numerous suppliers of cereals, livestock and general goods, his purchases offset in his accounts by sales of livestock and regular quarterly injections of cash from Hugo Worthington. For 1822 they reveal a detailed picture of the seasonal routine of the farm and park.[122]

Given the amount of meat supplied to the house, stock husbandry must have been an important aspect of the work, but it is rarely mentioned specifically and we are left to infer it from deliveries of straw for animal bedding (1,270 cwts in twenty deliveries at a cost of £123 19s at 2s per cwt) and livestock feedstuffs. These were mainly oats, barley, turnips and mangolds, but in addition there were two deliveries of carrots for the deer costing £198 and one delivery of French wheat for the partridges. Beans were purchased for mixing with oats for the horses and for the keepers for pheasant feed. The purchase of 12 bushels of acorns was also for animal feed, presumably the pigs.

Davenport submitted annual inventories of livestock (Box 32, opposite) as well as quarterly bills for the purchase of livestock (horses, sheep and cattle), which came to the substantial total of £783 8s (Box 33, below). These included the fat cows, Scotch cattle and wether sheep, which provided the main meat supply to the house. The Scotch heifers were bought in a single block from a dealer in Ormskirk market.

33

Livestock bought and sold by the home farm, Dunham Massey, 1822

EGR 7/12/3

Bought

	£	s
Horses – total spent	**£70**	
2 cart horse	£50	
A bay pony	£20	
Sheep – total spent	**£261**	**15s**
245 wether sheep	£231	10s
40 ewes in lamb	£30	5s
Cattle – total spent	**£457**	**13s**
19 feeding cows	£159	3s
10 fat cows	£120	
20 Scotch heifers	£170	
1 calving cow	£8	10s
Total livestock bills	**£783**	**8s**

Sold

	£	s	d
Cattle – total income	**£221**	**3s**	
11 fat cows	£216	18s	
3 calves	£4	5s	
Sheep – total income	**£55**		
18 ewes	£9		
10 small ewes	£6		
20 fat sheep	£40		
Pigs – total income	**£12**	**10s**	
2 old sows	£6		
1 fat boar	£6	10s	
Livestock products – income	**£179**	**5s**	**11d**
1644lbs wool	£89	1s	0d
3682lbs tallow	£46	0s	6d
30 cow hides	£29	3s	11d
230 sheepskins	£15	0s	6d
Total income from livestock	**£467**	**18s**	**11d**

Fat cows were bought singly: ten cows bought from ten men, mostly small-scale local farmers with whom Davenport seems to have kept in close contact, probably at local market days.

The home farm also sold livestock and stock products, providing it with an income which over the year amounted to £467 (Box 33, p.135). Surplus fat cows were sold to a butcher in Altrincham, William Berry, who also supplied feeding cows. There were two other buyers of livestock, both local farmers. The meat requirements of the house also produced substantial by-products. The cow hides were sold to William Whitelegg, the tanner in Altrincham, and the sheepskins to a farmer from Warburton, John Lowe. The tallow from the cattle-slaughtering went to the chandlers, sent in monthly loads and priced by weight. An earlier farm account book shows that between 1785 and 1799 an average of 2,174 tons of tallow were sent each year at a price of between 4d and 6d per ton. The only other sales were very small amounts of potatoes amounting to £10 in total value. Dan Shaw's enterprise in the park, of course, produced venison carcasses, though the record of these appears nowhere in the archives for 1822.

To judge by the bills from the veterinary contractors, the livestock were extremely well looked after, each given their specialist medical attendants. William Cooper, the horse doctor, was employed to care for the twelve heavy horses, which received thirty-five visits from him over the year, mainly for routine attention to their feet but also to administer drenches, embrocations, poultices and dressings. One was bled and one had an operation on the eye. This was in addition to the attention of the blacksmith, Daniel Parsons, who sent in a quarterly bill for his work at the three stables, again mainly for removing and refitting shoes. The heavy horses were worked harder than their more refined colleagues and needed more attention. They were, after all, a truly essential part of the farm team. Whether out of sentiment or because they were controlled largely by word, in Parsons' bills the heavy horses were given their simple, traditional but evocative names: Ragman, Robin, Rose, Sharper, Smiler, Tom, Whitefoot, Darling, Mishap, Flower, Boxer and Jolly – whereas the riding horses were identified merely by description.

A cow doctor called Robert Holt was paid for doctoring the cows and the bull, with ointments, drenches and dressings. In all he was paid for twenty-two visits to them over the year, much of this time being spent trimming and dressing their feet. Like other livestock at this time, cattle were still moved around the country along roads and green lanes by drovers, so their feet needed particular care, but frequent foot-trimming probably also indicates a high level of cereal feeding. The farm did its own doctoring of other livestock, buying 12 gallons of tobacco water for worming or de-ticking the sheep and 6lb of goose oil, probably for removing pig lice.

Field-work and work around the park was done mainly by the two separate groups of workers, the male farm labourers and the female casual workers. Their wage records show the seasonal round of jobs to be done. During January and February groups of farm labourers were employed in 'assisting the teams', by which was meant the wagoner and his heavy horses. The work involved loading dung from the farm buildings and carting sand and lime for mortar, as well as timber and bricks for Shaw's alterations to the house. Winter also saw major work on the installation of

Women labourers were used widely on landed estates. This photograph was taken early in the twentieth century on an estate in Staffordshire.

a main drain on Cockridge Moss. Most of the 9,500 drainage tiles and 180 pipes purchased at a cost of £47 went to this. Existing pools and watercourses, including the mill 'fleam' (the mill-race) were 'slutched' (cleared of mud), and the pumps in the well-house were overhauled. In the winter fields, the women worked at the turnip harvest, pulling them up by hand and 'fashing' them (cutting the tops off).

Later, the men washed the sheep ready for shearing. In April and May the women cut potato sets and helped in their planting and, a little later, weeded the early corn. One man worked on digging turves and stacking them in the newly repaired turf-house and in early June both male and female labourers turned to cabbage-planting and the hay harvest. This last took over a month in all and was done by a team of twenty-six women and eleven men, paid at 1s 8d, or 1s 9d a day, depending on their job. They needed new hay-making rakes and a new tedding machine was bought which cost £13. A thatcher was paid 6s for thatching the two hay-ricks which were built and the local baker supplied coarse common 'stoved' salt for dressing the hay to reduce risk of internal combustion. The whole hay-making team was supplied with a copious allowance of beer.

For the teams of male farm workers, summer meant topping thistles, cutting grass in the park, reaping corn, turning the dung heap and carting building materials for a new enterprise, the erection of a row of cottages at Streethead and in Millington. They also cut hedges, did some coppicing and fenced the new cottage gardens. One small team cleaned the Knutsford smithy and farm walks, a total of 300 roods charged at 3d per rood (a quarter of an acre). The women's work continued with weeding cabbages, mangolds and potatoes and binding sheaves during the corn harvest. In autumn and early winter, the male gangs levelled the pits which had been dug at Streethead for making the bricks for the cottages, generally landscaped and tidied the building site and, back at Dunham, harvested potatoes and mangolds

34

Cereals bought by the home farm, Dunham Massey, 1822

EGR 7/12/3

	Quantity bought	Price per bushel	Total cost		
Oats	3,098 bushels	3s 9d late summer before new harvest, 2s 10d after harvest	£536	18s	4d
Meal		between 23s and 30s a load, according to quality	£145	17s	10d
Beans	151 bushels	between 3s 6d and 6s 3d, according to quality and time	£36	18s	2d
Barley	300 bushels	3s 6d before new harvest, 4s- after harvest	£58	15s	10d
Wheat		46s before harvest, 36s- after	£328	10s	2d
Groats	?	?	£2	6s	3d
Bran	?	?	£8	7s	0d
Malt	30 loads	between 54s in Jan. and Feb. and 44s 9d in summer	£75	10s	
Hops	6 lb	1s		6s	
TOTAL			**£1,193**	**9s**	**7d**

along with the women, who also weeded turnips. The men cleaned ditches, marled the fields, turned the dung heap again and dug yet more drains. One of the farm labourers was paid separately for threshing barley and three others got on with the plough-driving.

Throughout the year, extra work was available for the women around the park: raking grass after mowing, weeding and brushing the walks and driveways, raking and burning leaves. According to the vouchers, the cash payments for all of the women were paid to one woman ganger, Mary Blease, who signed for the money with a cross since she could not write. She herself earned an extra £1 13s for 132 mornings spent picking dung off the carriage drives.

We can see from this and from the purchases of seed from three suppliers that the home farm grew its own crops of cereals and root crops, but no values of home production are recorded. It is clear, though, that the estate was by no means self-sufficient in cereals for either animal feed or human consumption, for a major item of expense was the purchase of oats, wheat, barley, meal and malt, totalling £1,193 9s 7d (Box 34, above). The oatmeal was purchased in Liverpool, for which the farm paid a bill from the Duke of Bridgewater for freightage of 131 sacks in four journeys on the Bridgewater Canal. Other purchases were made from local farmers and dealers.

All routine maintenance on the estate properties was carried out by the land steward, using wherever possible the estate's own labour force, notably the bricklayer, John Hope. Bills were paid for new paving stones, building-stone and gravel for drives and walks. Notably, there are no bills for bricks for the farm or park, though

The deer barn at Dunham Massey, built around 1740 and used for the winter feeding of the herd.

the gardens did buy in 700 for their own use. There was obviously a brick-making enterprise on the estate as there were several references to filling in brick-making holes and a payment for 'new barrows for the brickmakers'. Building sand was bought from a nearby sand-hole outside the estate, scaffold poles were provided by the carpenter and scaffold ropes were bought from Joseph Hesketh in Carrington.

On the estate, a major job for John Hope which lasted throughout the summer of 1822 was the building of the new cottages at Streethead and Millington. His work on the cottages was not detailed in the accounts, but the 85 gallons of beer bought for the labourers from the Dog Inn is recorded. There was plenty of other work for him and his men. They built a length of the new park wall near the Woodhouses Gate,

35

Account for travelling expenses from Thomas Burgess, wagoner, to John Davenport, land steward, October–December 1822

EGR 7/12/4/64

Account of Jorneys with the Earl of Stamfords Teams December 31st 1822 By me Thos Burgess

	£	s	d
To 121 Jorneys to Millington and Nags head With Brick Lime Sand Timber Slate flag and Other Building Meterials at 8d	4	0	8
To 2 Jorneys with Waggon to Crown in Peover for Straw -- at 3s	0	6	0
To two Breakfasts at 1/6 and two Dinners at 2s	0	7	0
To 5 Jorneys to Crown in Peover for Corn at 2/6	0	12	6
To five Breakfasts at 1/6 and five Dinners at 2s	0	17	6
To 1 Jorney to Northwich for Beans at 2/6	0	2	6
To One Breakfast at 1/6 and One Dinner at 2s	0	3	6
To 2 Jorneys to Wincham for Soyle at 2/6	0	5	0
To two Breakfasts at 1/6 and two Dinners at 2s	0	7	0
To 1 Jorney to Wincham for Smithy Coal at 2/6	0	2	6
To One Breakfast at 1/6 and One Dinner at 2s	0	3	6
To 2 Jorneys to Tabley for Trees -- at 2/6	0	5	0
To two Dinners at 2	0	4	0
To 3 Jorneys to Manchester for Corn at 3	0	9	0
To three Breakfasts at 1/6 and three Dinners at 2s	0	10	6
To 1 Jorney to Manchester with Wool at 3s	0	3	0
To One Breakfast at 1/6 and One Dinner at 2s	0	3	6
To 1 Jorney to Preston and at Preston and Back	2	6	0
To 12 Jorneys to Millington for Stone at 8d	0	8	0
To 1 Jorney to Warmisham for Cheese at 3s	0	3	0
To 17 Jorneys to Warrington with fat at 1s	0	17	0
To two ~~Breakfasts~~ Dinners at -- 2s	0	4	0
	£13	0	8

(Decr. 30) Settled By me Thomas Burgess.

repaired the roofs of the mill and the deer barn, worked on the dovecote and paved a yard at home farm, repaired an old stable and set up a new boiler in the poultry yard. The contractor from Stourbridge who installed iron spouting at the main house also fitted the same spouting at the farm. Gilgrass, the contract plasterer, whitewashed the dog kennels and the ice-house, and colour-washed (in a stone colour) the keeper's lodge, the deer barn and the water-house. John Pearson, the glazier and painter who was so useful in the house, was contracted to paint the Woodhouses Gate and the railings by the mill, the paddock, the lions and the obelisk in Langhams Grove. He made up his own paint, of course, from boiled oil, turpentine, crude litharge (red lead), lamp black and chocolate colouring.

Daniel Parsons was kept busy on the estate in an endless stream of jobs, over and above his work as a farrier to the horse teams. Thirty-five park and field gates were fitted with catches and locks, there were whitewash buckets to patch, wedges to make for cleaving timber for the carpenters, and for the gamekeepers he made branding irons for marking the dogs and hooks on which to hang their meat. There were chains, brushing-hooks and iron cart-fittings to be mended and pigs to be ringed. Working with the wheelwright, he 'shoed' a pair of wheels, probably fitting new strakes (strips of iron tiring nailed on) rather than complete tyres. For 'me lords carriage' he repaired the shoe on the drag-chain (part of the braking system).

The estate wagoner, Thomas Burgess, was kept continually busy. In addition to the work billed to the house, around the farm and plough-driving, Burgess's annual travel expenses claim itemised 169 journeys, 121 of which were carting building materials to Streethead and Millington (Box 35, opposite). The rest were off the estate, for which he was entitled to 1s 6d for a breakfast and 2s for dinners. They included trips to Peover and Northwich to collect straw, cereals and beans, to Tabley for trees and to Warrington to deliver the tallow to the chandler. Occasionally he was so busy that odd jobs were put out to contractors, such as carting alder poles out of a covert and filling in a marl pit. In a sophisticated and complex environment, such as Dunham was at this time, it is sometimes difficult to remember that the retail industry was relatively undeveloped and many goods had to be bought in the form of raw materials rather than in a manufactured state. When Burgess needed a new waterproof sheet for a cart, for example, he not only had to buy the materials (12 yards of linen, cord and 2 gallons of boiled oil) but he also had to find a tailor to make it up for him and then pay the painter for one and a half days waterproofing the sheet. The total cost was £1 12s.

The estate provided so much work that some of the regular contract tradesmen worked for Davenport almost full-time. The bills of John Leigh, the wheelwright, show that he worked between twenty and twenty-four days a month at 3s a day in an effort to keep the wagoner's teams on the road. The carts and wagons needed regular maintenance; during the year new iron fittings, ropes and paint were bought for them. The saddler, John Warmishaw, was kept busy by the grooms, the wagoner and the gamekeepers (Box 36, p.142). For the last he made dog whips, buckles and straps and kept the keepers' horses in tackle. For the heavy horses there were endless bits and pieces to be made or mended: collars, back-bands, belly-bands, croupers, whips and 'best double diaper red horse rugs'. For the grooms he supplied bridles and saddle parts as well as 'travelling boots for the colts' and twenty-five wash leather skins.

John Walton, the cooper, supplied various bits and pieces of new equipment including new wooden buckets which he painted and marked, and a new salting 'turnil'

36

Bill from John Warmishaw to John Davenport, land steward, for saddlery and harness work, January–March, 1822

EGR 7/12/1/12

The Earl of Stamford
1822

To John Warmishaw

	Groom	£	s	d	
Jany 25	mending head collor rain 4, web breast plate with leather				
Feby	martingle part and plated buckles 6/0	0	6	4	
20	best breaking cavison complete 12/0, new snaffle bridle for colts 10/0	1	2	0	
	4 traveling boots for colts 4/0, binding for do 6d	0	4	6	
March	new stuffing and covering cavison nose and new pads to do	0	2	0	£ s d
1	8 lb of best oil 12/0, 1 lb of best herds 1/2, 2 3 wash leather skins 2/6	0	15	8	2 10 6
	Game Keeper				
Jany 26	new strap to sadle 6, fine main comb 6	0	1	0	
March	stout new dog whip 4/6d, 1 lb of best herds 1/2d	0	5	8	
4	new buckles and straps to dog couples 5/0	0	5	0	0 11 8
Jany 1	**Cart Stables**				
	~~new strap to breachband and mending do 1/10d, new cap to do 10~~	0	2	8	
	mending cart bridle 4, 3rd pair of backband straps 10d	0	1	2	
9th	new nose to head collor 1/0, new stay and mending do 10d	0	1	10	
	new throat to head collor 1/0, new rope rain 10d	0	1	10	
10th	2 best curry combs 2/8d, whip cord 1/0d, mending collor 1/0	0	4	8	
16	mending cart bridle 6d, 17th new piece to cart bridle rain 8	0	1	2	
21	new collor with large housing boned and straps 36/	1	16	0	
	new cart bridle 2 In broad with double head and broad nose 20/	1	0	0	
	strong 9 In. backband with straps 28/	1	8	0	
	strong 8 do. backcrouper 18/ pad and straps to do 2/0	1	0	0	
Feby	new chain bellyband 5/6, new double headed cart halter 9/0	0	14	6	
2	strong rope rain 10d, 6th strong cart sadle and crouper complete	3	0	10	
	~~new broad breachband 7 Inches longer then common~~	2	0	0	
6	new lineing collor with woolen 5/6 new leather to collor 1/0	0	6	6	
8	1 thousand of nails 3/4d, 11th new backband strap 5d	0	3	9	
12	strong leather head collor 6/0d, new cart martingale 3/0	0	9	0	
March	strong rope rain 10d, 14th long housing lace 1/0, 26th mendg collor 1/0	0	2	10	
1	mending and stuffing 1/6, mending collor and sowing straps 1/0	0	2	6	
4	lash and keeper mending whips 6. 2 lb of best oil 3/0	0	3	6	
5	3 new straps to body rollor 2/0 new pad to ditto 1/3	0	3	3	
7	2 new 9 foot cart whips 9/0. 6th new lineing cart bellyband 2/0	0	11	0	
13	new strap to cart bellyband 1/0 new lineing collor 5/6	0	6	6	
	tying collor housing on 4d, new end to breachband 1/6	0	1	10	
	lineing breachband and new cap 1/0. 14th new piece to head collor 6	0	1	6	
15	4 best double diaper red horse rugs at 11/ each, binding ditto 4/	2	8	0	16 12 10
				Total	19 15 0

Settled March 30th John Warmishaw

(a common name for a large open-topped coopered vessel for salting meat) as well as mending a beer barrel (Box 37, opposite). The ironmonger supplied locks and a new key to the park gate and also two new 'stove grates' (small grates with cast-iron hobs), a boiler, furnace door and fire-bottoms, perhaps for the new cottages at Streethead.

Bill from John Walton to John Davenport, land steward, for cooper's work and new utensils, October–December, 1822

EGR 7/12/4/13

37

The Rt. Honble Earl of Stamford & Warrington
on a Count of goods for Farm
1822 — To John Walton Cooper
March 23 To a Seed Hoppet — 3..6
April 16th Repairing a Barrel part of a Head — 1..0
3 new Milk pails at 4/6 each — 13..6
May 3rd 9 lb of hoop Iron at 3d P lb — 2..3
10 4 Bee hives at 1/9 each — 7..0
a Basket 2/9 a Small Covered do 1/- — 3..9
23rd a Churn staff — 2..0
31st a hair sive 1/2 – a Botwoll 8 — 1..10
July 10th new Bottaming a Tub & 1 hoop — 3..0
Sepr 25 2 new Buckits painted & marked 5/ each — 10..0
Oct 10th a Stable sive — 3..0
5 a new Salting Turnil — 12..0
Decr 17th 4 a hair sive — 1..2
31st Settled by me John Walton — £3..4..0

Tree-planting, fencing and hedging were recorded in the accounts of the estate carpenter, Timothy Brownell, who had his own small team of skilled men supplemented by the farm labouring gangs. Getting out stakes and cutting rails were important jobs, especially during the colder months. Work in the woodlands, such as felling trees, thinning saplings and cutting out wind-blown boughs, seems to have been done mainly in the summer and autumn. Brownell's team of four men, each paid as day labourers, fenced the turnpike road, having first cut and shaped the posts and rails. Oak rails were sawn and charged at 3 farthings a foot. They also made and repaired field and hunting gates, mended the stable doors, made cow cratches and laid a floor in the new smithy. Tree-planting must have taken up an enormous amount of time. A bill dated March 1822 itemised huge numbers of young trees and bushes bought for setting in the park and estate: 3,500 alders, 2,000 hazels, 1,000 privets, 200 spruce, 200 Scots pine and smaller numbers of more specialist trees and shrubs. Forty apple trees were set in the new cottage gardens.

The woodlands yielded a variety of forestry products. Besides the valuable whole timber, brushwood was collected as a waste product and a casual labourer was paid to make it up into besoms. More detail of this activity was provided in earlier farm account books. In the 1780s, for example, the farm paid Mathew Smith, a day

The interior of the mill, which was converted to a sawmill in the mid-nineteenth century, replacing the earlier saw pit used by Timothy Brownell and his team.

labourer, to make the besoms in two qualities: house besoms were costed at 2d each and the more substantial stable besoms at 3d.[123] Surplus brushwood was sold outside the estate by the cartload at 1s per load. At this earlier date the farm also sold leaf-mould and bark as well as gathering acorns and crab apples, the last paid for at a ha'penny a bushel, presumably for making into jelly by the kitchen. An account of the sale of a single oak-tree blown down in 1802 shows the variety of timber products yielded (Box 38, opposite).

No doubt small timber was cut for fuel for the open fires in the house, and in 1822 a labourer was paid £6 13s for binding up 3,800 'kids', the faggots or bundles of small pieces of timber used for 'ovenwood', fuel for the bread ovens at the house and farm. In 1822, there are no accounts for the purchase of charcoal for the kitchen stoves, so it seems likely that the estate provided its own. Certainly earlier farm account books record charcoal-making in the woodlands. In the account book for 1780 the farm steward noted two clamp firings in which a total of 696 bushels of charcoal were made, the cost of which was calculated at 3d per bushel.[124] A surplus was sold off the estate at 6d per bushel.

The ovens and charcoal stoves had very specific fuel requirements, but for roasting and room heating the main fuel was coal. The home farm served as the main supplier of coal to the house, a task requiring a huge amount of cartage, loading and unloading. Coal was bought from the Duke of Bridgewater's mine at Worsley and paid out of Davenport's accounts on a single annual bill. In 1822 this was for 551 tons of common coal, 6 tons of cannel coal and 6 tons of slack, delivered on the Bridgewater Canal, costing a total of £306, plus a gratuity for the banksmen at Worsley. During the year there were sixty-two deliveries, often on consecutive days. For example, in November full boatloads were delivered on the 5th, 6th, 7th, 8th and 9th then again on the 29th and 30th. The home farm must have had a large coal-shed to store these amounts, from which Burgess carried deliveries to the house and farm when needed. The smithy had its own separate supplies of high-quality coal fetched by Burgess from Wincham. The responsibility of the farm for the coal supply was not new in 1822, for the farm steward ordered and stored all the coal used on the estate even in the eighteenth century.

Davenport not only paid staff wages but also organised beer allowances from the Dog Inn on all 'lowance jobs', specific tasks which carried a beer entitlement. These included the hay harvest, washing sheep and shearing, cleaning pools and the mill fleam and digging turves. The sheep-washers alone consumed 296 pints; this was in addition to the usual daily allowances of beer as the staple drink for those who lived on the farm. Supplies of malt were bought by the farm from John Barratt and

38

Oak tree blown down in Dunham Park, January 1802

The trunk of the large Oak Tree blown down in Dunham Park in January 1802 measured	321¼ sq. ft		
The large Tops or Branches measured	82¾ sq. ft		
Sir Robert Peel and Co bought the Trunk 321¼ and 52½ foot of the tops @ 6/6s a foot	£121	7s	9d
The remainder of the tops being 29¾ foot were used for charcoal @ 1s a foot	£1	9s	9d
1 ton and a half of postwood sold for	£1	10s	0d
Some very small tops and Cropwood sold for	£1	9s	0d
The Bark, in season, worth about	£8	0s	0d
TOTAL	**£133**	**16s**	**6d**

delivered directly to the estate brewer who made beer for the labourers as well as the house. Davenport paid other allowances too: the blacksmith, Daniel Parsons, lived in one of the cottages and received 5s a year for tending the smithy gate for a year, his wife acting as gate-keeper during the day. Another labourer was paid for tending the church walk gate. The wagoner needed his travel expenses, and the butcher was paid his vermin money of a penny ha'penny each for 144 rats' tails (this is the only documentary proof we have that one of the labourers acted as slaughterer/butcher, though the need was obvious).

Davenport himself was entitled to travelling and office expenses. Travel came to between £3 and £4 a quarter, chiefly for trips to Northwich, which seemed to be the main market centre, and also to Knutsford, Stockport and Manchester. Office expenses consisted of a large supply of paper and three ledgers to help keep his accounts straight. For John Thorpe, a long-serving gamekeeper, the estate provided not only work and home but also the ultimate support of family, for Davenport arranged for and paid his funeral expenses when he died in the autumn of 1822. These included bread as well as alcoholic liquor, a suit of coffin clothes, a coffin made by Timothy Brownell, the gravedigger's costs and the expenses of the sexton.

The farmhouse itself figures in the accounts for 1822. It was allocated a total of 2,510lb of meat for consumption by the steward's family and the farm servants.[125] This works out at an average of 48lb a week, of which twenty-five per cent was beef, the rest fairly evenly divided between sheep and pig meat. Both sheep and beef were eaten throughout the year, but the pig meat shows a strong seasonal concentration into the colder months; no pig was slaughtered for the farm between May and December. All the carcasses were of fully grown animals except for one lamb and one calf. For accounting purposes, all the meat was valued at 6d per lb, giving an annual value of £62 15s 0d. Other purchases included cheese (from a local grocer, not the house dairy), groceries for the farmhouse, 20 quarts of oil, 28lb of soap, candles and the materials for new bed sheets and towelling.

* * *

In 1822 the estate mill was another of Davenport's responsibilities, though it was worked by two men, Robert Booth who was a salaried employee and his assistant, Thomas Jones, whose wages accounted for most of the mill's costs of £36.[126] In terms of volume, the most important item milled was far and away malt (750 loads), followed by wheat (575 loads). By comparison, oats, barley and beans were negligible. However, oats and malt were easy to mill and were thus charged cheaply (2d and 4d per load respectively). Barley was charged at 1s per load, beans at 1s 4d and wheat at 2s. This means that by value wheat (£51 10s) was the most important grain, followed by malt (£18 14s 9d), barley, oats and beans. In addition, the mill charged to its accounts the cost of grinding toll corn, an annual amount of some 36 pecks at 1s 6d per peck. A further £24 15s 9d was earned from miscellaneous grinding and rolling of small amounts, including grinding 52lb of barley for the poor, presumably to make barley bread. It is not always clear when the milled flour was intended for the use of the house, though most of it probably was. Apart from the house, the largest single user was John Barratt, the supplier of malt to Dunham Massey. He

The kitchen garden at Dunham Massey. The wall on the left was heated for the cultivation of exotic fruit. A series of small stoves were built into the base, which led into long serpentine flues within the wall.

was paying for a regular processing of 12 loads of malt a week, presumably sold to other customers as well as the house and farm. The remaining costs were for a saddle, the annual supply of candles for the mill and a small amount of work done by the blacksmith. Profit was entered as £69 12s 8d, the only enterprise to be in such a happy situation.

The head gardener, Joseph Pickin, also worked under the departmental supervision of Davenport. An earlier kitchen garden without greenhouses was shown in one of the views by John Harris dated 1751. This was expanded in the 1770s when the house steward's account included items for joiner's, glazier's and painter's work on the 'new Wall & Green House'.[127] This was probably the heated back wall, which has internal flues built into it.

Pickin kept his own account book and vouchers.[128] Each month the gardens employed a more or less standard number of labourers, paid according to experience

39

Account for raking leaves at Dunham Massey, paid by Joseph Pickin, head gardener, September–November 1822

EGR 7/12/12/14

1822 Novr 30th Paid for raking Leaves

	days		£ s d
Betty Holt	11½	at 1s pr day	11.6
Betty Hunt	25	Do	1.5 —
Margret Greasty	7	Do	7 —
Jane Gibbon	4	Do	4 —
Nancy Holt	15½	Do	15.6
Phaeby Lingard	14	Do	14 —
Sarah Walker	10½	Do	10.6
Mary Holt	15½	Do	15.6
Sarah Garner	5	Do	5 —
Mary Blease	5	Do	5 —
Ellen Wareham	15½	Do	15.6
Cathrine Gibbon	15	Do	15 —
Martha Perceval	17	Do	17 —
Mary Bancroft	15	Do	15 —
Ellen Gibbon	10	Do	10 —
Betty Barlow	14½	Do	14.6
Mary Copack	17	Do	17 —
John Holt	16	Do	16 —
Tom Timperley	26	Do	1.6 —
Tom Chorton	6	Do	6 —
John Farnworth	18	Do	18 —
Fredrick Stubbs	12½	at 10d pr day	10.5
Saml Warburton	22	Do	18.4
Betty Clough	4	Do	3.4
Mary Padmore	9½	at 9d pr day	7.1
		£	16 2 2

and skill. Eleven men worked for 20d a day, one for 17d a day, two for 16d a day and two women for 12d a day, a total of fourteen men and two women. These worked full-time, that is anything between twenty-five and twenty-nine days a month, all the year round, a prodigious workforce by modern standards. The monthly wage bill came to around £30 to £32. In addition, extra labour was bought in, paid at 16d a day and totalling around £5 a month. Extra weeding and raking of leaves was done by teams of women and boys, many the same individuals who did field-work for the farm[129] (Box 39, above). In the summer, payments were also made for extra mowing around the island pool and a man was paid for 'serving the kitchen', that is, cooking in the mess-room or bothy. Pickin employed the usual craftsmen and tradesmen

40

Account of wasps killed at Dunham Massey garden, paid by Joseph Pickin, head gardener, May 1822

EGR 7/12/10/1

1822 May Account of Wasps destroyed in or near Dunham Massey Garden. at 1/ Pr Score

		£ s D
Thos Smith	136	6-9
Charlotte Warburton	20	1.–
John Dale	90	4.6
David Allen	40	2.–
Betty Ludlow	60	3.–
Joseph Wareham	120	6 –
Ellen Farnworth	20	1 –
Robert Holt	120	6
Wm Garner	70	3.6
Thos Burgess	20	1 –
Mary Ludlow	40	2 –
Mary Gibbon	42	2.1
Thos Hyam	80	4 –
Wm Bancroft	30	1.6
Alice Holt	60	3.
Wm Owen	60	3
Saml Holt	60	3
John Chorton	32	1.7
Amy Pickin	300	15 –
Ellen Wareham	40	2 –
George Perceval	30	1.6
		£ 3.13.5

over the year: the estate carpenter, the blacksmith, the bricklayers, the wheelwright and the glazier, for whom there was plenty of routine glass-replacement. The gardens also had work for a contract carter to supplement Burgess, a knife-grinder and, on two occasions, a man to destroy wasps' nests. The gardens waged wholesale and unremitting war on the latter, for it also paid its casual labourers for killing wasps at a rate of 1s per score. In May 1822 this bill came to over £3, paid to twenty one people (Box 40, above). One woman named Amy Pickin earned 15s, equivalent to more than fifteen days' work.

The record of goods purchased gives glimpses into the everyday life and work of the gardeners. Not surprisingly, perhaps, the first purchase in the year was an almanac. Thereafter followed a wide variety of goods: seeds, plants, trees, pots, nets, mats, baskets, heather besoms, rope, a saw, nails, bricks, colouring, gloves and, a reminder that gardeners at this level had to be highly literate, pencils. A major purchase was a new steam heating apparatus, costing £59, to heat the hot-houses or the heated walls. Fitting this was perhaps the reason for several items on Daniel Parsons' blacksmith's bill, including many entries for sharpening stonemasons'

The Dunham accounts for 1822 show that gardeners and labourers collected ice for the ice-house in the park. This unusual photographic record shows the ice harvest at Knole, Kent, *c.*1900, a strenuous job that was rewarded by large amounts of beer and ale.

chisels and brick-axes as well as providing holdfasts for copper piping and fixing and painting a 'steam pan'. Other items on Parsons' bill include a series of repairs, to the water-engine (probably a well-pump), the water-cart, barrows, ponds, hot walls and various door and gate locks, as well as the provision of new metal plates in the greenhouse floors and in the 'pine pits' (pineapple pits), and twelve new scythes for mowing. Sharpening edging tools was of course a regular job for him.

Routine garden purchases included monthly deliveries of bones for fertilising and spent bark and tan, probably for heating up the raised hotbeds where melons and winter salads were grown.[130] Ale was bought occasionally, one delivery being specifically mentioned as 'ale for the Icing' or ice harvest, the annual task of breaking up blocks of ice on a nearby pond or flooded meadow, carting and filling the ice-house. Strange to say, this was a very hot job, accompanied by generous allowances of beer and ale, the latter probably consumed at the informal celebration which usually followed. In most houses, the ice harvest was traditionally a job for the gardeners and obviously Dunham was no exception.

The quantity and variety of kitchen produce grown can be glimpsed from a single bill for over £13, paid to William Caldwell and Sons for plants in May 1822. This included eight varieties of cabbage and eight of lettuce, five varieties of broccoli, four different sorts of peas, and two of spinach as well as cauliflowers, sprouts, endive, cress, onions, turnip, radish and a variety of other vegetables, herbs and perennial flowers. There is no record of the amount of fruit produced, though clearly it would have been substantial. Some idea of the scale of the enterprise can be gained from records of the similar garden at Enville (see p.113). It was common practice at this time to reckon that if a kitchen garden were efficiently managed at a modest level, the value of fruit alone would cover most of the expense.[131] When the 7th Earl left

Dunham permanently, the kitchen gardens became a commercial enterprise with records of the regular sale of produce to the public beginning in 1859.[132]

In some months of the year, transport of produce became an important part of Pickin's routine. From January to April, usually one box of produce a week was sent from the gardens to Enville, costing from 2s 6d to 3s 7d a time. In May and June, when the family moved for the London season, these regular consignments were sent to London, now costing up to 6s 9d a time. In July all boxes ceased, as the family came to Dunham for the summer and autumn. Pickin's accounts total over £747. Both goods and services expenditure shows that March was a very busy month; bills for construction work were paid and the new steam apparatus installed. May and June were also slightly more expensive than other months, largely due to the increased cost of sending produce to London. As with the house, December was a busy month for the accounts, as several larger bills from tradesmen were paid off, presumably for work done over the year.

* * *

Farm, mill and garden accounts supply useful supplementary evidence about the running of the house as well as detail about the management of the home farm and the park; reading the household accounts on their own could result in an exaggerated impression as to the extent to which the estate met its own food requirements. The farm accounts show how much of the cereal supply came through the farm rather than being grown on it. Home production could not keep up with the need for straw and oats particularly, but other cereals such as barley and wheat also had to be bought in. Much of the demand was for feed for livestock, for work and recreational horses as well as high-quality Scotch cattle and fat cows. This was needed not just for winter subsistence to replace grass but also for fattening ready for slaughter at the time required by the family. Fuel, too, was provided via the home farm, which served as a large-scale storage facility for the house and gardens. Davenport's establishment was also the practical means by which many of the theoretical ideas of estate-building and park design achieved reality. He supervised not only the tree-planting which is so obvious a part of the landscape, but also provided the control centre for all those essential but often overlooked skills such as bricklaying, carpentering and metal-working. What emerges is therefore a complex picture. The home farm has to be seen not only as a producer of food and other goods needed by the house, but also as a storage depot, a processing and finishing plant and an environmental agency. Like the house itself, through its highly flexible but stable workforce and its purchases, the home farm provided a connecting point between the estate and the local community, and it is this aspect which will be explored further in the next chapter.

CHAPTER SEVEN

'The Labourers were bearers with Mourning Cloaks...'

A Community of Individuals

The concept of 'community' is nebulous and difficult to define, though historians and sociologists recognise some characteristics as typical. A community is united by a common purpose and a sense of belonging. It is not necessarily tightly knit geographically, though residential stability and a close relationship between work and home are often important, as are ties of kinship and the cement provided by cultural structures such as organised religion or recreation. The country house is an example of a community which, far from being homogeneous, was strengthened by the structural diversity of its parts. We can express this diversity diagrammatically as a series of concentric circles or 'ripples' moving away from the focus which is the Grey family (Diagram, opposite). The component parts are represented by a wide range of individuals, some of whom are the subject, albeit very briefly, of this chapter.

At the head of the Dunham hierarchy, and closest to the family in a social sense, were the land agents, the Worthingtons. Isaac Worthington, with his brother George, acted as the Dunham agent from 1760 to 1809 and was succeeded by his nephew Hugo Worthington, who was agent between 1809 and 1839.[133] With other partners, they formed a highly respected private practice as attorneys and land agents in Altrincham. Their house, later their office, was built in the 1780s in the most prestigious part of the town, in Market Street. The importance of the Grey business to the practice can be judged from the fact that at one point Isaac Worthington lived in the house at Dunham Massey; the Market Street premises is still the Stamford Estates Office as well as now being the Regional Office of the National Trust. In 1821 Worthington retained a room for occasional use at Dunham. For eighty years the Worthingtons ran the tenanted estates of the Greys and generally represented the family in their annual absence from Cheshire. The fact that they also acted as attorneys to Altrincham town council opens up a wide range of possibilities with respect to the Greys' influence within the town.

In 1822 Hugo Worthington was aged forty-four and married to Mary, who was exactly the same age. Hugo died in 1839, shortly after his resignation from the agency, and was outlived by his wife by fifteen years. They had at least one son, but the gravestone in Bowdon churchyard tells a tragic but not unusual story, for the couple had lost no less than four sons and two daughters in infancy.[134]

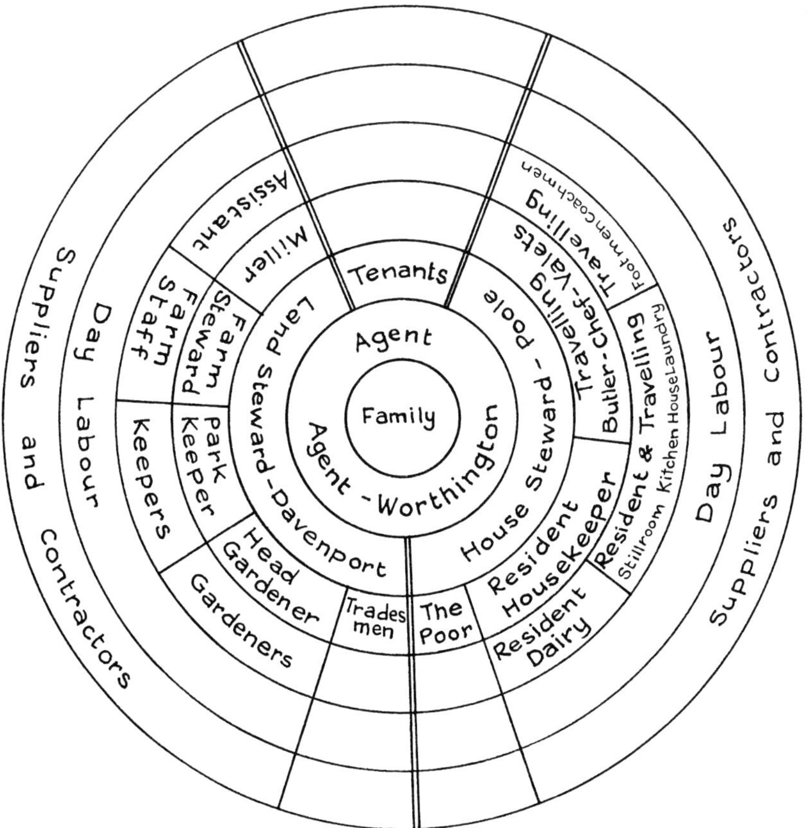

Diagram of the household and park labour structure at Dunham Massey in 1822 by G. Dale.

Both Isaac and Hugo Worthington left behind voluminous correspondence with the Earls of Stamford, mainly relating to estate administration, tenants' affairs and land purchases, but larded with local gossip about births and deaths, illnesses and disasters. One series of letters, however, is highly revealing of the relationship between the 5th Earl, Hugo, and an important supplier to the estate, the grocer and maltster, John Barratt. The correspondence highlights the fact that, important and responsible as Worthington's position was, Dunham was not a community of equals. Ultimately, the employer had the whip hand over his employees, no matter how elevated within the hierarchical structure. In 1814 the 5th Earl and John Barratt were competing purchasers for a desirable property, a cottage with a small field on the outskirts of Altrincham, which Barratt had rented for some years, paying £20 a year. It was put onto the market by the owner, the widow of a Mr Ashley, who had recently died. The Earl confided to his agent that he very much wanted to buy it and would be prepared to give £200 or £300 more than he had already offered, though he warned Worthington not to tell anyone of this fact.[135] Did Worthington know whether Mr Barratt realised the Earl was a potential purchaser? Yes, replied the agent, Mr Barratt did know, but, mindful of the warning about confidentiality, Worthington added that he had not been told by anyone connected with the agent's office. Word had got back, however, that Mr Barratt was also very keen to purchase the property but 'he certainly did not intend to oppose your Lordship in the purchase'. Correspondence between the Earl and his agent then degenerated into a series of recriminations and protestations about the reluctance on the agent's part to tell Barratt directly of the Earl's intention. The Earl thought that Barratt would not have dreamt of competing with him if he had been told of his interest early enough and that Worthington had been remiss in not telling him. The agent was perhaps more realistic:

> Your Lordship's wish to purchase land in Altrincham is too well known for Mr. Barratt to be ignorant of it and though he would not openly oppose your Lordship, it is plain that he had privately used every means in his power to purchase the property before his wish to do so became known.

Eventually the Earl implied the agent had hidden motives for his reticence, whereupon inevitably the agent conceded, writing a fulsome apology:

> I am extremely concerned that your Lordship should appear to consider my not having communicated with Mr. Barratt... to have arisen from a reluctance to do so founded on some other motive than that of serving your Lordship.

The Earl's reply was still recriminatory, but finished with a decidedly grudging recognition that 'I will give you credit for your good intentions'. Worthington, however, was not to get away from this brush so lightly. A couple of months later the Earl sent a very sharply worded note refusing his agent's application for an allowance towards the cost of the upkeep of a horse:

> I was very much surprised to receive your application for the keep of a Horse. It was a Privilege given by the late Countess of Stamford to the late Mr. Worthington, <u>because he then lived</u> in the House at Dunham Massey. I have received no advantage from the keep of the Horse.... I am most hurt, that you should be so very tenacious in making so very unreasonable a request. I will not comply with it.

The letter ended with a veiled threat: 'I wish you had specified all your expectations before you had received the Appointment.' In this case, the Earl came fairly close to accusing Worthington of having divided loyalties, a situation which must have been possible given Worthington's wider position within the town. Clearly, the Earl was pressing upon his agent that sense of common purpose which was at the heart of the Dunham community.

Within the next hierarchical circle the key figures were the two stewards, John Davenport and John Poole. John Davenport came from an extended local family and served first as farm then land steward at Dunham between 1801 and 1835. He seems to have gone through a difficult period in 1814, when some prolonged illness struck him. In May of that year Hugo Worthington remarked in a letter to his Lordship: 'Mr. Davenport seems now to be getting strength and I hope will soon be quite well – he has had a long illness which has pulled him down exceedingly.'[136] As we have seen, he recovered from this phase to be promoted by the 6th Earl to the wider responsibilities of land steward.

John Davenport died in 1835 at the home farm and, surprisingly for a man who was so well organised, his will was made on his deathbed on 31 December of that year.[137] By this time his wife was dead, but he was survived by two sons, John Davenport junior and George Sutton Davenport, as well as a daughter, Elizabeth Jones. In his will he left two sums of £1,450 and £1,000 in trust to provide annuities for George Sutton and Elizabeth. The rest of his real and personal estate went to the elder son, John. Witnesses to his will were the vicar of Bowden, Richard Broadbent, the surgeon/apothecary, and Mark Pierson, a Dunham employee. His total personal estate came to just under £4,000, plus properties left to John which are not itemised in the will. Davenport clearly groomed John to follow in his footsteps. John Davenport junior appeared on the list of casual labour in the gardens at Dunham in 1822, but in 1824 he was appointed agent at Enville, where he was still working in 1844. He died shortly afterwards in slightly mysterious circumstances. Although he was buried in the churchyard at Enville, rumour persists that he committed suicide, possibly because his wife was having an affair with the 7th Earl. Not only do we begin to see here a glimpse of the relative wealth and status of employees, but also the long-term commitment of employed families, which were building a tradition of passing key posts from father to son.

John Poole's situation seems to have been slightly less affluent. His family were not local, for in his letter of application he said he was a native of Shropshire. He worked for several employers before coming to Dunham and held some sort of post in an institution in Macclesfield. He remained as one of the longest-serving house stewards the Greys ever had, staying for fifteen years. Like the butler, Philip Osgood, he was married, though he seems to have had no children. In his will, he left all his personal and real estate to his wife, Anne, for her lifetime and thereafter in equal shares to a niece and nephew, the children of his sister.[138] The will states that he owned leasehold and freehold properties as well as mortgages, but unfortunately does not itemise them. Later on in his married life he lived in one of these houses with his wife, probably in the village of Dunham. He settled in the area and had what for then was a long retirement of twelve years. On his death he had accumulated a personal estate of around £800. He was obviously a careful man, for he made his will in 1831, fifteen years before he actually died.

Poole enjoyed something of a personal family life but for other long-serving professional servants the aristocratic household provided the security of surrogate kin. The death of the serving Dunham house steward in February 1799 throws interesting light on the nature of this relationship. Correspondence between Isaac Worthington and the 5th Earl illustrates the care with which lines of propriety and closeness to the family were drawn. The Greys were at Enville as usual during the winter when their house steward at Dunham Massey, John Arnatt, died.[139] The agent wrote of his shock and distress on hearing about 'the awful and sudden change in your Lordship's family by the death of Mr. Arnatt'. Since the steward was in charge of the Dunham household in the absence of the Earl, and had responsibility for large amounts of cash, such an event could potentially throw the whole system into confusion. But the crisis brought out the best in the rest of the staff:

> The keys of his Desk and Room were sealed up by Mr. Foster [Worthington's clerk] and will not be opened till Mr. Arnatt's Brother and I are together ... Mr. Pass [Nathaniel Pass was an auctioneer in Altrincham] went to Dunham as

> soon after Mrs Princep [housekeeper] sent word of Mr. Arnatt's death to have locked up his Desks and room, but Mrs Princep with Mr. Holland [the family's medical attendant] had done that before he got there.

Mrs Princep also took charge of the keys to the cellar but later gave them to the agent, together with all the other keys kept by the steward. She also sent an express messenger to notify the steward's nearest relative, his brother who lived in Nottinghamshire and she also fixed the day of the funeral at Bowdon church. But she did not think it appropriate to agree with the vicar where exactly in the church Arnatt's grave should be; this she left up to the agent to decide. He reported back to the Earl: 'As none but old servants have been laid in the Chancel and fresh ground must be broken I could not presume to take that liberty but shall order a proper burial place in the new part of the Church Yard.' Worthington was not belittling the status of the steward in this, for he later reported: 'I fixed on a burial place near my own in the new part of the Church Yard.'

Because of the seniority of the steward, things had to be done correctly. As it turned out, Arnatt's brother was delayed by bad weather and poor road conditions and he did not arrive from Nottinghamshire until too late for the funeral, so the agent and housekeeper did their best to take his place. The service was conducted with

> as much propriety as me and Mrs Princep could think of without his Brother's presence. I ... took Mr. Holland in my chaise to attend the Funeral. We had Hatbands and Gloves.... Mrs Princep and Mrs Staples had Gloves and so had all your Lordship's servants. Six of the Labourers were bearers with Mourning Cloaks and had Gloves. All your Lordship's menservants attended the Funeral.

The correspondence shows clearly, however, that the ties binding the community together might have been personal but they were also professional, especially towards that central sense of common purpose. The underlying message is that the even tenor of his Lordship's life must not be troubled by this occurrence: 'My brother and I will use every Exertion in our power respecting the Business immediately under Mr. Arnatt's direction, in order that your Lordship may be put to as little inconvenience as possible, until your Lordship can procure a proper person to supply his place.'

After the funeral, therefore, the agent set about winding up the steward's affairs: 'Yesterday and today I have spent with Mr. Pass in the presence of Mr. Arnatt's brother and Mrs. Princep, in examining his Accounts and Papers and I find in Cash and Notes £164 5s 1d.' Most of this was cash held in hand from the Earl, but there remained some £24 of personal money. An inventory of clothes and personal property was made and a copy given to the brother. The most valuable possessions were the two horses owned by the steward, which the brother took away with him. There were some savings, but not as much as was expected. Indeed, Arnatt's financial circumstances presented something of a mystery. Worthington explained:

> On the 9th March 1797 Mr. Arnatt laid out £104 13s on the purchase of £200 in the 3 p.cts [government stocks] and in November 1797 he told me that he had 100 guineas by him and wished me to purchase him £200 more stock, but in

> two or three days afterwards he told me that he had altered his mind and would not buy any more stock. Since that time I have paid him £75 for wages, so that I should have expected he would have more money or securities. His Brother was with him at Christmas and he says that Mr. Arnatt told him that there would not be much money found when he died, so that his Brother is satisfied.

This was puzzling since the steward had been in a succession of well-paid posts and should have accumulated more savings. According to his brother:

> he had saved £100 in Sir William Boothby's service and £70 afterwards with Mr. Eaton and ... his circumstances were full as good when he came to Dunham as when he dyed. His brother and indeed everybody are sensible that he must have saved a considerable sum of money in your Lordship's service, but at present it is not known what he has done with it.

This case shows that senior servants were expected to accumulate fairly substantial savings. That some did so is illustrated by a letter from the 6th Earl to his daughter in 1831, reporting how one of his father's old servants had died leaving property amounting to over £3,000 and legacies of £840, mostly to his only brother who lived in London.[140] Just as telling, many servants took personal lessons from the way they administered their master's affairs. This was obviously true of the steward Thomas Walton who, as we have seen, left substantial educational charities (p.88). Another interesting case is that of George Cooke, Dunham's house steward before Arnatt, who left in his will two amounts of money totalling £110 in trust to the 5th Earl. The interest was to be applied to the upkeep of the Sunday schools in Altrincham and in Carrington and to the purchase of religious books for Carrington chapel and 'such poor persons as most constantly attend divine service at Bowdon Church'. Cooke's will is a superb document which has much to tell us about the nature of family and household and the relationship between servants and employer (Box 41, p.158). He owned one freehold and two leasehold cottages in Altrincham and a substantial personal estate, out of which he made over £5,000 worth of bequests not only to his own family of brothers, sisters, nieces and nephews, but also to the Earl of Stamford, the Countess, their children, the Booth-Greys, the John Greys and Sir Henry Mainwaring, a Cheshire landowner. Even though Cooke had a wide circle of extended kin of his own, the Greys seem to have been his surrogate family and he obviously held the Earl and Mainwaring in very high regard, even to the extent that he left his late wife's gold ring to the latter. A childless widower at his death, he left £100 to his servant and two guineas each to all the residential servants at Dunham.

Some stewards to a great house or estate could consider themselves men of substance, but how did less exalted servants fare at Dunham Massey? The case of Timothy Brownell, the estate carpenter, is an illuminating one. The Brownell name was well known in the Altrincham and Bowdon area where there were at least four Timothy Brownells in the early nineteenth century, which makes the origins of 'our' Timothy confusing. One is buried in Bowdon churchyard with his wife Annie, and this couple may well have been our Timothy's parents. Another Timothy, listed in a census of Altrincham taken in 1801 as a carpenter and married to Ann, was

41

Extracts from the last will and testament of George Cooke, house steward at Dunham Massey, died 1791

Cheshire Record Office, ws 1791

... To my Brother Augustine Cooke the sum of three hundred pounds and my wearing apparel, silver watch, rasor case with the five rasors therein, one penknife, one pair of scissors, one large hone, and my money scales and weights in the shagreen case ...

To the right honourable George Harry Earl of Stamford the sum of one hundred pounds and my mare Tabinet ...

To the honourable Booth Grey the sum of one hundred pounds and half of my silver waiter given to me by him and the honourable John Grey and eight volumes of Ellis's modern husbandry...

To the said John Grey the other half of my said silver waiter, my picture of the late dear Earl of Warrington, my picture of old Driver, my amberheaded Cane, my Gun made by Barker of Wigan, my shot Belt, my large quarto volume of the late reverend Mr. Lancaster's work on the revelation of Saint John and my large quarto volume of the complete farmer...

To Sir Henry Mainwaring Baronet the sum of one hundred pounds, my silver Gill with arms engraved thereon, my large money scales and weights in a mahogany case, my late dear wife's gold ring and my silver seal with arms engraved thereon with red ground ...

And it is my desire that the Dunham Family and Sir Henry Mainwaring will accept of their respective legacies as token of my gratitude for the many favors they have been pleased to confer on me ...

To my said Nephew John Hodgkinson the further sum of twenty pounds, my two hand whips, my measuring chain and my Money weights and scales in a mahogany Case made by Gibson ...

To my Servant Hannah Leather the sum of one hundred pounds ...

To the servants of the said Earl of Stamford residing at Dunham Massey in the Winter Season and usually stiled the Dunham Servants and who shall be living in the said Earl's service at my decease the sum of two guineas each ...

And I give and bequeath all my books, pamphlets and manuscripts and my silver plate not by me herein before disposed of unto my said Brother Augustine, my said sisters Frances Saunders, Martha Hodgkinson and Ellen Garner and my said Nephew John Hodgkinson to be divided amongst them as equally in point of value as the said Isaac Worthington and John Foster can divide the same. And I give and bequeath all my household goods and furniture of what nature or kind soever unto my said Brother ... and my said Sisters to be divided amongst them ...

probably ours. Other Brownells in the area at that time were craftsmen and small dealers (leather-cutters and grocers). They must have been men of some means, for a Timothy Brownell was Mayor of Altrincham in 1793 and two were included in a list dated 1798 of people entitled by leasehold ownership to serve on juries.[141] Our Timothy lived in a house in Altrincham owned by the estate, a timber-framed thatched cottage which his family had held from 1746 on a long lease.[142]

Timothy Brownell became head carpenter on the Dunham estate in 1806, a position he held for sixteen years. He had then reached the pinnacle of his trade, for Worthington relied on him not just for day-to-day work but for advice about the state of property which the Earl was thinking of purchasing. When the Earl wanted to buy an old cotton mill in Altrincham with the intention of converting it into two houses, it was Brownell who was sent to give an opinion as to its viability.[143] Again, in a dispute over timber rights with the Bishop of Chester, Worthington sent Brownell to value the ornamental trees involved in the argument. He was also a crucial figure in the sale of timber and bark from the estate, which from 1792 consistently brought

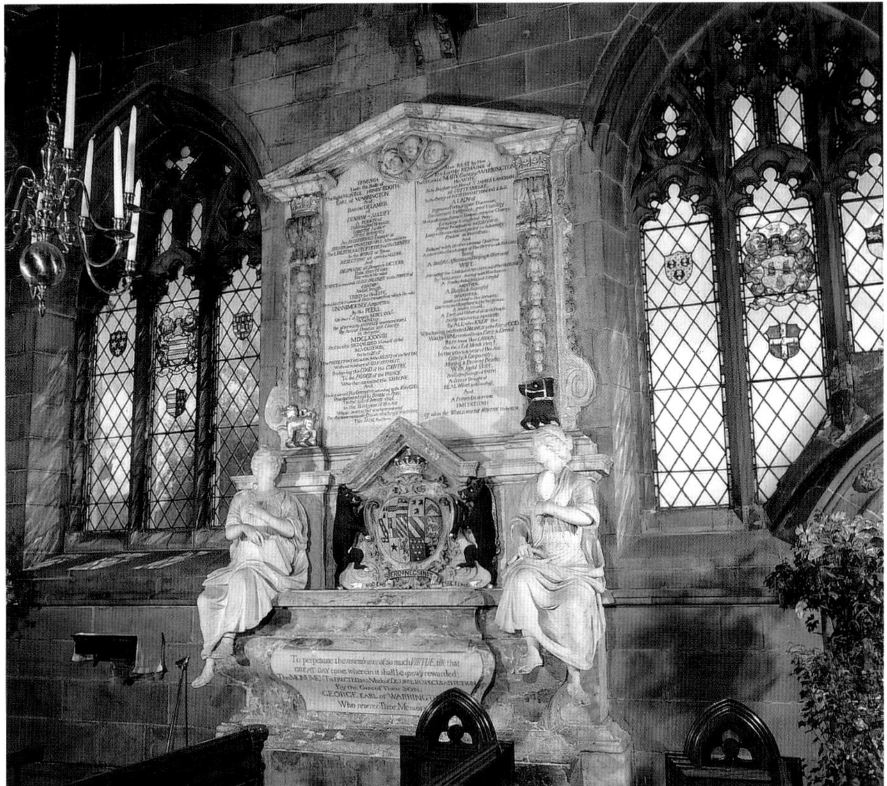

The monument to Henry Booth, 1st Earl of Warrington, who died in 1694, and to his Countess, in Bowdon church.

in over twenty per cent of total income.[144] In one auction at Ashton-under-Lyne in 1812, for example, several lots from Dunham fetched over £1,000 each. Brownell was a highly skilled man in his own right, however, and many of the floorboards which visitors to the house tread over so unthinkingly today will have been hand-sawn by him. He was by no means a cabinetmaker, however. Though he did joinery work in the parish church at Bowdon in 1822 in connection with the installation of the organ, previously in 1814 when the estate had arranged for its 'pewing', Brownell was involved simply in choosing the timber, the actual construction work having been carried out by a specialist firm.

On the face of it, 1822 appears to have been an extremely busy year for Brownell. Not only was he heavily involved in the preparatory work for Shaw's alterations and in maintenance jobs around the house, park, farm and garden, but in that year he was appointed Mayor of Altrincham.[145] This last appointment, of course, says a lot for the position of tradesmen and craftsmen within local society and of Brownell personally within Altrincham. In fact, although the carpentry bills for 1822 are signed by him and made out to his name, it seems likely that the practical work, which included a good deal of heavy sawing, was done by his son James. In true Dunham tradition James succeeded Timothy as estate carpenter for a further twelve years, between 1822 and 1834.

Timothy died only two years after retirement, in 1824, leaving Ann to live to the age of eighty-one. Unfortunately, only three months after Timothy's death his unmarried daughter Ann was buried alongside him in Bowdon churchyard, aged forty-four. The Brownells had already lost two young daughters, Sarah aged one year and Mary aged thirteen, both of whom were buried in the same plot at Bowdon.[146] It seems likely that his son James was buried nearby in 1854, aged sixty-nine, exactly the same age at death as his father. A later Timothy, buried at Bowdon in 1882, may well have been Timothy's grandson.

Daniel Parsons, the estate blacksmith, was another long-serving employee, though it is not clear whether this was the same Dan Parsons who was recorded at Dunham in the 1780s.[147] He was clearly a hard-working man and one who believed in the security of land and property. His will is a testament to the extent to which a successful estate servant could himself accumulate relative wealth.[148] On his death in 1840 he owned a long lease on a public house, the Bull's Head in Wilmslow, left to his son John, and a freehold house in Altrincham, which was rented out and which he left to his other son William. Two leasehold cottages in Wilmslow, also rented out, and a mortgage of £300, which he held on property in Altrincham, were left in trust to provide an annuity for his widowed daughter Hannah Smith. Apart from these he left a personal estate of £450.

Records of the travelling servants derive mainly from their work at Enville, which seems to have been their home more than Dunham. The head coachman, David Seammen, for example, was recorded at Enville on several occasions in the Torry journal.[149] In July 1836 he was discharged from service after thirty-six years with the Grey family, with a generous pension of £40 a year. He seems to have had at least three sons, one of whom, David, died in September 1830 after being injured in a heavy fall from his horse earlier that year. The other two followed their father into service with the aristocracy. Charles went to Lady Brooke's in 1833, and the following year Tubal found a situation with the Earl of Carlisle and later with the highly prestigious household of the Duke of Sutherland, where he is listed in 1841 as groom of the chamber.[150]

Moving on to those tradesmen and suppliers who worked for the family on a contract basis, their extent and distribution gives an indication of the geographical penetration of the influence of the Grey household and of the intricacy of relationships focusing on the estate. During the year 1822 alone, Messrs Poole and Davenport, with their various subordinates, dealt with a total of 188 separate individuals or firms. Many of these can be identified by their location, and not surprisingly Altrincham emerges as the single most important centre for the supply of goods and services to the estate, with Manchester and London only slightly behind. The smaller nearby towns of Knutsford and Lymm ranked next and equal in importance, with regional centres such as Warrington and Chester figuring fairly low down. There were also a small number of service suppliers based in Warwickshire, clearly relating to the family's connection with Enville. What is perhaps more surprising is the dependence on a network of suppliers from smaller centres, villages, hamlets and rural areas surrounding Dunham itself. Forty-seven in all, these are more numerous than those from any single urban centre.

Among the 188 individuals or firms identified, many (thirty-six) were used repeatedly by Poole or Davenport or both. Most of these were small-scale craftsmen offering a basic craft service such as coopering, turning, painting or clock repair.

Others were suppliers of provisions and goods such as textiles or iron spouting, and yet others were carriers who were used by different departments of the estate on a day in, day out basis. The vast majority were local to Dunham and Altrincham, but a few were more specialised tradesmen from further afield such as James Branthwaite, an ironmonger in Manchester who sold knives and cutlery to both the house servants and the farm and garden. Some provided different services for different departments. Peter Fletcher, the licensee of the Griffin in Bowdon, leased stable room and sold beer to Davenport, but for Poole he heated the pews in the parish church. John Johnson did tailoring for Poole but to Davenport he sold a small quantity of straw. John Wyatt, the clock man, also sold plants to Pickin the gardener. Even a house servant might have unlooked-for skills, for Davenport paid the footman at Dunham for mending the farm pump. Trivial details perhaps, but such is the evidence for an intricate, closely knit community where many people were multi-skilled and needed more than one activity to bring in money.

Poole and Davenport used many of the same tradespeople. The estate's regular contracting ironmonger, Edward Bolton of Warrington, for example, provided a huge variety of small goods as well as the staff to deliver and fit them. Yet each steward also had his own contacts who reflected the nature of their jobs. Davenport's suppliers of cereals, straw and livestock were almost all local, with only the Scotch cattle being bought from further afield in Ormskirk. They ranged from smallholders, selling perhaps one or two cows, to larger-scale corn merchants such as the Hardeys of Lymm or John Gibson of Northwich, and gentlemen's estates such as the Suttons of Timperley Hall. His staff bought apple trees from another gentry estate in Ashton-on-Mersey, dahlias from a seedsman in Altrincham, a large number of shrubs and flowers from William Caldwell's nursery in Knutsford and seeds from a druggist in Manchester.

Poole's purchases, on the other hand, show a strong bias towards town suppliers, especially Altrincham and Manchester. The latter he visited at least once a month, with a regular series of calls around the Market Street/High Street area where many of his contacts had their business premises: Richard Lovatt, a tobacco and snuff manufacturer, where he bought tobacco for the Earl; Samuel Thompstone, chemists in Cupid's Alley, who supplied the house with soda water; John Kaye, upholsterer and warehouseman, for carpets, paper and feathers; Ebenezer Thomson, bookseller and distributor of stamps; and Messrs Worthington, high-class drapers and silk manufacturers. Especially prestigious were Zanetti and Agnew, gilders, carvers and framers in Market Street, where a discerning gentleman could also buy barometers, thermometers and hydrometers. More workaday was Vickers, a firm of coppersmiths and brass-founders in St Mary's, who regularly repaired and re-tinned the kitchen copperware and boilers. Manchester seemed to offer Poole most of what he needed for the house. His only regular London supplier was Robert Hatton, a chandler in Paddington, from whom he bought spermaceti candles and white soap. Chester provided only newspapers and Liverpool only one high-class upholsterer.

The supply system as operated by Poole and Davenport was both hierarchical and specialised. In many cases there was only one supplier of the particular service or goods, but the household did use three newspaper-sellers for different papers – two

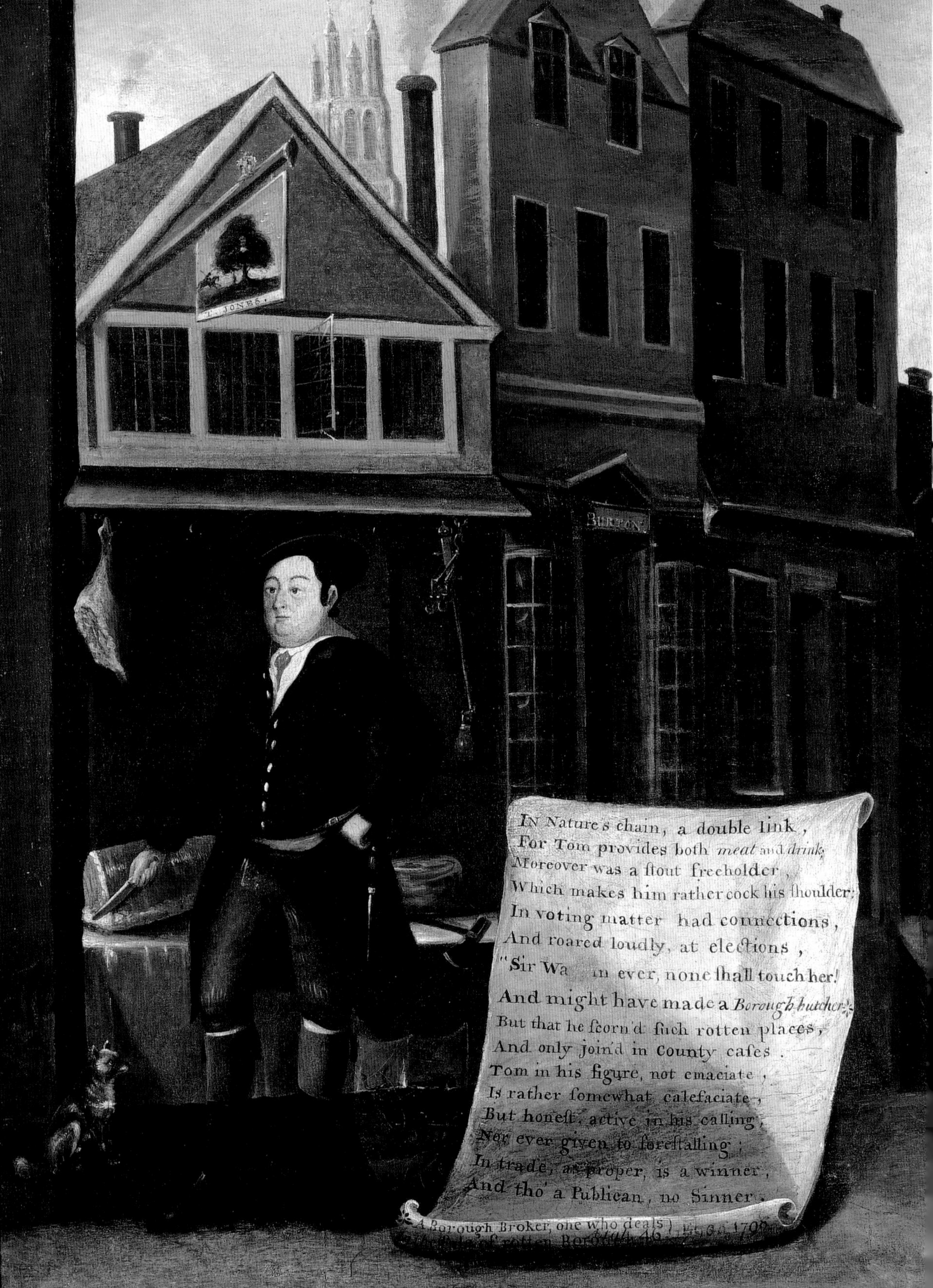
JONES
BURTON
IN Nature's chain, a double link,
For Tom provides both *meat* and *drink*;
Moreover was a ſtout freeholder,
Which makes him rather cock his ſhoulder:
In voting matter had connections,
And roared loudly, at elections,
"Sir Wa in ever, none ſhall touch her!
And might have made a *Borough butcher*
But that he ſcorn'd ſuch rotten places,
And only join'd in County caſes.
Tom in his figure, not emaciate,
Is rather ſomewhat calefaciate,
But honeſt, active in his calling,
Nor ever given to foreſtalling;
In trade, as proper, is a winner,
And tho' a Publican, no Sinner.
A Borough Broker, one who deals

in Chester and one in Manchester. They also patronised three millers, three tailors, three upholsterers and two joiners. Yet a careful reading of the bills shows that each was specialising in some way, perhaps supplying a different quality of goods. One of the tailors, for example, was paid to make clothes for the poor, another for the servants and another to work on the house furnishings. The fabrics supplied by the Misses Dean of Dunham were different from those bought from Satterfield's, mercer and linen draper in St Ann's Square, Manchester. One was for domestic linens and cotton, the other for fine furnishing fabrics. Generally, however, the family does not seem to have worried about spreading their custom to avoid favouring one tradesman, as some other country houses did. Account books from years both before and after 1822 show that many of the companies used by Poole and Davenport were long-term suppliers and this was especially true of the local trades. Having once found a satisfactory supplier or craftsman, wherever possible Dunham remained faithful for years, still true to the spirit of the dead 5th Earl. Such people provided a tried and tested pool of local skill, which was used to supplement the estate's own reserves. They were accepted into the community of the Dunham household, both literally and symbolically, as each year the 6th Earl invited them to the Master Tradesmen's dinner at Dunham.

For many of the contractors, of course, capturing the country-house trade must have lifted the scale of their businesses. So few records of private companies have survived that it is impossible to gauge the balance of advantage and disadvantage, the gaining of status and reputation as against the practice of credit-trading and exposure to family whim. John Pearson was part of a large extended family appearing in parish records throughout the eighteenth, nineteenth and twentieth centuries in Bowdon and Lymm. A young man aged twenty-five in 1822, struggling to raise a new family, John and his wife Jane had four children in the space of five years, only one of which, a daughter Jane, survived infancy. A plumber and glazier by trade, he was not just a craftsman in his own right: he employed several skilled and unskilled men, both for glazing work such as puttying windows at the house and for intricate painting. In 1822 he was extensively used by both Davenport and Poole, but such dependency led to great vulnerability.[151] What happened to such people when the 7th Earl decided to move to Enville permanently in the 1850s?

Yet some firms clearly made a success of targeting the landed estates and we can see a few examples amongst the Dunham suppliers. The estate's seed merchants were Caldwell's of Knutsford, a highly successful family firm. The Caldwells entered the nursery business around 1780, and thereafter six successive members continued in the trade. According to their customer ledgers, the firm supplied all sorts of gardening equipment from gloves to large-scale mowers and greenhouses, as well as seeds, vegetables, trees and shrubs. Clients included small- to medium-scale local gardeners such as Peter Holland, the Greys' medical adviser, who bought six damson trees for his garden in Knutsford in 1820, but also virtually every landed estate and park in the region, from Liverpool in the west, Blackburn in the north, Leek in the east and to the Trentham estate of the Duke of Sutherland in the south.[152] Over a period of many years the firm supplied the Earls of Stamford mainly with ornamental trees and shrubs, amongst them specimens which still grace Dunham Park today.

LEFT: Dunham was probably typical of many country houses that remained faithful to local tradesmen over long periods. In the 1790s the Yorkes of Erddig, near Wrexham, went so far as to commission a portrait of their butcher, Thomas Jones, which hung in the servants' hall.

The largest supplier to the estate in terms of value was easily John Barratt, the most important grocer and maltster in Altrincham. He was clearly a man of wealth and position locally, for his bills to Dunham alone for 1822 amounted to over £900 and his firm supplied the estate for decades. Given the prevalence of estate brewing, the country-house market was clearly one of his specialities, which meant that his business must have been substantial enough to carry a lot of credit accounts. Some of these accumulated over more than one year, as is shown by correspondence from the Langford Brooke family archive, relating to their estate at Mere. In 1829 their agent reported to his employer that he had paid two years' bills, a matter of over £600, which was owed to John Barratt for malt and groceries.[153]

In the 1820s Barratt's shop was in Market Place, and he later established a gentleman's house in Norman's Place on the outskirts of the town.[154] He was succeeded in the business by his son Samuel, who in 1871 was listed as owning property of almost forty acres, worth a gross estimated rental of £1,456, at this valuation clearly town property rather than farmland.[155] Yet unlike the Brownells, the Barratt family does not seem to be established in the town in the late eighteenth century, for it was not on the list of jurors in 1798, nor in the Altrincham census of 1801. John Barratt was mentioned in 1803, however, when Altrincham was required to send seven men for service in the army. The town decided to pay for the hire of suitable men, in place of the old method of choosing individuals by ballot, five to be paid for by the town, two by individuals. John Barratt, bent on establishing his position in the town, became one of these two individuals, contributing £43 to the total cost of the soldiers.[156] When Wellington finally succeeded in driving Napoleon out of the Iberian Peninsula, and Altrincham celebrated in traditional fashion with fireworks and a public feast held in the Bowling Green Inn, Barratt was one of four people who were asked to organise the event.

He appeared again in 1815 when the quarter sessions appointed a committee to meet with the magistrates and advise on a course of action regarding the poor state of local roads. John Barratt was a member of this committee alongside Hugo Worthington himself, only a few months after the affair of Mr Ashley's property.[157] Around this time Barratt was widowed, for he remarried in 1821.[158] By 1831 the family was truly established, as John Barratt was appointed as one of seven members of the trust administering the workhouse premises and land which had been donated back in 1755 by the Earl of Stamford.[159] On his death he left £200 for charitable purposes, the interest to be used to give bread to those poor who attended service at St. George's, one of several bread charities set up by Altrincham businessmen, in emulation of the Stamford bread charities.[160]

The family's medical practitioner, Peter Holland, also served the landed gentry and the aristocracy of the Knutsford area at the end of the eighteenth and well into the nineteenth century.[161] One of his nieces was Elizabeth Gaskell, the novelist, and it is generally supposed that the character of Mr Gibson, the country doctor in *Wives and Daughters*, was modelled on her uncle. Holland's first wife, Mary, was a niece of Josiah Wedgwood, and by this marriage he had seven children, three of whom died in infancy. One of his sons from this marriage became Sir Henry Holland, a famous physician amongst whose patients were numbered Queen Victoria, Prince Albert

A recreation of the sick room in the Apprentice House, Styal Mill in Cheshire. Here Peter Holland treated the apprentice boys and girls for minor accidents and illnesses.

and six prime ministers. Mary died in 1803 and Holland remarried in 1808, by which marriage he had a further three children. He was still alive at the time of the 1851 census, living in Knutsford with two unmarried daughters.

Born in 1766, Holland was apprenticed at seventeen to an eminent Manchester surgeon and obstetrician, Charles White, one of the founders of the Manchester infirmary. When Holland took up his own practice he moved to Knutsford, causing a breach in his relations with White as the apprenticeship agreement specified that he should work no nearer to Manchester than ten miles. White accused Holland of poaching his clients, a rift which was only settled by the good offices of Holland's most prestigious patient, the Earl of Stamford and Warrington. He succeeded in developing a large practice, which included most of the local aristocratic families such as the Egertons of Tatton, the Stanleys of Alderley, the Leicesters at Tabley, and, from 1803, the post of surgeon to the Earl of Chester's Yeomanry Cavalry.[162] At the other end of the social spectrum, Holland was employed to examine apprentices before they were taken into employment at Quarry Bank Mill, Styal. With this last appointment, recorded from 1795, Holland was entering into a new field, that of occupational medicine. Indeed his employment at Styal has been described as the earliest recorded example of an occupational health service in England.[163] By 1834 Holland was in partnership with Richard Dean, a son of one of Holland's early apprentices. Richard Dean became Holland's son-in-law, marrying his daughter Susan in 1844. By the time of his death in 1855, Holland was a wealthy man, who had invested in land, houses, cottages, church pews and a water corn-mill. In today's values he was a millionaire.

Holland was considerably more expensive than the Broadbents, a family of medical practitioners with a surgery in Market Place, Altrincham, who treated the main servant household. Richard Broadbent, described in directories as 'surgeon', came originally from Mere and was aged fifty-eight in 1822. He died eight years later and was buried in Bowdon churchyard alongside his wife Mary and was later joined by his son William, a Liverpool-trained doctor. A glimpse both of William's character and his place in the Dunham household comes in 1825, when he was called out by the Greys to attend to a 'hermit' who had fallen down some steps in the servants' corridor. At the family's insistence Broadbent stayed for a party which was just getting under way, being described by a friend of the family as 'the little smiling Esculapius', clearly a familiar figure around the house.[164] Another of Richard's sons, Richard, was described in the parish register as 'surgeon' and a further member of the family, Nathaniel, seems to have been an apothecary or perhaps simply the firm's accountant.[165] In the 1860s the business was still thriving in the hands of Richard junior, who had a surgery in the High Street and a residence in one of the best areas of Altrincham.[166]

Given the large number of tradesmen involved in the supply and maintenance of the house at Dunham Massey, transport was a critical element connecting the various circles of activity. The existence of excellent road carrier services from the centre of Manchester and the proximity of the Bridgewater Canal made life a great deal easier, especially when heavy goods had to be shifted. The household was not short of choice in carriers. A Manchester trade directory for 1821–2 lists 109 different land carrier services from Manchester, plus thirty-four canal carriers, twenty-three of whom plied the Bridgewater Canal.[167] Five local carriers were used by both Poole and Davenport to connect with the canal and to bring goods from Altrincham, Knutsford and elsewhere locally. Several of these were public carriers, that is, they ran scheduled routes open to all customers. Different firms ran daily services to different centres, depending on market days. John Warburton, for example, ran return vans from Bowdon to Manchester on Tuesdays, Thursdays and Saturdays and to Northwich on Mondays, Wednesdays and Fridays. He also ran a connecting service to Chester and thence to Wales. As we have seen, Poole also made extensive weekly use of a local boat carrier, Mary Allen, to bring goods to and from Manchester. These local carriers varied greatly in scale. Warburton's was fairly extensive, but others might be small-scale operators with perhaps only one or two wagons or carts or a single canal boat.

Most of the carriers used by the Dunham household were long-distance firms, both road and canal services. The Bridgewater Canal Company itself had a network of agents which ran a daily service from the Castle Quay in Manchester to Liverpool and this was used extensively by the Dunham stewards. Another private boat carrier was J. G. Ames, who ran from the Castlefield Warehouse to Kidderminster and Stourport and was used by the estate gardeners to send fruit and vegetables between Dunham and Enville.[168] Occasionally London carriers were contracted on private hire for a special job: Bryan & Co. brought the scagliola columns on the canal network and a carrier called John Mitchell delivered furniture.

The most extensively used network of carriers, however, was that run by Messrs Pickfords, by far the most important private firm in the history of British transport over a continuous period of 250 years and still in operation in the twenty-first century (Box 42, opposite). Providing almost seventy-five per cent of Dunham's

Pickfords: 'the first to deliver and the last to collect'*

The firm was founded in the 1750s, one of a large number of carriers who made up a well-developed and effective network of road services at that time. Through a system of offloading points which were usually inns, virtually every small town in the English countryside could be reached by efficient scheduled public or 'common' carriers, common in the sense they were licensed and thus obliged to accept the custom of all-comers and were fully liable for loss or damage. Smaller-scale private carriers with a single horse and cart could connect with the common services at the inns. Most covered an area not more than a day's journey, perhaps twenty to thirty miles, so goods were passed on from one carrier to another at the staging inns. One common feature was their impermanence. Firms came and went, leaving little or no record of their trade. In this respect Pickfords was the exception rather than the rule.

The Pickford family originated in Cheshire, near Prestbury and the first advert for the family carrier services appeared in the *Manchester Mercury* in 1756. Two years later the family owned six vehicles, each a broad-wheeled wagon able to carry perhaps 35cwt and working from a base in Poynton. This stock of vehicles represents a substantial investment of capital and James Pickford was an important man in the town and the owner of a sizeable farm.

It is no coincidence that the early Pickford trade developed around north-east Cheshire. Manchester was a growing industrial and commercial centre, an inland town which suffered from limited water-borne transport links even after the opening of the Bridgewater Canal in 1764 and the connection to Liverpool and London canal networks in the later 1770s. Many of the products of the Manchester area were high-value items such as silk, which were not happily trusted to the canal system but which needed access to the London export markets. Trade was booming, with both Manchester and Salford trebling in population during the last quarter of the eighteenth century and during that period the whole scale of Pickfords' operations began to change. In 1786 it became the first private firm to enter the canal trade in Manchester and a daily road service between Manchester and London was established in 1788. The firm began replacing inns by purpose-built carrier's depots, including one at Castle Quay, the terminus of the Bridgewater Canal.

Better road surfaces in the early nineteenth century led to the introduction in 1814 of Pickfords' fly-van services; high-speed vans could cover the ground between Manchester and London in thirty-six hours instead of the previous four to five days. Not only were these quick but they offered a smoother ride, being for the first time fitted with springs. Enclosed rather than covered with a tarpaulin, they were also secure. They were described as 'a large oblong vehicle, like an immense box, on springs, drawn by four horses, with coachman in front and a guard behind'. They had a payload of three tons and could travel at an average of six miles per hour. The service ran continuously through the night using relays of good-quality horses and had the specific aim of capturing the small expensive parcel trade which hitherto had been carried by the fast coach services, exactly that market provided by the great country houses such as Dunham Massey.

The early nineteenth century also saw expansion in Pickfords' canal services. In 1805 the completion of the Grand Junction Canal system opened up the routes from Manchester to London whilst in 1814 the Grand Union Canal created better networks around the Midlands. Canal traffic was specialised, suited to heavy, bulky or highly breakable goods where time was not of the essence, yet even here Pickfords introduced a scheduled fly-boat service which could travel at four miles per hour between locks, especially suited to cheap delivery of bulk groceries.

Pickford's overall aim was to be 'the first to deliver and the last to collect'. One of the keys to the achievement of this ambition was the firm's sophisticated organisation. Times during transit were pared to the bone by a system of fines levied on the boatmen and drivers for late arrival, a system which maintained a constant pressure on employees, many of whom worked an average sixteen-hour day. Turnaround times at the depots were reduced by forward planning. As soon as a boat left Manchester a detailed manifest of its cargo was sent to its destination by means of the company's fly-van service. This gave three days' warning to the receiving depot, allowing time for the clerks to allocate porters and delivery services. A second signal was sent en route, giving an estimated time of arrival within two hours. By the time the boat arrived at its destination a long line of porters, carts and wagons was waiting, each in the correct loading off order: light goods first, heavy goods last.

---

* This account is based on Gerard L. Turnbull, *Traffic and Transport: an Economic History of Pickfords* (George Allen and Unwin, 1979).

carrier requirements in 1822, their well-established network offered a daily connection from Knutsford through their van services to Macclesfield, Manchester, Liverpool and London. From their wharf near Oxford Street on the Bridgewater Canal in Manchester goods could be sent 'with the greatest dispatch' by their fly boat services to a wide area of the south and Midlands.[169] Dunham, like many other country houses, was quick to take advantage of the services offered by Pickfords. Secure, reasonably fast carrier services from London or between other country properties were essential to the elaborate lifestyle of the great aristocratic households in the late eighteenth and nineteenth centuries, a fact which has been obscured by the great myth of the self-sufficient household. However embattled the aristocracy came to regard itself, the country house was not an isolated stronghold bent on defending itself from the increasingly unpredictable industrial and urban world. On the contrary, communications were its lifeblood and, especially during those years immediately before the railway era, aristocratic households were pushing the available transport facilities to their extremes.

Reliant on good transport facilities they may have been, but successful great households were highly stable communities for many of those working in them. We can certainly see this in operation at Dunham, where the pattern of mobility versus stability has a logic to it. On the one hand, despite the problems faced by the 5th Earl at the end of the eighteenth century when he could not keep house stewards, most of the senior and outdoor staff stayed for many years. On the other hand, indoor domestic servants were notoriously mobile, and it is probable that many of the junior indoor staff moved on after a short time in post. Mobility amongst the junior female staff was inevitable. For them domestic service was a stage in their life, not a long-term occupation, a preparation for their real work of housewife and mother. In the nineteenth century and earlier it was unheard of for a woman to continue working as a full-time servant after she was married. For men there was no such stricture, though it might well mean the couple had to spend a good deal of their married life apart. If servants working in the same household married the result was inevitable: the man stayed, the woman left, as in the case of the still-room maid, Lydia Morton.[170] The long-term professional housekeeper was always single, despite her courtesy title of 'Mrs', whilst most of the stewards seem to have married, sometimes renting a cottage in the village in addition to their rooms in the house.

Providing cottage accommodation was one way in which the Greys encouraged their workfolk to stay, especially allowing them to buy long leases, usually of three lives (three named generations). The tithe map apportionment for the Dunham Massey estate dated 1839 shows this clearly.[171] Many of the estate cottages were entered under the names of lessees who were estate workers, and many labourers who appeared in the full-time or casual wage lists of the farm or the kitchen gardens held cottage leases. Most were occupied by the leasing family, but some were sub-let to other tenants. John Holt, for example, was a labourer at the home farm who held the lease of a cottage in Woodhouses that he occupied himself. The head groom, George Smith, leased both a house with garden and a field in Dunham Town. Elizabeth Cutler, widow of the house brewer, was the lessee of a cottage that she sublet to one of the farm labourers, William Lingard. The agents' letters indicate that

Fern and Rose Cottages, estate workers' houses in the village of Dunham Town, today still occupied by estate staff.

the estate was happy to let long leases, especially in return for capital investment. One example shows the estate accepting a proposal by Samuel Gregg, an existing tenant of the estate who became the owner of Quarry Bank Mill at Styal and who wanted to invest over £1,000 in building a house extension, stabling and a new Dutch barn in return for adding his son's life onto the lease.[172] It was one of the agent's regular tasks to send the Earl a list of 'lives lost', deaths of people who were leaseholders. By the early nineteenth century, many leases were into their third life, showing that the policy of letting long leases was not a recent one.

Not all the estate was let on leasehold. Areas of woodland and moss were, of course, managed in hand for timber and sporting purposes. Properties within the park itself would be exempt from the leasing policy, and by no means all the holdings on the wider estates were let long-term. George Royle, for example, one of the estate gamekeepers, had a short-term tenancy of a cottage in nearby Sinderland. Certainly,

43

Property and personal estate left by selected indoor and outdoor servants at Dunham Massey

Probate Records, Cheshire Record Office

Name	Post	Died	Personal estate	Real estate
George Cooke	house steward	1791	£5,000	Freehold and leasehold cottages in Altrincham
Elizabeth Byrom	kitchen-maid	1819	£300	Leasehold cottage in High Legh
John Holt	garden labourer	1826	£20	Leasehold cottage in Dunham
George Smith	head groom	1828	£1,000	Leasehold and freehold property
John Cutler	estate brewer	1830	£600	Leasehold cottage in Dunham Massey and a freehold cottage in Old Swinford
John Davenport	land steward	1835	£4,000	Unknown properties
John Royle	under-gamekeeper	1835	£100	-
Catharine Ainsworth*	head housemaid	1838	£200	-
Daniel Parsons	blacksmith	1840	£450	Leasehold pub and 2 leasehold cottages in Wilmslow, freehold cottage in Altrincham, £300 mortgage
Joseph Pickin	head gardener	1844	£4,000	Freehold and leasehold property
John Poole	house steward	1846	£800	Leasehold, freehold and mortgages
George Dean	house steward	1848	£100	?

*died intestate

there was no difficulty in letting cottages even on the shortest terms. In the early decades of the nineteenth century, when the local population was increasing rapidly, housing on the estate was in great demand. In 1813 the agent reported to the Earl that the miller at Dunham was having great difficulty in finding a suitable house and the estate needed to build more accommodation for its labourers.[173]

The policy of long leases meant not only that families stayed in place but also that individuals had various interests in property and therefore needed to make wills. This practice was obviously encouraged by the Worthingtons, who were attorneys as well as land agents. An unusual number of probate records have therefore survived for the senior and outdoor servants at Dunham, a selection of which are shown above (Box 43). Amounts of wealth left at death, either in the form of personal or real estate, clearly separate the senior servants from the juniors, for whom there are far fewer records, but also show that even head grooms and kitchen-maids could do well out of country-house employment. Most of the servants with substantial cash, investments or property set up annuities for their widows and children, or in the case of the childless John Poole, for his nephew. The unmarried kitchen-maid Elizabeth Byrom was still working at Dunham when she died in 1819, leaving her belongings to her sister, numerous nieces and a nephew. Though living in a room in the house,

44

Extract from the last will and testament of Elizabeth Byrom, kitchen-maid at Dunham Massey, died 1819

Cheshire Record Office, ws 1820

To my niece Martha Thomason ... the Bed with the Bolster and Pillow used therewith, the whitewood Box standing in my Bedchamber, the Chest of Mahogany Drawers ... my mahogany Tea Board and Tea Table, my Tea Spoons, and Tea Tongs and Brass Pestle and Mortar, two of my Brass candlesticks and all my Chinaware ... To my sister Phoebe all the rest of my household goods, furniture, wearing apparel ...

she owned a substantial amount of her own furniture, including her own bedding. The list of objects most precious to her evokes a picture which many working women of her day would envy (Box 44, above).

The Greys, consciously or not, used other more ephemeral ways of binding staff to the notion of the great family. Encouraging their outdoor workers to serve in the Cheshire Yeomanry increased their own standing in the local community and ensured their own safety in an increasingly turbulent time. In 1819 a new squadron of the Yeomanry was set up, made of two troops of cavalry, one of which was recruited from Altrincham, the other from Dunham Massey itself. The Yeomanry supplied the uniforms, horses and equipment for these men but not the good underwear needed. When one of the gardeners joined in 1822, the garden accounts itemised the purchase of flannel, linen, cambric thread, buttons and stockings and the labour of making up a set of underwear and shirts for him. The Dunham troop was limited to twenty-eight men, one horse and a man being recruited from every farm on the estate.[174] It was a popular undertaking. Not only were recruits given a set of clothing but they also had days off for practice and parades and were given occasional free meals. In February 1821, for example, the squadron held an exercise in the park at Dunham where 'after going through their field movements to the satisfaction of the officers, the men were regaled with strong ale by Captain William Egerton MP'. A few days later they met again in the same place to contest for two handsome swords, presented to 'the best and most expert swordsman in each troop'. Troop dinners were held at the Dog Inn, Dunham, paid for by Lord Stamford and the troop captain. The muster roll of 1839 shows that amongst the men were many members of the outdoor staff of the house, as well as villagers from the surrounding area. The Dunham Massey Troop was disbanded in 1856, when the house was abandoned by the 7th Earl as a regular residence.[175]

Worthington's account of the funeral of John Arnatt, the house steward, shows how important it was to display the correct outward signs of belonging. Households were turned out to mourn one of their own in a public display of the ethic of community, especially when the funeral was that of one of the Earls. At the death of the 5th Earl in May 1819, not only did major changes in staff take place but servants and tradesmen alike were called in to make preparations.[176] Timothy Brownell was paid 10gns for making two coffins, one for the Earl with an engraved brass plate, the second for the 5th Earl's wife, Lady Henrietta, aged eighty-two, who died eight years later. A local stonemason, Joseph Davies, made two large gravestones for the family vault in Bowdon church and the clerk and sexton were each paid a gratuity of 2gns. The process of going into full family mourning was elaborate and expensive. In 1819 an upholsterer, William Maskery, was paid £16 8s for lining the family coach with mourning cloth, and all the parish churches and chapels within the Stamford estates were decked out in heavy black cloth and cushions: not only Bowdon but also the churches at Carrington, and Ashton-under-Lyne, and the chapels at Stayley, Hey and Mossley. This involved four different drapers and upholsterers and a total cost of £731 19s 8d. Two firms of Altrincham drapers were paid for the supply of cloth for servants' mourning suits and dresses, a tailor for making them up and a Manchester hat-maker for crepe ribbon for the servants' hats – a total expense of just over £100. The cost of crepe supply and tailoring for mourning wear for the family itself came to £137 12s. Similar costs were incurred at Enville. When official mourning was ended in November, the black drapes were given to the rectors of the various parishes.[177]

Celebrations and entertainments were ways of conveying a sense of loyalty. Births and birthdays provided such opportunities, as in spring 1827 when the birth of George Harry Grey, heir to the 6th Earl, was commemorated at Enville by a celebration which lasted from 26–31 March.[178] The journal which recorded this event also noted that in the early morning of 5 November 1833, Samuel Timperley, one of the Dunham estate workers, cut his head badly in a fall whilst returning home from celebrating Lord Stamford's birthday in the Dog Inn, where he had raffled his donkey. At both Dunham and Enville there was a long tradition of the household paying for fiddlers to play at servant dances, unlike some houses where the servants had to pay themselves.[179] The dances were held in the servants' hall, which was cleared of the central table. Servants were allowed to bring guests to such events, though the occasion at Enville when Joseph Hardwick brought in his 'fancy woman' was sufficiently noteworthy to appear in Torry's journal.[180]

The general impression is that the Dunham household was a reasonably happy one for the servants. This is certainly the picture painted by an account of the celebrations for the marriage in 1825 of Lady Jane Grey, the second daughter of the 6th Earl, to Sir John Benn Walsh. The account comes in two letters written by Jane's brother Henry and her friend Harriet Inge, two days after the bridal couple had left Dunham for Enville.[181] Harriet first described how Jane's brother dressed the house dog, a mastiff called Lion, and a tiny spaniel with white satin ribbons round their necks. She went on to describe the story of an unexpected visit of a hermit from Oldham who arrived at the house intending to wish Jane good fortune. Hermits

A late eighteenth-century watercolour of Enville Hall, the Grey family home in Staffordshire.

This watercolour by Samuel Hieronymus Grimm, 1777, shows Henry, brother of the great naturalist, Gilbert White. He took delight in dressing as a hermit and greeting guests at The Wakes, the Whites' home in Selborne, Hampshire.

were a feature of rural society, rather like old wise women who could tell fortunes, and they were believed to bear good luck. They were also fashionable at this time and some great houses even employed their own to live in romantic landscaped grottoes. The Oldham hermit was greatly upset to find he was a day late, but was entertained firstly by the family and later in the kitchen, where unfortunately he was treated a little too well. He fell heavily from the top to the bottom of the steps in the corridor outside the steward's room, cutting his head so badly that 'a great deal of blood flowed'. The family called out Mr Broadbent, the apothecary, who put the old man to bed. He must have recovered for he left quietly at dawn the next day.

The letters go on to describe the evening celebrations. After dinner, at which the table was decked with more white satin ribbon, there was a display of fireworks at the front of the house, including one which lit up the sky in a fiery 'W', in honour of the bridegroom. The military band from Altrincham played on the front steps and two or three hundred people from the surrounding countryside watched in the park. The steward's room was taken over for a servants' dance, to which servants from other houses such as High Legh were invited. The family went to join in and decided to move the party into the Great Hall, so the servants' dance became a general ball with over fifty couples taking part. Harriet described how the housekeeper, Mrs Iveson, could not be prevailed upon to dance with the Earl, who partnered some of the maids instead. According to Harriet's taste, 'The best couple was old Mrs Jones from the Lodge and Mr. Hare the Cook!' The ladies and gentlemen left at two o'clock, but Jane's brother Henry stayed dancing with the servants until five in the morning. At one point the Earl's footman came into the Great Hall dressed up as an old woman 'with great effect'. Both Harriet and Henry were clearly thrilled: 'Such a lively, agreeable scene I have not witnessed for long and it was quite delightful to see everybody so happy. We have been talking it over this morning with great glee, I can assure you.' Henry's report of the same event gives a glimpse of household demarcation, for while the servants' ball was in progress, the farm labourers and gardeners, fifty in all, held a celebration dinner at the nearby Dog Inn, presided over by John Davenport and Joseph Pickin.

The journal kept by footman, later butler, William Torry shows that whereas family members might have been heavily committed to the conventional aristocratic sports of fox-hunting, horse-racing and shooting, servants and tenants at both Dunham and Enville enjoyed many other rural activities.[182] The journal records the occasional cockfight, badger-bait and hare-course, as well as bare-knuckle fights, and most numerous of all, foot-races. These last were usually hundred-yard dashes, often by two footmen, for a purse which varied between 2s 6d and £1. There were also a number of variations – foot-races over ice, racing whilst carrying a man on their backs, racing against the house dog cart and, on one occasion, an attempt to run five times round the New Park at Dunham in under forty-five minutes.

* * *

Academics have recognised the phenomenon of the 'closed village', a community run by the overriding power of the local great estate. In the case of Dunham Massey, the issue has been not of the closed village but of the closed town, and certainly until their retreat to Enville in the mid-nineteenth century the Booths and Greys dominated Altrincham. From the viewpoint of the town's burgesses, the relationship varied over time from a demand for complete servility to irksome control or even a welcome benefice. As late as the 1830s the government inspectors of the Municipal Corporations Act of 1832 were in no doubt, writing off the town as 'a mere appendage to the barony'.[183] This is a complex relationship which has been dealt with in many local studies of the area and could be further explored by painstaking examination of parish records and family histories.[184] Even a limited study shows an intricate network of relationships. The closeness of ties between the house and its hinterland is clear, and clear too is that sense of common purpose, the survival of a great house and its family.

Any oral historian who has talked to retired servants from the country-house world sooner or later comes across a remark such as 'It was a tough life but as long as you accepted the rules, it was good'. The 'rule' was that common purpose, which negated the idea of equality but in the best instances had in its place the notion of responsible care. In this circumstance there was no condescension, for people knew their place and on the whole accepted it. The community usually worked well, but it broke down when the lines between the hierarchical components were overstepped. It is interesting that at Dunham dislocation came in the mid-nineteenth century, when not the workforce but the 7th Earl broke the rules by marrying outside his class. This resulted in several decades of family absence from Dunham, followed later by a period of revitalisation and modernisation, all of which is the subject of the next chapter.

CHAPTER EIGHT

'We shall desire to introduce the telephone'

Survival and Conclusion

William Grey, 9th Earl of Stamford, as depicted in a cartoon by 'Spy' in *Vanity Fair*.

From the late 1860s to the early 1880s the house at Dunham was tenanted by Robert Platt, a highly successful entrepreneur in the cotton industry. By 1891 the only occupant was a living-in caretaker, sixty-two-year-old William Taylor from Prince Edward's Island. Taylor was still there in 1901, together with his wife, married daughter and three-year-old grandson. At the same time a twenty-three-year-old gardener, William Blease, lived in the stables with his widowed mother, brother and two sisters, while the home farm was occupied by John Hall and his family, two domestic servants and three farm servants. Gamekeeper David Laken, his wife and a lodger, keeper Peter Humphreys, were in the Stone Barn House.[185] The park was still ticking over though the house was all but empty.

By 1905, after twenty years of tenant household and a further ten of disuse, much of the servant furniture was in a poor state. The servants' hall showed signs of hard wear; an armchair was 'defaced' and an oak stool 'broken', though attempts had been made to cheer the place up a bit by hanging a couple of oil paintings and a stag's head. Furniture in the kitchen-maids' bedroom presented a sorry picture; the lamp-stand was 'imperfect', the painted washstand and the walnut occasional table were 'rickety and broken'. Other interiors had fallen out of use except for low-grade storage. The Platts did not keep up the family traditions of Dunham ale and the brew-house shared the fate of so many others, becoming a convenient store for awkward things which had seen better days but which no one wanted to throw away, like the old estate fire pump and a wooden sentry box for the watchmen. The same story was told in the cellars where a few derelict casks and stillages remained, and in the dairy, where only the heavy cheese-presses served as vestiges of a considerably more vigorous past.[186] The pheasantry and net room too were unused except for storage.

Other rooms, however, were provided with new equipment, either by the Platts or the trustees of the 7th Earl's Countess. The Platts employed a living-in laundress and the main laundry was still in use, though it had reverted to a multi-purpose washing-cum-ironing room and was made more comfortable by adding a round table, four chairs and a brown hearth rug in front of a small fireplace fitted within the larger bricked-up fireplace. A new ironing stove was fitted: the free-standing

Sketch by the author of the end wall of the dry laundry, showing the structural remains of two fireplaces, an old hotplate and the free-standing 'Pagoda' stove made by Thomas Bradford of Salford. This was fitted during the Platts' occupation of the house in the late nineteenth century.

'Pagoda', made by the premier manufacturer of laundry equipment, Thomas Bradford of Salford, who was also the supplier of the box mangle which has survived from that time. Yet other parts of the laundry were running down. The wash-house was not even listed in 1883, and in the backyard the clothes posts and copper wires were all imperfect. By 1905 the laundry and its equipment were derelict.

The most important technological change at this time was the installation of gas lighting. It is probable that a small private gas-making plant was installed at Dunham around 1880, and by the time of the 1883 inventory new lighting had been fitted in many of the family and a few of the servants' rooms. The living rooms, front corridors, staircases and landings had gasoliers. The dining room, for example, had an ormolu gasolier with ten ground-glass shades; that in the drawing room was crystal with sixteen shades. Most of the bedrooms were still lit only by oil lamps and candles, though both Lord and Lady Stamford's bedrooms had been fitted with gaslight.[187] A two-light gas pendant had been fitted into the housekeeper's room, which now had a decidedly more comfortable feel. She had a print-covered sofa, a couple of easy chairs, some pictures on the wall and a barometer. The two windows were dressed with heavy crimson curtains on brass poles and window-seat cushions to match, and the floor was covered with a green Brussels carpet and hearth rug.

The fitting of gas lights must have been an ongoing project. Gas lighting was not mentioned in the 1883 inventory in either the kitchen or the still room, though a photograph taken of the kitchen at some indeterminate date during the 1880s shows clearly a gas fitting in the middle of the centre table but no wall-mounted gas lights. Examination of the table reveals a patch where the hole for the light has been filled, so presumably gaslight was fitted into the existing table shortly after 1883. The 1905 inventory lists an 'antique Bronze Pillar light for 2 lights' in the kitchen, and by this time it was also fitted into the larders.

The Dunham Massey kitchen *c.*1900. The stone floor had been covered by a piece of diamond-patterned oilcloth and a small round table and an armchair had been provided for staff. The spits still hung by the fireplace, but the sink, which today sits under a window, had not yet been fitted.

The 1880s photograph shows that another important technical change had been made in the kitchen. Sometime during the 1880s the old open bar grate had been replaced by a closed range with a much narrower fire-basket, flanked by a hot closet which may well have survived from the 1770 refit. Roasting could still be carried out in front of the narrow fire but probably with vertical dangling spits rather than the long horizontal spits of the older bar grate. Presumably the small hastener at present in the kitchen was made to fit this smaller roasting fire. By this time, of course, fashionable food tastes had moved on, the roasting of meat in front of an open fire had become less important and kitchens were usually fitted with ranges which were capable of more flexible forms of cooking than were possible on the old open bar grate. Yet the kitchen as shown in the photograph is still slightly ambiguous. A state-of-the-art range is accompanied by an older fitment and sits side by side with obsolete spits and displays of pewter, kept for sentiment and decoration. The kitchen had already become an historic record rather than a purely functional work-place. As a result, the overall impression is much cosier than previously, especially as the old flagged floor is covered with oilcloth. The general scale of operations seems to be reducing. Most of the specialist functions, such as washing-up, meat preparation and pastry-making, were now centralised into the main kitchen area. The only larder mentioned in 1883 contained a strange mixture of fittings, the cook's pantry was furnished very sparsely and no mention was made of the pastry or scullery. The still room was flourishing, however. It had become almost a second working kitchen, complete with preserving pans, omelette pan and saucepan, tea kettles, pastry moulds and fully fitted closed range. It is possible of course that it had replaced the main kitchen as the real working area.[188]

Levels of comfort in the servants' living quarters seem to have polarised by 1883. The seniors did very well, the lower servants less so. Considerations of hygiene were beginning to dictate a change from wooden to iron bedsteads, which were easier to scrub down and protect against fleas, bedbugs and cockroaches. Unfortunately, as a result some servants had to put up with the old redundant bedsteads being stored in their rooms. Yet the male cook now had a dressing room as well as a bedroom. Both rooms had carpets and, though it was made of birch, the four-poster bed was hung with crimson moreen drapery with window curtains to match. There were several chairs, an oak wardrobe, chests of drawers in mahogany and oak and an antique inlaid table. In the dressing room was a dressing-table with toilet set, both a toilet mirror to stand on the dressing-table and a hanging mirror, a japanned footbath, towel rail, a walnut commode and a painted cupboard.

As we have seen, various degrees of modernisation had taken place over the centuries, but a wholesale refurbishment was embarked upon by William Grey, 9th Earl of Stamford, who inherited Dunham Massey on the death of the dowager Countess of Stamford and Warrington in January 1905. Once again, at the beginning of a new century a new Earl was prepared to take on a dilapidated house and turn it into a home. It was the 9th Earl's vision of the future, as well as his inheritance from the past, that ensured the survival of the house. Without that input, Dunham might have gone the way of many great houses such as Trentham, which was sold piecemeal at auction and dismantled.

In August 1905 the Earl commissioned a scheme of restoration and modernisation at Dunham and gathered together a team including the architect Joseph Compton Hall. Internally, this involved the installation of new sanitary and water supply systems, a fire protection system, electric lighting, telephones and central heating as well as a new dining room and an enlarged entrance hall. Externally, a new roof was needed, the 1820s corridor across the inner courtyard was removed and the south front remodelled with a lowered roofline and a new neo-Caroline frontage.[189] The project was started with modest aims and high hopes. In the summer of 1905 the Earl laid out an indication of the level of services required: 'Provision is to be made for hydrants, electric light, bells and gas piping and piping for hot water and radiators. We shall desire to introduce the telephone. We should wish to have a portion of the house rendered habitable as soon as possible – say by next summer.'[190] Inevitably the project grew in scale, ending up costing four times the original estimate (Box 45, opposite). For well over twelve months the house resembled a major building site and, for those servants who remained, life must have been full of noise and apparent chaos. Even the architect admitted to Lady Stamford that Dunham appeared to be in 'hopeless confusion', with dust everywhere. Security, particularly of the lead on the roof, was a constant worry. As with the 6th Earl nearly a century before, the

Modernisation of Dunham Massey, 1906

The team assembled by the 9th Earl was: architect Joseph Compton Hall from London, main contractor William Saint of Cambridge, interior designer Percy Macquoid and decorator Morant and Co. of London.

First estimate from Compton Hall, 1905

EGR 7/20/1/2

Work to the Mansion:	
Reconstruction of the roof and repairs to walls, floors, windows and chimneys.	
New drainage, water supply, fire prevention system and sanitary fittings.	
New entrance hall.	£5,550
Offices:	
Reconstruction of roof, repairs to floors and walls	£1,200
Stabling:	
Ditto	£800
Mill:	
Ditto	£500
Total estimate	**£8,050**

Second estimate, 1905

EGR 7/20/1/3

A revised scheme was adopted, which added to the above:

A new dining room on the site of the old servants' hall and maids' room
A new drawing room, servants' hall and butler's pantry
Reconstruction of the kitchens with new ranges, scullery and other fixtures.
Additional work outside on the moat, lodges and cottages

New total estimate **£21,845**

Summary of actual expenditure by Compton Hall, 1907

EGR 7/20/1/8

William Saint, main contractor		£30,409	11s	0d
Drake and Gorham, electrician		£1,284	11s	3d
Altrincham Electric Supply Co., laying cable		£132	7s	6d
Mr. Faraday, electric fittings		£92	10s	7d
Clements Jeakes, fitting up kitchens, ranges etc		£605		
William Smith, glazing and iron casements for hall		£359	14s	10d
Mr. Chubb, jewel safe		£16	0s	3d
Mr. Merryweather, hose		£19	16s	4d
Compton Hall:	architect's fees	£1,738	7s	6d
	clerk of the works	£455	10s	0d
	out of pocket expenses	£177	3s	0d
Total for Compton Hall		£2371	0s	6d
TOTAL		**£37,661**	**12s**	**9d**

9th Earl and Countess were closely involved in detailed decision-making, as shown by notes made by the Earl to himself:

> Reserve the right to get rid of any Workman disapproved of. Prevent men from roaming about park and grounds. Board round building yard and keep men out. Policemen probably required to keep people within bounds; especially if more than 100 men employed. Rockets for testing chimneys. Try all fireplaces. Every drain to be tested before passed ... Sewing maid in telephone room always rings for footman. No-one else allowed to listen to messages – she receives and sends them. Fire appliances, hand pumps, galvanised buckets in tank with ball cock ... Fill leather buckets with sand. Lodge gates – as close as possible to Lodge. Electric plant – get on public supply if possible. If private plant put in, agreement must be strict, ie reference approved in case of dispute.[191]

On the whole, the project worked out well and to everyone's satisfaction. The 1912 inventory provides an overview of the effect of all the changes. From the servants' point of view, one of the main alterations was the creation of a new servants' hall in the middle of the centre wing. This was refurnished with a round mahogany dining-table and leather-bottomed chairs, which in themselves speak volumes about the Edwardians' new attitude towards their servants. Difficult to recruit, and even more difficult to keep, efficient servants now had to be actively wooed, given a reasonable level of status and comfort, and provided with good furniture, silver or plated cutlery and decorated ceramics.

The housekeeper's room also experienced a general increase in status goods. The mahogany furniture was described in the 1912 inventory as 'antique' and her desk was now a bureau, 'internally fitted, with five drawers under and ornamental brass furniture'. The chairs too had moved upmarket to rosewood, though the seats were covered with functional American cloth rather than hide. The eight-day clock in a mahogany case and the barometer in a 'Chippendale case' were retained, as was the carpet. The fireplace now had an embroidered cloth mantel beneath a new walnut-framed mirror. One of the tables was covered with a crimson worsted cloth to match the curtains. There were two rise-and-fall electric light fittings and a telescopic table-lamp, and, though the furniture had perhaps improved in quality and status, the room had become more professional, more business-like. Large linen cupboards and a rug chest now lined the walls. Several items added a touch of family identity; there were pictures and photographs on the walls and in the corner stood a cage for a parrot, a favourite pet at Dunham over many years.

The old steward's room where the senior servants dined was swept away entirely, the space taken up into the new family dining room. The Edwardian servant household was smaller in size and senior servants dined in the housekeeper's room. By this time the whole idea of house stewardship had been replaced by housekeeper and butler, with a secretary taking over the personal side of family administration. The rise of the butler as the senior manager of the household was reflected in the new butler's pantry, built on the site of the old servants' hall and the only room where we have evidence of a senior servant's preference being accepted over that of the

In 1906 the butler's pantry became the control centre for the new internal communication system, which combined telephone and electric push buttons connected to a flag board.

Countess. The latter wanted the floor to be made of 'segalith', a new composite stone-like surface used elsewhere. The butler, however, expressed a strong desire for a wood floor and he seems to have won the argument. The new position of the butler's pantry was central for both butlers and footmen to work from. It was neatly fitted with cupboards for the storage of glassware and china, and two new sinks for washing glass and ceramics separately. A supply of soft water was collected from the roof and piped to a third tap, for rinsing. The room was also the hub of the new telephone communication system installed in 1906. To the right of the door was the switchboard, which connected to most of the family rooms as well as the lodge, giving warning of the arrival of family cars so that the front door could be opened

The still-room range, fitted *c.*1906 and supplied by Clements Jeakes.

and the butler ready to greet them. Visitors arriving unannounced at the front door had to rely on an electric bell system. This last was installed at the same time and appears to have been more successful than the telephone, which suffered from inadequate battery power. The butler's pantry has a homely feel to it and it is not surprising that in his later years the 10th Earl liked to take his tea here, sitting to the right of the fireplace in a large Windsor chair – perhaps the old butler's chair which appeared in past inventories of the servants' hall.

A new servery was designed by Compton Hall immediately outside the butler's pantry. A fine hot cupboard was supplied by Clements Jeakes of London. A hatch allowed the kitchen staff to pass the dishes through to the footmen without requiring the latter to trespass into the kitchen, which was a common source of irritation for chefs. The whole was screened off from the door into the main house, which helped reduce noise levels.

Changes had taken place in the kitchen too. The old stone floor was replaced by quarry tiles and the gas lighting by three pendant electric lamps and two rise-and-fall

RIGHT: The insulated cold store in the wet larder supplied by Clements Jeakes, *c.*1906. Ice blocks from the ice-house were placed on one side, pies, fish and cheese on the other.

CLEMENTS JEAKES & CO
LONDON

Close-up of the maker's nameplate in ceramic.

wall lights. The list of contractors used in 1906 includes an item for work by Clements Jeakes for kitchen fittings and a range for over £600 (Box 45, p.179). This must relate in part to the repair and conversion to gas of the old charcoal stoves, but the first of the two larders was also completely refitted by Jeakes as a wet larder, with new slate stillages and two beautifully made slate sinks for washing meat and salting. The same firm supplied the elaborate grained insulated meat-closet that remains today, as well as the refrigerator that now stands in the cook's room. The new range referred to was probably the 'Turpin' range in the still room and it seems likely that the kitchen range was left intact, though supplemented by a small free-standing gas cooker of this date which still stands in the fireplace archway.[192] Unfortunately, all Jeakes's work was subcontracted by the main contractor William Saint, so details of his bills have not survived, though the firm was well-known as a contractor to the aristocracy (Box 46, opposite). Adding together his £605, an estimated amount for Saint's bills and for electrical fittings, it is probable that the family spent between £1,500 and £2,000 on modernisation of the kitchen suite in the period 1906 to 1908.

William Jeakes: emulating the country-house lifestyle

One London firm which served the country-house market for over a hundred years was William Jeakes, the supplier of Dunham's new kitchen and larder equipment in 1906. Emulation was an important feature of the whole country-house ethic, as is illustrated by the story of William Jeakes.

The Jeakes family was established as carpenters and builders in Little Russell Street, Bloomsbury from around 1810 until at least 1829. William Jeakes branched out on his own as a general smith, soon expanding into an office frontage in 51 Great Russell Street, opposite the present British Museum entrance. Rebuilt in the 1880s, No. 51 remained Jeakes's office address until the 1920s, though the workshops were removed from Great Russell Street to Macklin Street.

We know little about the early history of William Jeakes's engineering firm, except that there is a tradition that he made all the lamp posts in the City of London. By the 1830s he was specialising in the manufacture of cooking apparatus and appeared in the official catalogue of the Great Exhibition of 1851 where he was described as an inventor, a claim borne out by the list of patents taken out by him spanning the period from the 1820s to the 1850s. A patent for a hotplate dated 1822 is especially interesting in the context of the Dunham Massey kitchen and its charcoal stoves. Even eighty or more years later, the Dunham Kitchen had nothing as sophisticated or as safety-conscious as this. Although no catalogue or trade card of the Jeakes's manufactory is available, equipment bears eloquent testimony to his ingenuity, workmanship and reputation. Many large-scale country houses that were built or refurbished during the nineteenth century were supplied by him. His clients included many famous families and individuals, including Charles Dickens and Florence Nightingale, for whom he designed a drying-cabinet and spin-drier for the hospital at Scutari. Perhaps the most important and complicated contract was for Sir Charles Barry, working on the kitchens of the refreshment rooms of the House of Lords and the central heating of the new Palace of Westminster in the 1840s and 1850s.

William remained as the driving force within the firm of Jeakes until his retirement in 1861. Thereafter his energies were transferred to the care of his own scaled-down version of a country house, a large red-brick mansion called Winchester Hall, on the corner of Highgate Hill and Hornsey Lane. Here Jeakes became a major figure in the community and earned a place within the local gentry. Earlier he had raised a company of the 37th Middlesex Rifle Volunteers from his own workforce and in Highgate he was always known as Colonel Jeakes. At Winchester Hall, William Jeakes lived in some style. He bought adjacent land, extending the original four acres to fifteen, which included meadows, a stream and some pastureland. The land was well screened by trees, the lawns studded with cedars. The more formal gardens were graced by terraces and hedges, ornamental pools and a grotto, as well as hot-houses for pineapples and grapevines.

William Jeakes died suddenly in 1874. His son John William lived at Winchester Hall for a while but the house was soon demolished to make way for residential streets. The contents listed at the sale included one and a half miles of iron park-fencing, a wrought-iron heating system in the pineapple house, a fernery, octagonal beehive, an aviary and a summer-house with stained-glass windows. Inside the house was adorned with delights befitting a minor stately home: paintings by Zucchero, Kneller, Hilliard and Lely.

John William Jeakes does not seem to have been interested in carrying on the family firm and sometime shortly after William's death his friend Edward Clements took over the company, which thereafter traded under the name of Clements Jeakes. The spirit of William Jeakes survived in the new company, which turned out work of high quality though it was no longer innovative. The firm was finally wound up in 1927.

For further reading see Joan Schwitzer, 'Some Victorian Business Men and their Residences: Winchester Hall, Highgate', *Bulletin of Hornsey Historical Society*, No. 19, n.d. pp. 40–49, Holborn Local History Centre; British Library, Patent specification No. 4687, 1822, Postans Improved Cooking Apparatus, p. 2; and British Library, George Tomey, 'Report of the Banquet given by Major Jeakes of the 37th Middlesex Volunteer Rifles, to his Artizans, Foremen, Clerks and Assistants on his retiring from Business', London, printed James Horsey, 1861.

Dunham Massey's huge Aga, fitted *c.*1936, one of the earliest and largest examples ever made.

The present Aga stove was fitted later, in 1936, during the time when Mrs Millington was cook. According to her daughter, she started work on a purely temporary basis to help out, but stayed seventeen years and it was during her time that the Taylor range was taken out and replaced by the Aga.[193] The Dunham Aga is one of the earliest and largest ever made, a caterer's range with three double ovens, simmering-plates and ample warming space.[194] Interestingly, Dorothy Millington used to go into the kitchen to help her mother and always remembered it as a cold room, even with the fire going. This is not surprising as it was originally designed to work with a huge open fire which deliberately threw most of the heat into the room to be reflected back by the hastener onto the roasting meat. The Aga was more efficient at heating hotplates and ovens and thus lost much less heat to the room. This is not to say the old open range was 'inefficient', rather that it was designed to do a different job from the Aga and did it superbly.

Since they were already used only for storage, both the dairy and the laundry were little changed by the 1906 modernisation scheme. The dairy did, however, solve a difficult problem. The new heating system required a fuel store for 50 ton of coal, but the only cellar available was some distance from the boiler. Using this would have involved a lot of hand labour, even if a trolley were used, which could have been noisy. At the Earl's insistence the old dairy house was used as a fuel house, fitted with a chopping-block and a new lean-to store for firewood outside the back wall. In the laundry the only change was the installation of electric lighting, for when the 9th Earl set up his new household the washing was sent out to a cottage laundry in Charcoal Lane.

Similarly, the alterations impacted little on the stable block. The saddle room remained in use and the lofts were filled with discarded furniture and small amounts of hay and corn in use. One of the coach-houses became home for a mare and a pony, as well as four large cricket screens, an oil tank and a new Merryweather fire cart, hoses and stand-pipes. Another coach-house was converted into a 'motor house' for three motors, complete with an inspection pit. The brew-house was cleared and fitted with a drained floor to become the 'wash' for cars.

In 1906 the servant living accommodation was overhauled, so that by 1912 the maids' rooms had what appears on paper at least to have been a fairly standard level of furniture and fittings. More iron 'French beds' were bought, fitted with wire spring bases topped with thick 'bordered mattresses', doing away with the need for unhygienic piles of flat mattresses and feather beds. For the family, however, feather beds were still considered desirable, and the feather room of 1912 still contained both ticking and paper bags full of feathers as well as a wool mattress worth £35. One particularly comfortable servant's room was probably occupied by the lady's maid. It had crimson carpeting, an oriental hearth rug, a high wire fireguard and a single-size French bedstead with a wool mattress, feather bolsters and pillows. The brand new oak dressing-chest had a toilet mirror and two small drawers on top. The washstand was made of birch and had a marble top. Another chest of drawers was described as antique oak and there was a painted wardrobe, a stuffed ottoman and pretty bamboo-pattern cane chairs. Despite this comfort, the maid's room doubled as a workroom in the old tradition, for she had ready to hand the tools of her trade: an ironing board, a dress form and a Singer sewing machine.

Besides the investment of capital in the fabric of the building, the arrival of the 9th Earl and his wife in 1905 saw the re-establishment of a full-scale servant household. Despite the growing attractions of careers other than domestic service, Dunham was not short of applicants for vacancies, even for menservants. In February 1909, for example, twenty-five letters of application were received for the post of second footman at a salary of £24.[195] Parlour-maids were replacing footmen generally, so positions as footmen were unusual and all the applicants were young men in their late teens or early twenties, of some experience in the service. Appearance was important and all the letters gave their height, all but one being 5ft 10in tall or more. The successful applicant was James Bell, aged twenty-two and 6ft tall. Accompanying the letters of application were references, sometimes a letter from the applicant's present employer, often the butler rather than the family

47

Character reference for a footman. From Mrs Hunt, a servants' employment agency, to Dunham Massey, 1909

EGR Restricted Box 14/11

In respect to Capt Wood's kind application, Mrs. Hunt begs to forward the particulars of a Servant at £ 24. 8. 2. 1909.

Register F.

As 2nd footman.

Name Sidney S Oswell.

Address 147 Ebury Street. Westminster. London SW.

Age 21.

Denominⁿ Ch of Engd.

Height 5ft 10.

Character 6 months

with Mrs Hall.

Previously 8 months.

with Mrs Henderson.

1 year with Mrs Eden.

Oswell was footman under butler with Mrs Hall. 8 servants kept. 6 in family, & obtained the situation through Mrs Hunt.

Mrs Hall wrote Mrs Hunt that Sidney Oswell was a clean nice looking boy & clean

KINDLY RETURN THESE PARTICULARS TO MRS. HUNT IF NOT REQUIRED. T.O.

C.I

in his person & work.

Previously he was footman under butler with Mrs Henderson, which situation he also obtained through Mrs Hunt's recommendation.

Formerly hall boy with Mrs Eden whose butler spoke very well of him when writing.

Oswell can valet wait table clean silver & lamps. also understands hunting & shooting things.

Is of good appearance fresh looking.

Free now.

He has since been with the Marquis of Ailsa as 2nd footman of 2, 3 in family, 10 servants kept but is leaving after having been there 2½ months as the situation is unsuitable.

head, and sometimes a *pro forma* from a servant agency, one of which was based in Leeds (Box 47, above).

Notes kept at Dunham outlined the conditions of employment which servants generally expected at this time and to which the house was prepared to adhere.[196] The salary commenced on the day service began and not on the date of engagement, though if the agreed starting date was delayed by the employer, the servant was entitled to the agreed wage, board and lodging for the intervening time. In addition to salary, women staff were entitled to tea, sugar and beer allowances plus washing expenses, men to tea, sugar and beer only. Servants were allowed travel expenses to get from their home to Dunham at the start of their employment and likewise the return fare at the end if they had left through no fault of their own. From 1911 the law required that either party give notice before the end of the second week if employment was to be terminated at the end of the first month. Thereafter a full month's notice was required on either side, or one month's wages in lieu of notice.

48

A tax on servants

A tax on servants was first introduced in 1777 to help finance the War of American Independence and to encourage men to enlist in the Navy. It was originally set at one guinea per annum for every male indoor servant, later changed to a sliding scale, rising steeply with larger numbers in the household. It was adjusted many times subsequently. In 1785 Peel temporarily extended it to cover female servants and at one time bachelors were double-rated. It continued until 1937.*

Stewards and bailiffs were classed as male servants and so were included in the tax. Thus in 1813 the 5th Earl was liable for tax of £2 each on six senior managers on his various estates, as well as on his more junior servants.† In 1818 the tax was a considerable burden; the annual total paid by the Greys amounted to the equivalent of slightly under half the total year's wages for Dunham's permanent resident servants.

Servant tax paid by the Earl of Stamford in 1818

EGR 11/2/6/7

1818		£ s d
April 25	Mr Worthington paid me for the Earl of Stamford and Warrington one hundred and fifty five pounds fifteen shillings and six pence for a half years duty on Male Servants	155 : 15 : 6
	Additional D°	7 : 13 : 0
	Joel Hobson	
Nov. 2	Also one hundred and fifty nine pounds and twelve shillings for the like purpose	159 : 12 : 0
	Joel Hobson	
		£ 323 : 0 : 6

* J. Jean Hecht, *The Domestic Servant Class in Eighteenth Century England* (Routledge and Kegan Paul, 1956), p.33.

† EGR 4/1/8/3/30 Letter from Hugo Worthington to 5th Earl of Stamford, 17 January 1813.

Setting up a household from scratch required expenditure over and above servant wages, of course, and invoices from the early years of the twentieth century record the expense of buying servant uniforms as well as kitchen and family linen.[197] Further expense and paperwork was required to obtain the necessary licences. Until 1937, a licence was needed to keep menservants, carriages, motor cars, armorial bearings and hunting dogs, an interesting amalgam of what were considered to be the distinguishing luxuries of the aristocracy. Prosaically enough, the form was obtainable from the post office and in January 1909 cost the 9th Earl £10 16s.[198] It shows that the Earl employed six indoor menservants, a substantial number for the time, but modest compared to the numbers employed in the nineteenth century (Box 48, above). Outdoor servants such as gardeners and female servants were not liable for tax as they were considered essentials not luxuries.

49

Turnover of women servants at Dunham Massey, 1935–9

EGR Restricted Box 53/2

	Number who held the post 1935–9	Average length of service (in months)	Average salary (£s per year)
Housekeeper	2	?	87
Head parlour-maid	1	?	49
2nd parlour-maid	4	12·5	36
Head housemaid	3	14·3	58
2nd housemaid	5	9·2	44
3rd housemaid	6	7·6	34
4th housemaid	9	4·6	27
Cook	5	7·4	86
Kitchen-maid	3	9·3	38
Scullery-maid	7	7	26

In the early twentieth century the family were fortunate in finding two individuals who became key to the household's future serenity, helping it weather both the cataclysm of a world war and routine desertions by junior servants. Both had begun their employment with the Greys in the establishment of the 7th Earl's Countess at Enville. Isabella Collins was set on at the beginning of March 1898 at a salary of £29 and went on to become housekeeper at Dunham with thirty-five years' service. Charles Hughes was set on at Enville in 1901 and was to remain as butler at Dunham for thirty-seven years.[199] Both left within a couple of years of each other, Mrs Collins retiring with a life pension in 1936 and Charles Hughes in 1938. Their departure is recorded in the staff wages book for 1935–9, which also details the employment of fifty-three other female servants. The average length of service was fairly short and seems to relate to wage levels, the poorer-paid moving on quickly (Box 49, above). The 4th housemaids, for example, stayed on average just over four months. Even the longest-staying servants, the head housemaids, stayed only a year and a couple of months. In the face of such instability the two senior staff must have seemed like a rock.

The wages book, kept by Lady Stamford personally, includes notes against some of the servants, written when they left. Some were positive, as with one housemaid: 'Nice girl, sorry she leaves' and again 'very nice, left to be married'. Mrs Collins' replacement earned a regretful: 'Left through bad health, excellent in every way'. But many were not missed, despite the bother of having to find replacements: 'Began well, but later most unreliable and untruthful'; 'good hearted but untidy and unmethodical, very childish'; and a short but intriguing: 'naughty girl!' All the cooks seem to have given disquiet. One was described as 'not clean and mysterious', another: 'not to be recommended'; another: 'good cook but queer and temperamental' and the final one: 'Impossible, walked out!'

50

Work for the housemaids before breakfast, Dunham Massey in the 1930s

EGR Restricted Access Boxes

Housekeeper

Dust the marble tops and other tables in the Great Hall, the Saloon and the Chapel.

Head housemaid

Sweep and dust Lady Stamford's Parlour, the Saloon, the family side of the Chapel, the Grand Staircase, the Summer Parlour and the Chintz Drawing Room.

2nd housemaid

Clean the grates in the room swept by the Head Housemaid

Sweep and dust His Lordship's Study, the Breakfast Room, the servants' side of the Chapel, the Great Hall and the Saloon staircase.

3rd housemaid

Clean grates in Breakfast Room, Billiard Room, Housekeeper's Room

Sweep and dust the Housekeeper's Room, the Front Hall, the Billiard Room, the Long Corridor, her Ladyship's lavatory and the Red stairs

Dust the Saloon floor.

4th housemaid

Clean the grates in His Lordship's Study and the Servants' Hall

Sweep and Dust the Anti room, His Lordship's lavatory, the corridor outside the Breakfast Room, the bottom of the Red Stairs and the Garden Entrance.

Scrub all the steps

Get the kettle on in the Housekeeper's Room by 7·30am.

The 1930s were, of course, at the very tail end of the highly structured servant household. Smaller establishments were badly hit by the First World War, but the great households recovered to a large extent, except that they were even more dependent on female labour than before. Many carried on, however, with the same structure of hierarchical work routines as previously. This is illustrated at Dunham by the tradition of daily Chapel attendance, which took the form of ten minutes of family prayers. Even in the 1930s, every morning at five minutes to nine the housemaid or butler rang a bell, which still hangs high above the kitchen roof, calling the whole indoor household (the gardener on his morning visit to the kitchen or to arrange flowers used to disappear quietly). Family and guests sat in the raised pew at the far end of the Chapel, the indoor servants below, men on the right and women on the left, in order of precedence.[200]

The hierarchical nature of the household in the twentieth century is also evidenced by a notebook written by the housekeeper in the 1930s (Box 50, above).

Minnie Hulme, née Ackerley, was housemaid at Dunham Massey during the 1930s. Here she is with other Dunham servants (*far right*).

This lists the housemaids' daily morning work, before the family rose for breakfast.[201] The work was divided between the maids on the basis of seniority of experience. The housekeeper trusted no one but herself to dust the most precious objects, whilst the 4th maid learnt her trade by cleaning interiors fitted with plain, everyday furniture and few ornaments. This meant that as far as furniture was concerned she was restricted largely to service rooms or corridors, though she also did heavier, dirtier jobs such as cleaning grates and scrubbing floors.

For a more personal, anecdotal account of what it was like to work as a housemaid at Dunham in the 1930s, we need to turn to servants' memories. Born in 1916, Minnie Hulme (née Ackerley) was third of four housemaids at Dunham during her late teens and early twenties, earning 15s a month. Her reminiscences were recorded at Dunham in 1998, when she was eighty-two years old.[202]

The summary of Minnie's early career is a typical story of the early twentieth century. In the nineteenth century it was the usual thing for country girls to go into service, but by the 1930s so many other forms of employment were open to women that most of those who chose the life had been born into it as a family tradition. Minnie was no exception. Her parents 'lived under the Cholmondeleys', whose estates were in south Cheshire, and they later went to live 'under the Graggington estate' near Bangor-on-Dee. One of her brothers worked his way up the servant ladder from pantry-boy to footman and butler, but finally gave it up during the Second World War to drive lorries for McAlpines. Minnie's first job was to help Mrs Wilson, the daughter of Lady Carver and wife of the brewery magnate, a woman who took a long-term interest in the girl and her family. Later, after a short break at home to help her mother who was pregnant, Minnie was found another position by Mrs Wilson, at Enville, then inhabited by the 10th Earl of Stamford's second cousin, Sir John Grey. However, both Mrs Wilson and Lady Cholmondeley came to believe

Minnie Ackerley, housemaid, (*right*) in her best dress.

that the Enville household was not a suitable position for the young girl and she was found another place at Boughton, the Northamptonshire house of the Duke of Buccleuch. Here again Minnie did not stay long, this time from her own choice, as the housekeeper at Boughton was 'an absolute terror' and regularly reduced the maids to tears. After Boughton, Mrs Wilson found her a place at Dunham, where she worked as 3rd housemaid, and where she stayed until she was 'poached' by Lady Stamford's best friend, Mrs Wrigley.

Minnie recalled Dunham as a household of twelve or thirteen full-time living-in servants, still rigorous in its hierarchies and division of labour. Walking around the house she could remember clearly for which rooms she was responsible and which were cleaned by senior maids. In practice as in theory, the division seems to have been based on experience and status. Minnie cleaned the housekeeper's own room, the front hall, the Summer Parlour, the nurseries, the billiard room, the Queen Anne Stairs and the south corridor where, as Minnie herself said: 'I dusted this, because there is not much value to worry about is there?... If they are priceless things they are not going to have a young girl handling them are they?' She was not allowed into the Saloon, the Earl's study, the dining room, the chapel, the Stone Parlour or the Great Hall. She also helped clean most of the family bedrooms, but here the work was differentiated even further. Each room was cleaned to strict standards and in a strict order. The lower housemaids cleaned the fireplaces and the carpets, but the head housemaid dusted 'the tops', that is the mantelpiece and furniture surfaces with their ornaments. Carpets were done first (time would have to be left for the bits to settle), then the surfaces dusted and lastly the wooden floors. Simply lifting an ornament to dust underneath it was not allowed; all ornaments were removed first and placed somewhere safe under a cover. Minnie could not remember scrubbing steps, and her memory is accurate, for according to the housemaids' written worklist

(Box 50, p.191) this was to be done by the 4th housemaid. Any alteration to this set routine (one servant helping out another, for example) precipitated a confrontation with the housekeeper. The kitchen and house staff were also clearly differentiated from each other, the housemaids not being allowed into the kitchen, even to fetch their meals.

Despite the fact that Dunham had changed from footmen to the more modern practice of keeping parlour-maids, it was still a traditionally run house. The maids used tried and tested equipment rather than new-fangled gadgets, stiff brushes rather than vacuum cleaners, and the grates were cleaned with old-fashioned burnishers made of fine metal chain. The internal telephone system was not used and the pantry staff were still called by room bells, though these were now electrified. Servant breakfasts were taken in the servants' hall, with the housekeeper, Mrs Collins, sitting at the head of the table and Mr Hughes, the butler, at the bottom. Time off was still half a day a week, though as the park gates were locked at 9pm they all had to be in by then, plus one week's holiday a year, when Minnie would go home to her family at Cholmondeley. This was always during the hay harvest so she helped with this and also cleaned the house from top to bottom, so 'it was no holiday'.

Lady Stamford was a strict disciplinarian with high expectations of the way the house was run. One maid gave notice when she was not allowed leave to be a bridesmaid at her aunt's wedding. She was also a busy practical housekeeper; she herself insisted that blinds were drawn evenly, stair-rods were level, no chairs were across a corner and that in the Great Hall all the chairs were the same distance away from the wall. Other houses might still adhere to strict rules, but at Dunham they were enforced in the old eighteenth-century way, by her Ladyship, not the senior staff. Yet Minnie was clearly not frightened of Lady Stamford, even though she would come into the maids' bedroom to tell them off for laughing. All the servants respected and liked her, though she had the reputation of snobbery amongst the locals of Altrincham, perhaps because old-fashioned traditions of deference were kept up. Boys living on the estate were still taught to touch their cap when the family passed by and girls curtseyed, as did the lodge-keeper, Mrs Seniscall, when she opened the gates for the car to sweep through.[203]

The maids had bedrooms on the first floor. Minnie shared hers with another maid and though the head housemaid had her own room, it had a door into the girls' room so privacy was limited. The bedrooms were uncarpeted except for a small rug, and were unheated, for although there were fireplaces they were never used. They did have the luxury of a bathroom. Not all the servants lived in the house itself. The two men lived out; Hughes, the butler, lived in one of the park cottages with his wife and sister-in-law, and the odd-job man lived in a lodge.

Minnie held Lady Stamford in high regard until disappointed at the treatment she received after she had decided to leave Dunham. In Minnie's words 'she turned awkward when I would not stay', and the indignant little scene which followed etched itself in the young woman's memory. Holding a note in her hand, Lady Stamford went into the maids' bathroom while she was in the bath, accused her of throwing away a good job and said she was sure that Mrs Wilson, Lady Cholmondeley and her mother would not want her to leave. After this she flicked

The garden party held to celebrate the official homecoming of the 9th Earl and Countess of Stamford and their children in August, 1906.

the piece of paper at Minnie and swept out, leaving the girl speechless. Through the following days, the maid tried to 'dodge' her, preferring to give her final notice through the housekeeper, but Lady Stamford again caught her in her bedroom with a final admonishment about her reference: 'Well, I can't say anything about your work, but I will say you don't stay in your places.'

In Minnie's memory, Dunham contrasted with Enville, which was home to a much smarter and racier household. Sir John Grey lived not with his wife but with a Mrs Aldridge and although this meant more work in clearing up after late-night dinner parties and unpacking guests' clothes, the girl enjoyed her stay. She was, however, prey to a vague sense of unease and sometimes slept with the lady's maid as a safeguard against the menservants. The Duke of Buccleuch's household at Boughton was different again. This was a huge establishment with thirty-three servants, but run with a lighter hand by the family. Being seen to run down a corridor was not a problem at Boughton, but at Dunham it would have been punishable by sacking. Dunham she characterised as a sombre house, not jolly but not unhappy or miserable, just rigid in its routines and old-fashioned.

Servants still had their little rebellions, though, both personal and collective. In the afternoon when the two younger housemaids were supposed to be occupied with their routine of cleaning the larger floor areas, they would smuggle in their knitting and sit behind a piece of furniture, talking and knitting. When the head housemaid discovered them she never reported them, even though she was a niece of Mrs Collins, the housekeeper. As was often the case, the servants' hall was home to family cast-offs, in this case a grey and red parrot relegated from her Ladyship's parlour. The bird was not popular with the under-housemaid, Florence, who had to clean the cage every day, but the parrot survived her dosing it with strong mustard, which, it turned out, the parrot loved.

On one memorable occasion the house servants went on strike over the poor food, one of very few records of this level of insubordination. Though breakfast was taken together, the senior servants at Dunham dined separately from the housemaids and parlour-maids, who had all their meals in the servants' hall. One day the hall was presented with rabbit stew (a very frequent dish for servants) which had bits of newspaper in it. Minnie described what happened next:

> So we all decided to give our notices in, all of us. The pantry and the housemaids.... So Lady Stamford was waiting for us all to go into the housekeeper's room.... We were going down that passage and there was no carpet on it then ... and the feet of everyone going down those steps set me off with the giggles. Mr. Hughes I remember, pushed me in the back and said: 'Minnie, do get a grip on yourself', but when I got to the top of those stairs and saw Lady Stamford's face, that was enough, you know... to keep me serious. But she went to each one of us. The head servants were there, but they had not given their notice in and she said 'Why?'... and then she sacked the cook and she wished us all to withdraw our notices except the head of the parlour-maids.

This would have been unthinkable a hundred years earlier, but by the 1930s servants had come to have a higher sense of their own worth. Clearly it was not just the food which set off this dissatisfaction. Minnie recalled a vague sense of being hemmed in, a humdrum existence which contrasted to her previous houses and an isolation from the outside world, represented by Altrincham. Though the house had a green Raleigh bicycle, the servants were forbidden to ride it and had to walk to town across the park, for the bus service was very infrequent. Minnie kept in touch with her mother through all her employment. Every week on her half day off, if the weather was fine, she would go to sit under a special old tree in the park and write a letter to her mother, then walk into Altrincham to post it. The pleasures she recalled were simple. In the old days the servants' hall might be the venue for dances and impromptu sing-songs, but in the 1930s it was provided with records and a gramophone, and Minnie enjoyed the experience of teaching Florence to dance. Minnie's words echo those of many girls in service in the great country houses: 'You had to make your own fun, there was nothing otherwise.'

Minor rebellion about inadequate food presaged a more permanent and widespread withdrawal of service from the great country houses. For centuries, domestic service had been one of Britain's most important industries. Even at the beginning of the twentieth century, it was still the largest single form of employment for women and, perhaps more amazingly, it was the second largest source of employment for all workers, men and women.[204] Yet within a few decades (certainly by the 1950s) even the most elaborate and tenacious form of domestic service, employment in the country house, was dead.

Signs of decline were discernible much earlier for those who cared to look for them. One academic writer has identified the 'servant problem' as 'an ageing chestnut even in 1700'.[205] By 1880 contemporary journals and monographs show that middle- and lower-middle-class employers were obsessed with what they also called 'the servant problem'. By this was meant not only the growing shortage of good servants, but also the 'restlessness, intractability and general cussedness' of the servant classes.[206] At a higher social level, however, the traditional country house could still offer training and conditions of work sufficient to lull masters and mistresses into thinking they were above such difficulties. In colourful imagery, Clive Aslet described many late-Victorian and Edwardian country houses as 'grazing on a savannah of cheap labour and cheap fuel' and 'basking beneath a sky in which the filmy clouds of income tax and death duties had only just begun to appear'.[207] Statistics gave the lie to such complacency. Between 1881 and 1901 the number of female servants in employment still rose, by eight per cent, but this rise was far below the general increase in population.[208] More importantly, the numbers of young girls employed in the industry actually fell in real terms during those twenty years. Servants were not only becoming scarcer, they were becoming older and therefore more expensive. This boded ill for the country house, which relied on a continual supply of young girls. Looking back from 1951 the Marchioness of Bath thought that country-house life was at its zenith between 1880 and 1914; she further stated that 'it never returned to its full splendour after the first World War'.[209] Some, like Dunham, were treated to a pleasant if deceptive Indian summer.

* * *

Although many books and papers have been written about country-house servants, there exist few detailed studies of single households based on the type of records used here, at least from the eighteenth and nineteenth centuries.[210] From more general writings on servants, however, a couple of overall characteristics stand out. Firstly there seems to have been a consistency in servant structures between houses. In view of the general mobility of servants, it was important that individuals could move to a new house and pick up the routine quickly. Work differentiation between ranks of housemaids, kitchen-maids and footmen, therefore, was largely standardised. Such a system worked to the advantage of both employer and employee, though how it came about is slightly puzzling, given the absence of cheap instructional handbooks until the nineteenth century and of formal colleges of training until the twentieth. One explanation lies in the second interesting characteristic, the conservatism of the country-house system. Until the second half of the nineteenth century domestic service in the great houses had changed relatively little over centuries. Staff conformed to patterns of behaviour established hundreds of years before. The division of labour between footmen cleaning downstairs furniture and housemaids cleaning upstairs, for example, harked back to a much earlier age, to the great medieval households which were based on a military model in which women played but limited roles, either as washerwomen or body-servants to high-ranking ladies.[211]

Yet country-house structures did experience change over time, especially with the growing expectations of privacy by landed families during the eighteenth and nineteenth centuries. The development of specialised servants with specialised workplaces has been seen as a strategy of control and distancing in response to such expectations, and the 2nd Earl's development of a formal kitchen court and separate stable blocks was a good example of this.[212] The improvement of communications within the house was an essential prerequisite of such distancing. Early techniques

depended solely upon personal contact with footmen, one of whose duties was 'close waiting', the de-personalisation of footmen being achieved by dressing them in elaborate formal uniforms. By the mid- or late eighteenth century most country houses had invested in wire bell-pull systems that enabled footmen and housemaids to respond from within the servants' quarters, which could now be sited at a greater distance from the family rooms. The nature of the sprung bell system gave five or ten minutes' response time. By the early twentieth century wire-operated bell-pulls had been replaced by electrical boards and telephone systems, which were a source of pride to owners but were detested by servants themselves. Provided with more privacy and control over their work spaces, they were now continuously interrupted by the ringing of bells which required immediate answering.[213] Perhaps it was not simply inadequate batteries that led to the under-use of Dunham's internal telephones in the 1930s.

Was Dunham conservative in its use of technology? Compared to an innovative house such as Cragside, it was not at the cutting edge, but neither was it a laggard. It had heated walls in the kitchen garden in the eighteenth century and water-closets in the house early in the nineteenth. The water supply was powered by the mill by 1860 and a private gas plant was installed in the 1880s.[214] The refurbishment of 1905–6 provided the house with modern plumbing, heating and communication systems. These features were far from pioneering, however, and the gas plant as well as the new closed range in the kitchen may have been forced on the family by Robert Platt, a successful industrialist who may have persuaded the Stamford trustees to invest in such basic amenities during his tenancy. Dunham is best characterised as being representative of the solid achievement of country-house technology, part of its fascination being the way in which modernisation has been carried out with a light touch, the remains of the redundant systems left to mark their passing.

The conservatism of Dunham existed in its workpeople rather than its technology. The estate formed a highly stable community. In the absence of long runs of servant wage books it is impossible to be sure about indoor servants, but it is highly unlikely that the junior indoor staff were any less mobile than others in similar households. Yet their overall context was secure and relatively unchanging. Usually the length of service of managerial-level staff can be measured in years rather than months, and indeed Dunham had a tradition of occasionally throwing up faithful family servants who become far more than servants to their masters. In the eighteenth century, the 1st Lord Delamer had a servant called John Andrews who was buried next to his master in Bowdon church, and in the twentieth century history repeated itself when, on the instructions of the 10th Earl, his long-standing servant/chauffeur/friend Piers Davenport was buried alongside him.[215] Certainly, as far as outdoor workers were concerned, we have seen how the same families were involved in the estate over generations as posts were passed from father to son. This feature of outdoor servants and casuals was common to many households, but it is particularly marked at Dunham.[216]

The distinction between managerial and menial staff has been identified as the 'principal line of cleavage' within the country-house servant hierarchy, and in the context of Dunham it is hard to disagree with this, at least at a superficial level.[217]

LEFT: A service corridor showing the internal systems of communications. At the end of the corridor is the old wire bell-pull system. On right and left walls are receivers for the internal telephone, which operated on a coded number of rings for different people. The hand bell called servants at meal times.

Our reading of the work of the steward and housekeeper has highlighted features which distinguished their work from that of lower servants: they were subject to little or no direct supervision, they were expected to make decisions and to use initiative in emergencies, they handled large amounts of cash and other valuables and they had to budget and plan ahead on behalf of others. In short, they represented the master and mistress in their absence. Since at Dunham this amounted to half the year, this delegation of power constituted a very high level of trust. As such the managerial staff were distinguished by their title. In the apothecary's bills the senior servants were identified as, for example, Mrs Calder and Mr Osgood. Middle servants were given their full name, as John Cutler (the brewer) or Thomas Shawcross (the coachman). The junior servants were identified by their Christian name and occupation, for example, as Anne Housemaid, William Footman, Ann Laundrymaid. This last practice confirms evidence in servants' diaries of around this time that even servants referred to each other in this way.[218]

The importance of managerial staff is one of the features distinguishing country-house service from other levels of domestic service. In London households, for example, the most significant line of separation between servant and servant has been seen to be not hierarchy but gender, a demarcation which 'fractured' relationships within the household from top to bottom.[219] Within the country-house context, gender presented a powerful line of demarcation too, but it was inextricably bound up with hierarchy. Men and women usually did different work in different, specialised places, supervised by different managers, but where work was similar, as in the case of footmen and housemaids polishing furniture, it was differentiated by the status of goods and their position within the house, whether in the public rooms downstairs or the private bedrooms upstairs.

It is possible to see gender as a means of defining the public and private roles in the work of steward and housekeeper. From the 1822 records we can see that Mrs Calder as well as Poole were closely involved with estimating, ordering, handling and paying for goods and services from the world beyond the park walls. But Poole made regular trips to Altrincham, Warrington and Manchester, presumably to visit tradesmen and suppliers to leave instructions. Mrs Calder does not seem to have made such excursions. It was the usual tradition in many country houses for regular local suppliers such as grocers to come up to the house themselves, in routine visits at which they would be offered a glass of port or sherry by the housekeeper in her sitting room, followed by a discussion of her needs and perhaps a joint inspection of her storerooms. This was one of the ways in which a diligent housekeeper could keep up to date with new products coming onto the market. In the nineteenth century, as more and more branded goods became available, it was the competent tradesman who was best-placed to advise and instruct her. So, unlike Poole, Mrs Calder might well have been able to organise her supplies without setting foot outside the house. For her, goods and provisions linked the domestically enclosed world of the housekeeper with the wider, more public world of industry, design, innovation and commerce. She had to achieve an accommodation between an internally oriented domestic structure and an increasingly proliferating material world.[220]

Steward and housekeeper were united in their dependence on communications

RIGHT: A housemaids' closet on the first floor at Dunham Massey, fitted with a sink and slopsink in 1906. The sink originally had three supplies of water – cold, hot (*right*) and soft (*centre*), from the roof. The floor is made of a composite material called 'Segalith'.

outside the household. This is perhaps the most important point made by the analysis of Poole's accounts, and it is one which has been hardly mentioned in most previous studies of the country house.[221] Perhaps Dunham had a particular pattern to its deliveries, given its proximity to a growing industrial complex and to the Bridgewater Canal, but a heavy reliance on transport facilities must have been a feature common to most great households. In houses such as Shugborough in

Staffordshire, which were the venues for parties with hundreds of guests, the demand for an ever more sophisticated lifestyle pushed the infrastructure of non-electrical communications to their limit.[222] Again, the importance of communications can be seen in the amount spent personally on travel by the 6th Earl of Stamford in 1822 (Box 51, opposite). The country-house use of new methods and equipment was generally highly conservative in some areas, but in this respect at least the Greys and the Ansons of Shugborough and their like were knocking at the door of technology with some impatience. Their demand makes nonsense of the idea that the country house was a monolithic structure isolated from its surroundings except on days of special celebrations. A dependence on local and distant labourers, suppliers, tradesmen and skilled craftsmen meant the household was truly embedded into a network of multi-directional contact. At Dunham this seems not to have been linked to the presence of the Earl, for in his absence the bureaucracy of senior servants continued. Servants interceded between family and community, and correspondence from agent to Earl ensured the regular conveyance of local gossip and news. How far such networks continued after the 7th Earl quitted Dunham permanently is unknown; from this viewpoint the Platt tenancy, usually seen as a blank interlude in the story of Dunham, takes on a new, though perhaps impenetrable, interest.

The Greys' involvement in charitable support of the poorer members of the local community was a strategy commonly adopted by the country house both to create links into the community and to emphasise its own status and separateness. Back in the eighteenth century, in addition to their bread doles, educational and bedding charities, the Greys had established a tradition of regular cash donations to the poor of surrounding parishes; later they gave land in Altrincham for the building of the Workhouse at Broadheath and the Lloyds Fever Hospital.[223] We have seen, however, that by 1822 senior household staff were responsible for the practicalities of much of the charitable giving except for subscriptions, and it is hard to escape the conclusion that the process of charitable support had been largely bureaucratised. This may well not have been the case earlier. Lady Mary Booth, the 2nd Earl of Warrington's daughter, probably spent a good proportion of her time dealing with the various school and bedding charities. The delegation of the mechanics of charitable donation to managerial staff did not necessarily mean that commitment had waned, though it must have had a slightly less personal touch. More generally, much of the charity donated by the landed gentry was channelled in personal and private directions, towards retired servants or old tenants.[224] This was perhaps less the case at Dunham where the educational and bedding charities were well developed. Annual bills for healthcare for the local poor also indicate that the 5th and 6th Earls' commitment in this area, though far from unusual, was perhaps greater than average.[225] The Greys' charities were never indiscriminate, however. As was common practice elsewhere, donations other than those made at the back door were conditional upon regular church attendance and preference was given to those who had not 'bothered the parish', that is, received poor relief.[226] Particularly after the 1820s there was a widespread concern that indiscriminate giving was bad for the poor, but the Greys seem to have practised selection long before, with their clear commitment to self-help through education and religion.

51

6th Earl of Stamford's personal expenditure, 1822

EnvArch 1/8/1

Clothing	£173	6s	7d	
Travelling Expenses	£592	19s	11d	
Carriages and repairs	£82	3s		
Wages	£25			(for 2 women, probably lady's maids for the Countess.)
Servants' clothing	£488	4s		
Stables	£312	4s	4d	
Presents	£961	2s	11d	
Charitable contributions	£747	5s	5d	(mainly subscriptions)
Sundries	£2,626	2s	9d	(wide variety – books, theatre boxes, club subscriptions, personal purchases)
TOTAL	**£6,008**	**8s**	**11d***	

* This excludes the Racing Account.

It is unwise, however, to assume that all donations to the poor were motivated by altruism rather than self-interest. At a time of great unrest in the early nineteenth century, the agent Worthington reported that the assistance given to the poor in Altrincham had done much good and the town remained peaceful. It would be a good idea, reported the agent, to build on this by donating a further £50 to the poor of Ashton-under-Lyne.[227] In the same vein, the family's determination to keep out of national or local disturbance was exercised in 1842 when a group of Chartist rioters visited Altrincham. Alfred Ingham, writing in 1879, described the Greys' reaction: 'In order to prevent a descent on Dunham Hall, the Earl of Stamford at that time ordered several barrels of beer, cheese and baskets of bread to be placed on the fringes of the park, near the present Green Walk Gate, which good things the rioters eagerly consumed.'[228]

In any case, it is easy to overstate the country house's commitment to charity, partly because it has been well documented both in family archives and in published literature. For the landed gentry as a whole it has been estimated at 'seldom more than 5 per cent, and commonly less' of their total expenditure.[229] For the Greys in 1822, charity seems to have made up around twelve per cent of John Poole's cash accounts (see p.81) and of the Earl's personal expenditure (Box 51, above). These two accounts totalled something below £10,000 per annum during the early nineteenth century, and thus represent only a small part of the family's total annual expenditure, which might be five times that amount. The remaining housekeeping expenses, salaries and wages, educational expenses, garden upkeep and so on need to be added to the equation, giving a final percentage figure for charity of way below twelve per cent. In general, aristocratic commitment to the poor and disadvantaged was heavily outweighed by an indulgent lifestyle and the Greys were no exception. Hospitality, entertainments and equestrian sport came high on their priority list. Throughout the early nineteenth century the two largest sectors of expenditure were the Earl's 'sundries' account (personal purchases, theatre boxes, clubs and so on, making up thirty per cent of his expenditure) and the housekeeping costs at Dunham, Enville, London and other houses (which made up a further twenty-five per cent). It is salutary to compare such expenditure with the commitment made by less well-known individuals of a much lower social origin such as Sir Smith Child, a Victorian benefactor of the Potteries. Over a period of some sixty years this very private man donated around a £1,000 a year to local charities, which is also roughly the amount spent on charity by the Greys. Given the relative incomes, however, Smith Child's commitment represents a personal dedication of a totally different order.[230]

In 1822 the Greys' total expenditure on horse-racing was also around £1,000 a year. In this case, however, the expenditure was offset against income from prize money and betting, resulting sometimes in a profit, sometimes in a loss, usually of several hundred pounds. The second decade of the nineteenth century seems to have been a bad period; only four of the ten years showed a profit. The account was run jointly by the 5th Earl and his eldest son, but the family's involvement with racing was long-standing and fairly extravagant. Their expenditure in 1818 was not far short of that of the 1st Earl of Lichfield a few years later, a man who was characterised as 'rather deep in the Turf'.[231] The early nineteenth century was a critical time in the development of the sport and the Greys could not have avoided contact with some highly dubious characters, such as Jack Mytton, a notorious gambler and sportsman to whom the 5th Earl sold his horse Jupiter in 1818 for £315.[232] Similarly, the fox-hunting world of the 1820s, in which the Greys were involved, was notorious for its wild living. It became much more respectable in the late 1830s.

The country house was an indulgent consumer of food, and one feature which appears to emphasise the isolation of the great household was the deliberate effort to be self-provisioning, especially in food supply. We have seen how in both the 1740s and the 1820s Dunham met a large percentage of its food requirements from within its own parklands. This choice was probably based more on philosophical concepts than sound economics. In theory, the degree to which households could practise self-sufficiency depended upon scale and status, though Alan Crosby has shown that other characteristics such as family history and religion also entered into the equation.[233] A study of an early eighteenth-century gentry household at Kildwick Hall near Skipton, in North Yorkshire, seems to support the idea that the greater the household the less the reliance on bought foodstuffs. Unlike the situation at the much larger establishment at Dunham, supplies of beef at Kildwick were a mixture of home produce and purchases.[234] These were differentiated by season; winter slaughter saved fodder costs and provided meat until March, when purchases of butcher's meat began. Similarly, Kildwick did not make all its own bread at home, whereas there is not a single reference to buying bread at Dunham. So the higher up the social scale, the more self-sufficient and exclusive was the household. Yet our reading of the household and farm accounts at Dunham during both the eighteenth

The mill at Dunham Massey was built in 1616 for corn-grinding. According to John Davenport's records, it was fitted with a new water wheel in 1814, when breakdowns were so common that the steward feared it would fail while the Earl was present.

and nineteenth centuries tells us this is simplistic nonsense. The beef may have been provided by the home farm, but even in the 1740s the farm was dependent on local farmers and markets for supplies of young livestock and feedstuffs, and other luxury foods and drink were delivered from an ever-widening circle of tradesmen and provision merchants by road and boat. The reality of self-provisioning, therefore, served not to isolate the household but to forge closer links with the local rural economy.

The desire to be self-provisioning was especially noticeable in respect of two foodstuffs, beef and beer. At other levels of society these may have been luxuries, but at Dunham they were staples on which the household diet was based. The country-house dependence on beer has a venerable history stretching back to medieval times. Its importance generally in the wealthy household can be gauged from expenditure; in 1634, for example, the single most expensive item within the lavish domestic economy of the Cecil household at Quickswood in Hertfordshire was the provision of small beer, the staple drink of the household.[235] In a social sense, alcoholic malt liquor performed several roles, binding together the household and easing relationships – as at the Dunham Leasing Days. In a close-knit society where it was important to draw boundaries between different groups, alcohol was a clear internal marker of hierarchy. While the servants drank most of the beer and ale, and the family and guests drank most of the wine and spirits, senior servants drank both on a regular basis, confirming their intermediate position in the ranking order. Alcohol also defined the household in relation to the outside world, who were 'let in'

An eighteenth-century painting of Dunham's house mastiff with puppy, by an amateur artist. Dunham traditionally kept a guard mastiff, usually called 'Lion' – William Torry noted that a Lion died in 1832 and was replaced by a young dog of the same name. The small barrel can be seen today in the south corridor.

occasionally. For this reason, drink was given to the poor on family birthdays, to visiting workmen and to estate labourers doing particularly difficult or dirty jobs. Finally, alcohol provides us today with a key with which to unlock some of the complexities of life in the house. How else would we know about the Earl's dinner for the master tradesmen, an event which speaks volumes about their importance to the family and household?

Again, dependency on a high-protein meat diet was by no means unique to Dunham. Any study of the food provisioning system of the country house, great or small, will arrive at the same conclusion. In the eighteenth century meat was cheap in relation to butter, for example, which, weight for weight, was twice the price.[236] The Currers of Kildwick lived on a diet which was 'firmly based on a plentiful supply of high-protein meat and fish', and at Canons, near Edgware, servants of the Duke of Chandos were given formally structured allowances of meat: 21oz of beef each on Tuesdays, Thursdays and Sundays, 21oz of mutton on Mondays and Fridays and 21oz of pork on Wednesdays and Saturdays.[237] In the 1850s the household of the Earls Fortescue at Castle Hill in Devon allowed the servants one and a half pounds of meat each per day, plus a pound of flour, a quart of ale and a pint of small beer. The amount of meat consumed at Dunham was in line with other houses, therefore, but it certainly set the household apart from its local and less wealthy community. The point was emphasised by the dispensation of beef to people who would normally be classed as outsiders. Beef was given away as presents to tenants, labourers and gardeners to commemorate the birth of the Prince of Wales in 1841, beef was dispensed to people on errands, and gifts of venison and game were used to cement relationships with local individuals and groups. Thus the great traditional household developed subtle forms of inclusion and exclusion, control and acceptance.

All families have kinship myths which build bonds and ties of communal memory and the Greys and the Booths had more reasons than most to engender and nurture such beliefs. As James Rothwell has explained:

> The Great Hall had a particular potency for the family, because it was here on 14 September 1682 that Charles II's illegitimate son, the Duke of Monmouth, who was trying to promote himself as heir to the throne, 'sat at meat' and, according to a contemporary account, 'the doors were set open and the rabble suffered not only to gaze into the room but to come in and view the Duke, entering at one door and going out at another'.[238]

Such a vivid picture provokes many questions, about notions of privacy, power structures or mass manipulation but also about the potency of conspicuous food consumption. Is it fanciful to see that food (the use of the word 'meat' in this context is unspecific), and particularly red beef and venison, has held an enduring and affective place in the family's past? Its position is attested to not only by such word pictures but also by the long-term devotion to the deer park, the prominence of the slaughterhouse, the generosity with gifts of beef, the 'historic' character of the great kitchen with its arches and spits, as well as the careful weekly recording of cattle, feedstuffs and slaughterings.

Some questions are, of course, impenetrable. In the early nineteenth century in particular there was a huge world of discontent of which the household records provide only occasional echoes, but which must have caused uneasy vibrations within the Dunham community. Only one solitary twentieth-century voice from inside the house (the housemaid Minnie with her food strike) attests to a dissenting counter-culture which must have existed amongst the servants, but the journal kept by the Earl's butler provides rare glimpses of an external world where not everyone doffed their caps to the Earl: Thomas Smith 'shot at' in the New Park (1826); Daniel Shaw 'illused at Altrincham' (1827); Samuel Timperley 'illused by poachers' at Dunham (1828); 'a thief taken in the stables at Dunham Massey' (1831); and 'Mr Davenport's saddle and bridle and Thomas Foster's great coat stolen from the farm' (1833). Even amongst the estate workers themselves, the record was far from unblemished. On one occasion, William Johnson, together with one of the Royles and one of the Warburtons, all families employed by the Earl of Stamford for many years, was convicted of 'rioting and fighting in the public street'.[239]

Is it mere cynicism which prompts worries about the wealth left by some of the senior employees of Dunham? Amounts such as £5,000 could not legitimately have accrued from the wages of such people and, though some wealth may have been inherited from previous generations of established farming or service families, many individuals were in a position to abuse the trust placed in them. Corrupt agents and stewards were, after all, by no means uncommon. At a lower level, the closeness of local families and the widespread use of day labour were features that writers of manuals of domestic service warned the unwary employer against, as these were well-known routes of 'leakage' of consumables, especially food. With the prolonged absence of the family from Dunham in the early part of each year, it would be amazing if substantial amounts of food and drink did not find their way out of the household, if only tucked into the voluminous clothing of charladies and washerwomen. Perhaps this was countenanced by the Greys as an informal contribution to the local economy. After all, many nineteenth-century households accepted the 'percentage' system, whereby servants received a gratuity from tradesmen for pushing trade their way. There were surely many clandestine ways for servants to boost their incomes.[240]

It is the personal documentation of individual servants that provides the best example both of the innate conservatism of the Dunham regime and its commitment to the idea of community. We have seen how in the eighteenth century loyalty and stability were fostered by the letting of long leases. Wills dated as late as the 1830s which include references to leasehold tenancies passed on to a later generation show that this system was still operating at that time, and indeed new lives were being added to leases. According to John Hodgson, the cataloguer of the Warrington and Stamford Papers, leases for lives continued on the estates until 1845, though it was not until the end of the century that all such leases expired.[241] By the 1840s many other estates had long since abandoned this practice in favour of an annual or six-monthly agreement. Long leases were seen to inhibit agricultural improvement and the consolidation of smaller holdings.[242] From both the landlord's and the tenants' viewpoint they were inflexible of market fluctuations in rent. Generally, by the early nineteenth century such leases were regarded as 'standard practice only for the larger farms, and even there were not universal'.[243] The retention of long leases at Dunham must have been a conscious policy, aimed at encouraging a stable workforce and strengthening ties of community, family kinship and loyalty.

* * *

The intention of this book was to explore the rings of interaction which radiated from the country-house family like the ripples on the surface of a pool when a stone is thrown in. It is justified if it has given even a glimpse of the relationships which were in place over a very limited period of time. Aristocratic networks have long been familiar to historians and genealogists; but within and around the great house at Dunham Massey were other families, business associations and individuals who together built a community which, far from domestic, was of a scale and sophistication reminiscent of a great institution or business. Yet the land agent to the Sutherland estates, James Loch, famous as one of the perpetrators of the Scottish Highland clearances, would not have agreed with this analogy. He likened the running of a great estate to ruling a small country:

> The property of a great English Nobleman must be managed on the same principle as a little kingdom, not like the affairs of a little Merchant. The future and lasting interest and honour of the family as well as their immediate income must be kept in view – while a merchant thinks only of his daily profits and his own immediate life interest.[244]

As a statement of the sense of common purpose which bound the community of Dunham Massey together this can hardly be bettered. It was in the nature of the ancient country-house family, however, that building for their future also entailed building for others.

Notes

Select bibliography

List of Plates

Index

Notes

CHAPTER ONE

1. See James Rothwell, *Dunham Massey, Cheshire*, official guidebook (National Trust, 2000).
2. J.V. Beckett and Clyve Jones, 'Financial Improvidence and Political Independence in the early 18th century: George Booth, 2nd Earl of Warrington, 1675–1758', *Bulletin of the John Rylands University Library of Manchester*, Vol. 65, No.1, 1982, pp.8–35. The first part of the introduction and the quotations used in it are based on this paper, Rothwell, *Dunham Massey*, and on Littler, Joyce, *The Protector of Dunham Massey: the Dunham Massey estate in the 18th century. A study in the management carried out by George Booth, 2nd Earl of Warrington* (Altrincham, 1933).
3. The evidence that Lord Warrington fathered offspring outside his marriage is discussed by James Rothwell in his forthcoming book on the collection of silver at Dunham Massey.
4. The inventory of 1693–4, taken at the death of the 1st Earl of Warrington, does not reveal a derelict or empty house. The brew-house, for example, appeared to have been well equipped and the cellars well stocked. See p.51.
5. EnvArch G/1/3/1820, 24 December, wages paid at Enville.
6. EGR 3/6/2/1/2 Inventory 1693–4; EGR 7/17/1, 1758; EGR 7/17/3, 1819; EGR 7/17/5, 1883; EGR 7/17/6, 1905 and EGR 7/17/9 and 10, 1912. Note that until 1752 the English used the Julian Calendar in which each year began on March 25th, Lady Day. Thus the year ending 25th March 1694 by present reckoning is now usually referred to as 1693–4, though the inventory made on the death of the 1st Earl was correctly dated at the time as 29th January, 1693.
7. Beckett and Jones, 'Financial Improvidence', p.17.
8. See for example Tom Arkell, Nesta Evans and Nigel Goose (eds), *When Death Do Us Part: understanding and interpreting the Probate Records of early modern England* (Local Population Studies Supplement, Department of Humanities, University of Hertfordshire, 2000).
9. The Dunham inventories have been painstakingly worked on by James Rothwell, for whose help in identifying rooms and changes in layout I am extremely grateful.
10. This alphabetical record is signed only with the initials 'W. T.' The earliest dated record, however, is of the death of Mary and John Torry; William Torry was footman during the 1820s and butler in the 1851 census so it is likely that he was the author, perhaps beginning his journal with the death of his parents. It has therefore been attributed to him in the references.
11. Census Enumeration Books for Dunham Massey for 1841, 1851, 1861, 1871, 1891 and 1901.

CHAPTER TWO

12. Description of the manor of Dunham Massey from the Manorial Extent of 1410–11.
13. EGR 3/6/2/1/2 Inventory 1693–4.
14. Mark Girouard, *Life in the English Country House: a social and architectural history* (first published 1978, Book Club Associates, London, 1979), p.276.
15. Collection of architectural drawings of Trentham by Sir Charles Barry, now in the Potteries Museum, Stoke-on-Trent.
16. Most of this chapter is based on the house inventories EGR 3/6/2/1/2, 1693–4; EGR 7/17/1, 1758; EGR 7/17/3, 1819; EGR 7/17/5, 1883; EGR 7/17/6, 1905 and EGR 7/17/9 and 10, 1912.
17. EGR 7/19/2/1 to 5 Alterations at Dunham Massey, 1821–9.
18. Edited transcript of taped interview with Minnie Hulme, recorded 19 May 1998 at Dunham Massey, made available by James Rothwell, the National Trust, Stamford Estates Office, Market Street, Altrincham.
19. C. Anne Wilson, 'Stillhouses and Stillrooms', in Pamela Sambrook and Peter Brears (eds), *The Country House Kitchen, 1650–1900: Skills and Equipment for Food Provisioning* (Sutton Publishing in association with the National Trust, 1997), pp.129–143.
20. EGR 7/14/1/7 House Steward's Quarterly Accounts, George Cooke to the Earl of Stamford, April 1774.
21. For a fuller explanation of footmen's work see Pamela Sambrook, *The Country House Servant* (Sutton Publishing in association with the National Trust, first published 1999).
22. William Torry, footman and butler, manuscript journal of events at Enville and Dunham, 1820s to *c.*1850, loaned by James Rothwell. No pagination.
23. Torry, manuscript journal.
24. EGR 4/1/8/11/23 Letter from Worthington to the Earl of Stamford, May 1814.
25. Sambrook, *Country House Servant*, p.51.
26. The use of the wagon was described in H.J. Leech, *Tales and Sketches of Old Altrincham and Bowdon* (1880), p.15.
27. Pamela Sambrook, *Country House Brewing in England, 1500–1900* (Hambledon Press, 1996), p.231.
28. EGR 7/14/1/6 March 1774; EGR 7/14/1/7 April 1774; EGR 7/14/1/25 June–Sept. 1779; EGR 7/14/1/73 House Steward's Quarterly Accounts, George Cooke to the Earl of Stamford.
29. Information from Tim Martin of Context Engineering, Petworth House, and Peter Brears.
30. EGR 7/19/1 Account of the Expenses of the Alterations at Dunham Massey in 1821, 1822, 1823.
31. Torry, manuscript journal.
32. EGR 7/12/8/10 Bill from Daniel Parsons for blacksmithing, December 1822.
33. Torry, manuscript journal.
34. EGR 7/14/8 Bundle of Housekeeper's accounts, 1842.
35. EGR 7/12/8/10 Bill from Daniel Parsons for blacksmithing, December 1822.

36. EGR 7/19/2/6 Account of the Expenses of the alterations at Dunham Massey in 1832.
37. For an idea of the variety and richness of dairy produce in aristocratic diet see Robin Weir, Caroline Liddell and Peter Brears, *Recipes from the Dairy* (National Trust, 1998).
38. Sambrook, *Country House Servant*, pp.120–27.
39. Reference to building the wash-house was made in EGR 4/1/10/5/5 Letter dated 27 April 1800 from the land agent Isaac Worthington to Lord Stamford.
40. Santina Levey, *An Elizabethan Inheritance: the Hardwick Hall Textiles* (National Trust, 1998), p.33 and Sambrook, *Country House Servant*, p.106.
41. For further detail on the brewing process, the importance of brewing in the country-house economy and a full glossary of archaic brewing terms see Sambrook, *Country House Brewing*.
42. Eleven thousand gallons in the cellars at Shugborough in 1824 and 12,000 gallons at Trentham in the 1830s, see Sambrook, *Country House Brewing*, p.157.
43. EGR 7/17/6 Inventory 1905.
44. EGR 7/14/1/19 George Cooke's Accounts to the Earl of Stamford, 1777.
45. EGR 4/1/8/11/5, 9, 23 Letter from Worthington to the Earl of Stamford, March–May, 1814; Compton Hall, J., *Dunham Massey Hall: an account of its history and a brief description of the recent Restoration* (private publication, 1909), p.5.
46. EGR 7/19/2/1 Account of the Expenses of the Alterations at Dunham Massey, 1821.
47. EGR 4/1/8/11/1 Letter from Worthington to the Earl of Stamford, 4 December 1813.
48. EGR 7/19/2/2 Account of the Expenses of the Alterations at Dunham Massey, 1823. The narrowing of chimney-throats was advocated by Count Rumford; see G.I. Brown, *Count Rumford: the Extraordinary Life of a Scientific Genius*, (Sutton Publishing, 1999), pp.100–104.
49. EGR 7/19/2/1 Account of the Expenses of the Alterations at Dunham Massey, 1821.
50. EGR 7/19/2/4 Account of the Expenses of the Alterations at Dunham Massey, 1827.
51. Sara Pennell, 'The Material Culture of Food in Early Modern England, 1650–1750', in Sarah Tarlow and Susie West (eds), *The Familiar Past?* (Routledge, 1999), pp.42–3.

CHAPTER THREE

52. The 6th Earl's establishment prior to inheriting Dunham was at Atherstone Hall, Warwickshire, EGR 4/2/6/1.
53. EGR 11/2/8/60 Wages paid by Hugo Worthington to the Earl of Stamford and Warrington's servants resident at Dunham Massey due 25 December 1819; and EGR 11/2/8/61 Wages paid by Hugo Worthington to the Earl of Stamford and Warrington's travelling servants due 25 December 1819.
54. EnvArch G/1/3/1820, 24 December, wages paid at Enville.
55. SRO, Leveson-Gower Papers D593 R/11/12 Wages Books, 1840–54.
56. EGR 11/2/5/4 Wages at Dunham Massey, 24 June 1819; EGR 11/2/8/9 Account of Money paid … for Mourning for the late Earl at Dunham, 25 May 1819; and EGR 11/2/8/43/1 Legacies to servants on the death of the Earl of Stamford, paid 2 July 1819.
57. EGR 11/2/5/5 Wages at Dunham Massey, 24 June 1817.
58. Enville Archive, G/1/3/1820, 24 December 1820.
59. Parish Register of Marriages for Bowdon St Mary's, March 1822.
60. For example, the footmen in the service of the Duke of Sutherland, SRO, D593 R11/12, 1840.
61. EGR 11/2/8/61 Wages paid by Hugo Worthington to the Earl of Stamford and Warrington's travelling servants due 25 December 1819.
62. Pamela Sambrook, *The Country House Servant* (Sutton Publishing, 1999), p.25.
63. William Torry, footman and butler, manuscript journal of events at Enville and Dunham, 1820s to *c.*1850, loaned by James Rothwell. No pagination.
64. Charles W. Cooper, *Town and Country, or Forty Years in Private Service with the Aristocracy* (Lovat Dickson, 1937), p.26.
65. Ibid. p.56.
66. Pamela Sambrook, *Country House Brewing in England, 1500–1900* (Hambledon Press, 1996), p.209.
67. Torry, manuscript journal.
68. EGR 4/1/8/3/8 Letter from Worthington to the Earl of Stamford at Enville, 22 February 1799.
69. Torry, manuscript journal.
70. EGR 7/19/2/5 Account of the Expenses of the Alterations at Dunham Massey, 1829.
71. EGR 7/19/2/4 Account of the Expenses of the Alterations at Dunham Massey, 1827 and EGR 7/19/2/2 ditto for 1823 and EGR 7/19/2/7 ditto for 1833.

CHAPTER FOUR

72. This section is based on correspondence between the 5th Earl of Warrington and Hugo Worthington, EGR 4/1/8/4/33 19 March 1813; EGR 4/1/8/4/34, 1813; EGR 4/1/8/3/36 March 1813.
73. EGR 7/19/1 Account of the Expenses of the Alterations at Dunham Massey 1821, 1822, 1823. Equivalent value of the pound: the amount of money required in 2000 to purchase goods worth £1 in 1820 is approximately £35 (excluding the cost of real property or wages).
74. *A New Directory of Manchester and Salford, 1821–2* (Pigot and Dean).
75. EGR 7/8/1 House Steward's Cash Book, 1822 and EGR 7/1/12 House Steward's Account Book, 1821–32. Most of this chapter is based on EGR 7/8/1.
76. EGR 7/12/5–8 Bundles of House Steward's Quarterly Accounts, January–December 1822.
77. 'Papers of the Grey Family, Earls of Stamford, from Dunham Massey Hall. EGR 7 Household Records, Introduction' catalogue compiled by John R. Hodgson (John Rylands University Library of Manchester, 1995).

78. EGR 7/4/4 Mill Account Book, 1818–39.
79. EGR 7/5/3 Farm Stock Book, 1822.
80. Charles Balshaw, *A Stranger's Guide and Complete Directory to Altrincham, Bowdon, Dunham, Timperley, Baguley, Ashley, Hale and Bollington* (1860s, reprinted by E.J. Morten, Manchester, 1973), p.48.
81. Alfred Ingham, *A History of Altrincham and Bowdon* (first published 1879, reprinted by Prism Books, 1983), p.144.
82. An apothecary was the nineteenth-century equivalent of a modern general practitioner.
83. Staffordshire Record Office D1287/3/23
84. Diaries of Sir John Walsh, later 1st Baron Ormathwaite, National Library of Wales, Aberystwyth, entry for 25 April 1845. H.J. Leech, *Tales and Sketches of Old Altrincham and Bowdon* (1880), p.13.
85. This account of the Thomas Walton Charity is based largely on 'Papers of the Grey Family, Earls of Stamford, from Dunham Massey Hall, EGR 8 and 9, Introduction', catalogue compiled by John R. Hodgson (John Rylands University Library of Manchester, 1995).
86. This section is based on EGR 8/4/7 State of the Poor with Respect to their Bedding, September 1786; EGR 8/4/6/5 Bedding Register for Altrincham, 1822; and EGR 8/4/2/12 Bedding Register for Altrincham, 1818.
87. William Torry, footman and butler, manuscript journal of events at Enville and Dunham, 1820s to *c.*1850, loaned by James Rothwell. No pagination.
88. Leech, *Tales and Sketches* p.13.
89. EGR 7/1/4 House Book, 1760–67.
90. Gerard L. Turnbull, *Traffic and Transport: an economic history of Pickfords* (George Allen and Unwin, 1979), p.12.
91. EGR 4/1/10/5 Correspondence of the 5th Earl of Stamford regarding the postal services.
92. Roy Lewis, *Royal Mail in Staffordshire*, Staffordshire County Council Education Department, Local History Source Book No. G18, n.d., pp.9 and 12.
93. This was normal practice. Local delivery networks were financed separately from the national mail services which operated between London and major receiving offices, in this case Knutsford. The local services worked from the receiving offices through a highly variable mixture of horse-posts, mail carts and footposts and usually the extra cost was levied per letter, occasionally per house delivery. See for example C.M. Beaver, 'Newcastle Potteries: the Evolution of Postal Provisions in N.W. Staffordshire', in *Postal History: the Journal of the Postal History Society*, No.235 (1985, 3rd Quarter), pp.17–27.
94. See for example Lewis, *Royal Mail*, p.31.
95. This section is based on EnvArch 1/8/1, 6th Earl's private accounts, 1822, 1st and 2nd bundles.
96. See Leech, *Tales and Sketches*, p.15.
97. Staffordshire Record Office, D593/N/2/8/1 Regulations for the Lodge-keeper at Trentham, 1810.
98. Ingham, *Altrincham and Bowdon*, p.194.

CHAPTER FIVE

99. This chapter is based on EGR 7/1/12 Household Account Book, 1821–32 and EGR 7/12/13/1–7 Bundle of Housekeeper's Accounts, 1822.
100. EGR 7/1/1 House Book, 1743.
101. Kate Mertes, *The English Noble Household, 1250–1600; Good Governance and Political Rule* (Basil Blackwell, 1988).
102. EGR 7/8/1 House Steward's Housekeeping Cash Book, EGR 7/12/8/3 Bill from John Hewitt for cheese, 1822 and EGR 7/12/8/9 Bill from W. Heyward for cheese, 1822.
103. EGR 4/2/7/17 Game lists.
104. EGR 7/11/2 Venison Book, 1826.
105. EnvArch 1/8/1, 6th Earl's private accounts, 1821, 2nd bundle.
106. EGR 7/12/8/9 Bill from William Heyward for cheeses etc., 1822.
107. EGR 7/14/5 Bundle of bills from Barratt, 1830s.
108. EGR 7/14/5 Bundle of grocery bills from Barratt, 1837.
109. EGR 7/8/1 House Steward's Housekeeping Cash Book.
110. For details of country-house beer types and strengths see Pamela Sambrook, *Country House Brewing in England, 1500–1900* (Hambledon Press, 1996).
111. Diaries of Sir John Walsh, later 1st Baron Ormathwaite, National Museum of Wales, Aberystwyth, entry for 25 April 1845; H.J. Leech, *Tales and Sketches of Old Altrincham and Bowdon* (1880), p.15.
112. EGR 7/9/3 Cellar Book 1820–31.
113. H. Warner Allen, *A History of Wine* (Faber and Faber, 1961), pp.197–9. This provides a summary of the importance of bottle shape and well-fitting corks to the development of the European wine trade in the eighteenth century.
114. The strength of the Earl's feeling for family ritual is shown here, for he maintained the traditional ale allowance for the Rev. Law's birthday, despite his strong antipathy to his daughter's marriage to him.
115. EGR 7/10/2 Wine Bin Book, begins August 1819.
116. For the change in the eighteenth century from buying wine in the cask to wine by the bottles see Allen, *History of Wine*, pp.182–3.
117. EGR 7/1/1 House Book, 1743.
118. Sambrook, *Country House Brewing*, p.233.
119. *Receits transcribed from a Book of the Right Honourable the Earl of Warrington's, 1730* in two volumes, currently at Dunham Massey House.
120. EGR 4/2/12/9/12–28 Accounts of the Company at Dunham, 1826–42.
121. Leech, *Tales and Sketches*, pp.14–15.

CHAPTER SIX

122. EGR 7/12/3 Bundle of Farm Steward's Accounts, 1822. Most of the section on the farm is based on these accounts.
123. EGR 7/3/1 Farm Steward's Account Book, 1789.
124. EGR 7/3/1 Farm Steward's Account Book, 1789.

125. EGR 7/2/4, Farm Steward's Cash Book, 1814–31.
126. EGR 7/4/4 Mill Account Book, 1818–39.
127. EGR 7/14/1/6 House Steward's Quarterly Accounts, 1779.
128. EGR 7/7/4 Garden Account Book, 1812–22.
129. It was normal to use women weeders in gardens, for further examples see Craig W. Thornber, 'The Langford Brooke Family of Mere, near Knutsford, Cheshire: Genealogy from 1612 to 1872 and Estate Correspondence from 1828 and 1829' (unpublished typescript, January 2000), p.33, letter from the agent Alex Ogilvie to Langford Brookes in Naples, dated 25 October 1828.
130. For descriptions of kitchen-garden techniques, including hotbeds, see C. Anne Wilson (ed.), *The Country House Kitchen Garden, 1600–1950* (Sutton Publishing in association with the National Trust, 1998), Chapter 5.
131. Thornber, 'Langford Brooke Family', p.33.
132. EGR 14/25 Cheshire Estates Cash Book, 1859–1943.

CHAPTER SEVEN

133. Janet Hardman, *A Study of Altrincham and its Families in 1801 and 1851* (pamphlet privately published, 1989), p.2.
134. Anon, 'Monumental Inscriptions of Bowdon Parish Church', Family History Society of Cheshire, typescript M26 in Alderley Edge Family History Centre, pp.19, 283.
135. EGR 4/1/8/3/38–48 Correspondence between Worthington and the Earl of Stamford, December–April 1814–15.
136. EGR 4/1/8/11/5 Correspondence between Worthington and the Earl of Stamford, 23 May 1814.
137. Cheshire Record Office, Probate Records, WS 1837.
138. Cheshire Record Office, Probate Records, WS 1840.
139. EGR 4/1/8/3/4,5,6,8 Correspondence between Worthington and the Earl of Stamford, 15, 17, 20 and 22 February 1799.
140. EGR 4/10/14/2 Correspondence between the Earl of Stamford and Charlotte Law, 20 December 1831.
141. Hardman, *Altrincham*, p.16; Alfred Ingham, *A History of Altrincham and Bowdon* (first published 1879, reprinted by Prism Books, 1983), p.176.
142. EGR 4/1/8/6/5 Letter from Worthington including a list of houses in Altrincham owned by the Earl of Stamford.
143. This paragraph is based on correspondence between Worthington and the Earl of Stamford, EGR 4/1/8/3/10 16 December 1807; EGR 4/1/8/5/5 2 March 1804; EGR 4/1/8/3/26 18 December 1812; and EGR 4/1/8/11/1 and 13, December–June, 1814.
144. James Rothwell, *Dunham Massey, Cheshire*, official guidebook (National Trust, 2000), p.49.
145. Ingham, *Altrincham and Bowdon*, p.85.
146. Anon, 'Monumental Inscriptions', p.8, 100.
147. EGR 7/14/1/66 Statements of Accounts, 1788.
148. Cheshire Record Office, Probate Records, WS 1840.
149. William Torry, footman and butler, manuscript journal of events at Enville and Dunham, 1820s to *c.*1850, loaned by James Rothwell, no pagination.
150. Staffordshire Record Office, Leveson-Gower Papers D593 R/11/12, Wages Book 1840–54.
151. Anon, 'Monumental Inscriptions', p.56, 737.
152. Cheshire Record Office, DDX 363 Caldwell's Nurseries, Customer Ledgers, 1789–1926.
153. Craig W. Thornber, 'The Langford Brooke Family of Mere, near Knutsford, Cheshire: Genealogy from 1612 to 1872 and Estate Correspondence from 1828 and 1829' (unpublished typescript, January 2000), p.38.
154. Charles Balshaw, *A Stranger's Guide and Complete Directory to Altrincham, Bowdon, Dunham, Timperley, Baguley, Ashley, Hale and Bollington* (1860s, reprinted by E.J. Morten, Manchester, 1973).
155. *Return of Owners of Land in Cheshire*, 1871. Vol. 1.
156. Ingham, *Altrincham and Bowdon*, p.187.
157. Ibid., p.180.
158. Parish Register of Marriages for Bowdon, 9 August 1821.
159. Ingham, *Altrincham and Bowdon*, p.203.
160. Ibid., p.204.
161. Craig W. Thornber, 'Peter Holland – Knutsford Surgeon', *Cheshire Ancestor*, Vol. 30, issue No.2, December 1999, p.27 ff. The following summary of Holland's career is based on this paper.
162. Frederick Leary, *The Earl of Chester's Yeomanry Cavalry, 1797–1897* (Ballantyne Press, 1898), p.10.
163. Robert Murray, 'Peter Holland: a pioneer of occupational medicine', *British Journal of Industrial Medicine*, Vol. 49, 1992, p.377, quoted in Thornber, 'Peter Holland'.
164. EGR 4/10/1a Letter 9 November 1825 from Harriet Inge, Dunham to Jane Grey.
165. Parish Register of Marriages, Bowdon church, 1822.
166. Balshaw, *A Stranger's Guide.*
167. *A New Directory of Manchester and Salford, 1821–22* (Pigot and Dean, 1822).
168. 'Goods went to Dunham [from Enville] by water for the 1st time, 19th July, 1831'. Torry, manuscript journal.
169. Pigot and Dean, *New Directory*, pp.196–200.
170. Parish Register of Marriages, Bowdon church, 1822.
171. Cheshire Record Office, Tithe Map and Apportionment, 1839–40.
172. EGR 4/1/8/3/2 Correspondence between Worthington and the Earl of Stamford, 4 August 1798.
173. EGR 4/1/8/3/31 Correspondence between Worthington and the Earl of Stamford, 16 March 1813.
174. H.J. Leech, *Tales and Sketches of Old Altrincham and Bowdon* (1880), p.13.
175. Leary, *Yeomanry Cavalry*, pp.85, 101, 107, 157, 266.
176. EGR 11/2/8 Vouchers for 5 June–31 December 1819.
177. EnvArch G/2/2/2/17/6, letter from John Beckett to Lord Stamford, 6 November, 1819.

178. Torry, manuscript journal.
179. EGR 7/14/1/25 House Steward's Quarterly Accounts, George Cooke to the Earl of Stamford, July 1779.
180. Torry, manuscript journal.
181. EGR 4/10/11 and 12 Correspondence, 9 November 1825.
182. Torry, manuscript journal.
183. Don Bayliss (ed.), *Altrincham: a History* (Willow Publishing, 1992), p.36.
184. For a collection of local history papers see Bayliss, *Altrincham.*

CHAPTER EIGHT

185. Census Enumerator's Book, 1901, Dunham Massey.
186. EGR 7/17/6 Inventory, 1905.
187. According to Maureen Dillon in a report on the lighting at Dunham dated September 2000, gas lighting is a rare survival in country houses. Whilst surviving equipment may be rare, household accounts show that private gas-making plants were common in this context.
188. EGR 7/17/5 Inventory 1883.
189. 'Papers of the Grey Family, Earls of Stamford, from Dunham Massey Hall. EGR 7 Household Records, Introduction', catalogue compiled by John Hodgson (John Rylands University Library of Manchester, 1995).
190. EGR 7/20/1/1 Correspondence between the Earl of Stamford and Compton Hall, 7 August 1905. This section on the 1905 alterations is based on correspondence between the Earl of Stamford and Compton Hall, EGR 7/20/1/1-8; EGR 7/20/2/3-18; EGR 7/20/3/12-14; and between Lady Stamford and Compton Hall EGR 7/20/5/18; EGR 7/20/4/8/1-5; and EGR 7/20/5/5.
191. EGR 7/20/2/27 Rough Note by the Earl of Stamford, n.d.
192. EGR 7/20/1/10 Summary of Contractors and Sub-Contractors Accounts, October 1908
193. Edited transcript of taped interview with Minnie Hulme, recorded 19th May 1998, p.19 at Dunham Massey kindly made available by James Rothwell.
194. Christina Hardyment, *Home Comfort: a History of Domestic Arrangements* (Viking in association with the National Trust, 1992), pp.134-5.
195. EGR Restricted list, 9th Earl's Records, Box 14/11, Letters of application for jobs.
196. EGR Restricted list, 9th Earl's Records, Box 26/3.
197. EGR Restricted list, 9th Earl's Records, Box 14/3, Invoices.
198. EGR Restricted list, 9th Earl's Records, Box 26/29, Licences, 1909.
199. EGR Restricted list, 9th Earl's Records, Box 11/4, Staff Wages Book 1898-1906.
200. James Rothwell, *Dunham Massey, Cheshire*, official guidebook (National Trust, 2000), p.19; and Minnie Hulme tape transcript.
201. EGR Restricted List, Housemaids' Work, n.d.
202. Minnie Hulme tape transcript.
203. Transcript of lecture by Oliver Turnbull at Dunham Massey, 1992, p.3, kindly made available by James Rothwell.
204. Lecture by Turnbull quoting from Board of Trade, *Report of Miss Collett on the money wages of indoor domestic servants*, British Parliamentary Papers, 1899, XCII, p.iii.
205. Amanda Vickery, *The Gentleman's Daughter: Women's Lives in Georgian England* (Yale University Press, 1998), p.141.
206. E.S. Turner, *What the Butler Saw*, (Michael Joseph, 1962), p.232.
207. Clive Aslet, *The Last Country Houses* (Yale University Press), 1982, p.3.
208. Ibid., p.85.
209. Marchioness of Bath, *Before the Sunset Fades* (Longleat Estate Co., 1951), p.7.
210. A still-excellent study is Merlin Waterson, *The Servants' Hall: a Domestic History of Erddig* (Routledge and Kegan Paul, first published 1980). See also Adeline Hartcup, *Below Stairs in the Great Country Houses* (Sidgwick and Jackson, 1980) and more recently for a gentry household Peter Brears, *The Compleat Housekeeper: a Household in Queen Anne Times* (Wakefield Historical Publications, 2000).
211. C. Anne Wilson, 'Keeping Hospitality and Board Wages: Servants' Feeding Arrangements from the Middle Ages to the 19th Century' in C. Anne Wilson (ed.), *Food for the Community: Special Diets for Special Groups* (Edinburgh University Press, 1993), p.44; Kate Mertes, *The Noble English Household, 1250-1600* (Basil Blackwell, 1988); C.M. Woolgar, *The Great Household in late Medieval England* (Yale University Press, 1999), p.34.
212. For a discussion on this point see Tim Meldrum, *Domestic Service and Gender, 1660-1750: Life and Work in the London Household*, (Longman, 2000), pp.76-83.
213. Eric Horne, *What the Butler Winked At* (Werner Laurie, 1923), p.258.
214. For examples of early water-driven pumping systems and private gas plants see Marilyn Palmer, 'Comfort and Convenience in the English Country House' in Malcolm Airs (ed.), *The Edwardian Great House* (Oxford University Department for Continuing Education, 2000), pp.19-28; also Aslet, *Last Country Houses.*
215. Transcript of interview with Dorothy Millington, recorded on 18 May 1988, p.21, kindly made available by James Rothwell.
216. Jessica Gerard, *Country House Life: Family and Servants, 1815-1914* (Blackwells, 1994), p.179.
217. J.J. Hecht, *The Domestic Servant in Eighteenth-century England* (Routledge and Kegan Paul, 1980), p.35.
218. Pamela Sambrook, *The Country House Servant* (Sutton Publishing in association with the National Trust, 1999), pp.56 and 58.
219. Meldrum, *Domestic Service and Gender*, p.127.
220. Sara Pennell, 'The Material Culture of Food in Early Modern England, *c.*1650-1750' in Sarah Tarlow and Susie West (eds), *The Familiar Past? Archaeologies of later historical Britain* (Routledge, 1999), p.47.
221. For the exceptional mention of trade routes used by country houses see Brears, *Compleat Housekeeper*, p.65.
222. Pamela Sambrook, 'Aristocratic Indebtedness: the Anson Estates in Staffordshire, 1818-1880' (unpublished Ph.D. thesis, Keele University, 1990), pp.217-8.

223. Alfred Ingham, *A History of Altrincham and Bowdon* (first published 1879, reprinted by Prism Books, 1983), pp.202–3.
224. G.E. Mingay, *Land and Society in England, 1750–1980* (Longman, 1994), p.29.
225. Mingay, *Land and Society*, p.76.
226. Ibid., p.96.
227. EGR 4/1/8/2/34 Correspondence between Worthington and the Earl of Stamford, 19 May 1819.
228. Ingham, *Altrincham and Bowdon*, p.200.
229. Mingay, *Land and Society*, p.29.
230. Unpublished information kindly provided by Betty Cooper.
231. Sambrook, 'Aristocratic Indebtedness', p.243.
232. EnvArch Racing Account Book, 1795–1818.
233. Alan Crosby, 'The Squire and the Poacher: some thoughts on Self-Sufficiency', *Regional Bulletin*, Centre for North-West Regional Studies, Lancaster University, New Series No.10, Summer 1996, p.56.
234. Brears, *Compleat Housekeeper*, pp.45–8.
235. Pamela Sambrook, *Country House Brewing in England, 1500–1600* (Hambledon Press, 1996), p.193 and Lionel M. Munby (ed.), *Early Stuart Household Accounts* (Hertfordshire Record Publications, 1986), pp.3–76.
236. Jennifer Stead, 'Georgian Britain' in Peter Brears et al. (eds), *A Taste of History: 10,000 Years of Food in Britain* (English Heritage in association with British Museum Press, 1993), p.237.
237. Brears, *Compleat Housekeeper*, p.45; Hecht, *Domestic Servant*, p.112.
238. Rothwell, *Dunham Massey*, p.15.
239. Ingham, *Altrincham and Bowdon*, p.175.
240. Anon., *The Servants Practical Guide: a Handbook of Duties and Rules* (Frederick Warne, *c.*1890), p.15.
241. 'Papers of the Grey Family, Earls of Stamford, Introduction', catalogue compiled by John Hodgson (John Rylands University Library of Manchester, 1995), Vol.1, pp.27–8.
242. See James Loch, 'An Account of the Improvements on the Estates of the Marquis of Stafford in the Counties of Stafford and Salop and on the Estate of Sutherland, with Remarks', private pamphlet dated 1820.
243. G.E. Mingay, *Rural Life in Victorian England* (first published 1976, Sutton Publishing, 1998), pp.47–8.
244. Mingay, *Rural Life*, p.136.

Select bibliography

Manuscript Collections

Alderley Edge Family History Centre
Parish Register of Bowdon, 1822

Cheshire Record Office, Chester
Census Enumerators' Books, 1841–1901
Papers of Caldwell Nurseries
Probate Records and Wills
Tithe Map and Apportionment for Dunham Massey

Dunham Massey House, Cheshire
Receit Books of Lady Mary Booth

Enville Hall Archive, Stourbridge, Staffordshire
6th Earl of Stamford's accounts and correspondence (EnvArch)

John Rylands Library, University of Manchester, Deansgate, Manchester
Stamford Papers (EGR)

National Trust, Stamford Estates Office, Altrincham, Cheshire
Journal of William Torry.
Transcript of recording by Minnie Hulme

Printed Sources

ALLEN, H.W., *A History of Wine* (Faber and Faber, 1961).

ANON, 'Monumental Inscriptions of Bowdon Parish Church', Family History Society of Cheshire, typescript M26, Alderley Edge Family History Centre

ANON, *The Servants Practical Guide: a Handbook of Duties and Rules* (Frederick Warne, n.d., *c.*1890).

ASLET, C., *The Last Country Houses* (Yale University Press, 1982).

BALSHAW, C., *A Stranger's Guide and Complete Directory to Altrincham, Bowdon, Dunham, Timperley, Baguley, Ashley, Hale and Bollington* (1860s, reprinted by E. J. Morten, Manchester, 1973).

BAYLISS, D., (ed.), *Altrincham: a History* (Willow Publishing, 1992).

BECKETT, J.V. and JONES, C., 'Financial Improvidence and Political Independence in the early 18th century: George Booth, 2nd Earl of Warrington, 1675–1758', *Bulletin of the John Rylands University Library of Manchester*, Vol. 65, No. 1, 1982, pp.8–35.

BOWDON HISTORICAL SOCIETY, *Images of England: Bowdon and Dunham Massey*, (Tempus, 1999).

BREARS, P., *The Compleat Housekeeper: a Household in Queen Anne Times* (Wakefield Historical Publications, 2000).

COMPTON HALL, J., *Dunham Massey Hall: an account of its History and a brief description of the recent Restoration* (private publication, 1909).

CROSBY, A., 'The Squire and the Poacher: some thoughts on Self-Sufficiency', *Regional Bulletin*, Centre for North-West Regional Studies, Lancaster University, New Series No. 10, Summer 1996.

GERARD, J., *Country House Life: Family and Servants, 1815–1914* (Blackwells, 1994).

GIROUARD, M., *Life in the English Country House: a social and architectural history* (first published 1978, Book Club Associates, London, 1979).

HARDMAN, J., *A Study of Altrincham and its Families in 1801 and 1851* (privately published pamphlet, 1989).

HARDYMENT, C., *Behind the Scenes: Domestic Arrangements in Historic Houses* (National Trust, 1997).

HARTCUP, A., *Below Stairs in the Great Country Houses* (Sidgwick and Jackson, 1980).

HECHT, J. J., *The Domestic Servant in Eighteenth-century England* (Routledge and Kegan Paul, 1980).

HORNE, E., *What the Butler Winked At* (Werner Laurie, 1923).

INGHAM, A., *A History of Altrincham and Bowdon* (first published 1879, reprinted by Prism Books, 1983).

LEARY, F., *The Earl of Chester's Yeomanry Cavalry, 1797–1897* (Ballantyne Press, 1898).

LEECH, H. J., *Tales and Sketches of Old Altrincham and Bowdon* (John Heywood, 1880).

LEVEY, S., *An Elizabethan Inheritance: the Hardwick Hall Textiles* (National Trust, 1998).

LITTLER, J., *The Protector of Dunham Massey: Dunham Massey estate in the 18th century. A study of the management carried out by George Booth, 2nd Earl of Warrington* (Joyce Littler Publications, Altrincham, 1993).

MARCHIONESS OF BATH, *Before the Sunset Fades* (Longleat Estate Co., 1951).

MELDRUM, T., *Domestic Service and Gender, 1660–1750: Life and Work in the London Household*, (Longman, 2000).

MERTES, K., *The English Noble Household, 1250–1600: Good Governance and Political Rule* (Basil Blackwell, 1988).

MINGAY, G. E., *Land and Society in England, 1750–1980* (Longman, 1994).

MINGAY, G. E., *Rural Life in Victorian England* (first published 1976, Sutton Publishing, 1998).

MUNBY, L. M., (ed.), *Early Stuart Household Accounts* (Hertfordshire Record Publications, 1986).

MURRAY, R., 'Peter Holland: a pioneer of occupational medicine', *British Journal of Industrial Medicine*, Vol. 49, 1992.

PALMER, M., 'Comfort and Convenience in the English Country House' in Malcolm Airs (ed.), *The Edwardian Great House* (Oxford University Department for Continuing Education, 2000), pp.19–28.

PENNELL, S., 'The Material Culture of Food in Early Modern England, *c.*1650–1750' in Sarah Tarlow and Susie West (eds), *The Familiar Past? Archaeologies of later historical Britain* (Routledge, 1999).

PENNINGTON, M. E., *Our Village: Dunham Massey* (private pamphlet, n.d.).

PIGOT and DEAN, *A New Directory of Manchester and Salford,* (Pigot & Dean 1821–22).

ROTHWELL, J., *Dunham Massey, Cheshire,* Official Guidebook (National Trust, 2000).

SAMBROOK, P. and BREARS, P., (eds), *The Country House Kitchen, 1650–1900: Skills and Equipment for Food Provisioning* (Sutton Publishing in association with the National Trust, 1997).

SAMBROOK, P., *Country House Brewing in England, 1500–1900* (Hambledon Press, 1996).

SAMBROOK, P., *The Country House Servant* (Sutton Publishing in association with the National Trust, first published 1999).

STEAD, J., 'Georgian Britain' in Peter Brears et al. (eds), *A Taste of History: 10,000 Years of Food in Britain* (English Heritage in association with British Museum Press, 1993).

SWARBRICK, J., *Dunham Massey Hall* (private pamphlet, 1925).

THORNBER, C. W., 'Peter Holland – Knutsford Surgeon', *Cheshire Ancestor,* Vol. 30, issue No. 2, December 1999.

THORNBER, C. W., 'The Langford Brooke Family of Mere, near Knutsford, Cheshire: Genealogy from 1612 to 1872 and Estate Correspondence from 1828 and 1829' (unpublished typescript, January 2000).

TURNBULL, G. L., *Traffic and Transport: an economic history of Pickfords* (George Allen and Unwin, 1979).

TURNER, E. S., *What the Butler Saw* (Michael Joseph, 1962).

VICKERY, A., *The Gentleman's Daughter: Women's Lives in Georgian England* (Yale University Press, 1998).

WALSH, Sir John, later 1st Baron Ormathwaite, *Diaries* (National Library of Wales, Aberystwyth).

WATERSON, M., *The Servants' Hall: The Domestic History of a Country House* (Routledge and Kegan Paul, first published 1980).

WEIR, R., LIDDELL, C., and BREARS, P., *Recipes from the Dairy* (National Trust, 1998).

WILSON, C. A., (ed.), *Food for the Community: Special Diets for Special Groups* (Edinburgh University Press, 1993).

WOOLGAR, C. M., *The Great Household in late Medieval England* (Yale University Press, 1999).

List of Plates

Please note that figures in **bold** refer to page numbers.

NTPL – National Trust Photographic Library
NT – National Trust Archives and Regional Libraries
NMR – National Monuments Record, English Heritage

Boxes

Index

Note:
Page numbers in *italics* refer to illustrations

Family members

Friends and contemporaries

Locations

Place Names

Posts

Servants and employees by name

Topics

Tradesmen, contractors and architects by name and trade